NATIONALITY, MIGRATION RIGHTS AND CITIZENSHIP OF THE UNION

Nationality, Migration Rights and Citizenship of the Union

by

Stephen Hall
Australian Government Solicitor,
Attorney-General's Department,
Sydney Office

MARTINUS NIJHOFF PUBLISHERS
DORDRECHT / BOSTON / LONDON

A C.I.P. Catalogue record for this book is available from the Library of Congress.

ISBN 0-7923-3400-0

Published by Martinus Nijhoff Publishers,
P.O. Box 163, 3300 AD Dordrecht, The Netherlands.

Sold and distributed in the U.S.A. and Canada
by Kluwer Academic Publishers,
101 Philip Drive, Norwell, MA 02061, U.S.A.

In all other countries, sold and distributed
by Kluwer Academic Publishers Group,
P.O. Box 322, 3300 AH Dordrecht, The Netherlands.

Printed on acid-free paper

Printed in the Netherlands

To Liang Mun Tong

Ecce ego quia vocasti me

ABBREVIATIONS

CMLR	Common Market Law Reports
CML Rev	Common Market Law Review
CLR	Commonwealth Law Reports
Court of Justice	Court of Justice of the European Communities
DR	Decisions and Reports of the European Commission of Rights
ECHR	(European) Convention on the Protection of Human Rights and Fundamental Freedoms
ECSC	European Coal and Steel Community
ECSC Treaty	Treaty establishing the European Coal and Steel Community
EC	European Community
ECR	European Court Reports (Reports of Cases before the Court of Justice and the Court of First Instance)
EC Treaty	Treaty establishing the European Community
EEC	European Economic Community
EEC Treaty	Treaty establishing the European Economic Community
EHRR	European Human Rights Reports
EL Rev	European Law Review
Euratom	European Atomic Energy Community
Euratom Treaty	Treaty establishing the European Atomic Energy Community

GAOR	General Assembly Official Records
ICCPR	International Covenant on Civil and Political Rights
ICLQ	International and Comparative Law Quarterly
ILO	International Labour Organisation
ILR	International Law Reports
IR	Irish Reports
JO	Journal officiel (des Communautés européennes)
LIEI	Legal Issues in European Integration
LNTS	League of Nations Treaty Series
OJ	Official Journal (of the European Communities)
Rec des	Recueil de la jurisprudence de la Cour de Justice Communautés européennes
RIAA	United Nations Reports of International Arbitral Awards
UKTS	United Kingdom Treaty series
UN	United Nations
Union Treaty	Treaty on European Union
UNTS	United Nations Treaty Series
US	United States Supreme Court Reports
YEL	Yearbook of European Law

CONTENTS

SELECT BIBLIOGRAPHY

Bleckman, Albert, "The Personal Jurisdiction of the European Community", (1980) 17 Common Market Law Review 467.

Boehning, W.R., "The Scope of the EEC System of Free Movement of Workers: a Rejoinder", (1972) 9 Common Market Law Review 81.

Bonner, David, "British citizenship: implications for United Kingdom nationals in the European Communities", (1982) 7 European Law Review 69.

Burrows F., *Free Movement in European Community Law* (1987), Oxford University Press.

Closa, Carlos, "The concept of citizenship in the Treaty on European Union", (1992) 29 Common Market Law Review 1137.

Closa, Carlos, "Citizenship of the Union and Nationality of Member States", in O'Keeffe, David and Twomey, Patrick M (eds); *Legal Issues of the Maastricht Treaty* (1994), Chancery.

Coenen, Harry, and Leisink, Peter, *Work and Citizenship in the New Europe* (1993), Edward Elgar Publishing Company.

Coppel, Jason and O'Neill, Aidan, "The European Court of Justice: Taking Rights Seriously?", (1992) 12 Legal Studies 227, (1992) 29 Common Market Law Review 669.

Donner, Ruth, *The Regulation of Nationality in International Law* (1983), Societa Scientiarum Fennica.

Durand, Andrew, "European Citizenship", (1979) 4 European Law Review 3.

Edens, D.F. and Patijin, S., "The Scope of the EEC System of Free Movement of Workers", (1972) 9 Common Market Law Review 322.

Edwards, Geoffrey, "Europe and the Falkland Islands Crisis 1982", (1983-84) 22 Journal of Common Market Studies 295.

Evans, A.C., "European Citizenship", (1982) 45 Modern Law Review 497.

Evans, A.C., "European Citizenship: A Novel Concept in EEC Law", (1984) 32 American Journal of Comparative Law 679.

Evans, Andrew, "Nationality Law and European Integraton", (1991) 16 European Law Review 190.

Evans, Andrew and Jessurum d'Oliveira, Hans-Ulrich, "Nationality and Citizenship", in Cassese, Antonio, Clapham, Andrew and Weiler, Joseph (eds), *Human Rights and the European Community: Methods of Protection* (1991), Nomos Verlagsgsellschaft.

Green, Nicholas, Hartley, Trevor C. and Usher, John A., *The Legal Foundations of the Single European Market* (1992), Oxford University Press.

Greenwood, Christopher, "Nationality and the Limits of the Free Movement of Persons in Community Law", (1987) 7 Yearbook of European Law 185

Hall, Stephen, "The European Convention on Human Rights and Public Policy Exceptions to the Free Movement of Workers under the EEC Treaty", (1991) 16 European Law Review 466.

Harhoff, Frederik, "Greenland's Withdrawal from the European Communities", (1983) 20 Common Market Law Review 13.

Hartley, T.C., The Foundations of European Community Law, 3rd ed (1994), Oxford University Press.

Heater, Derek, *Citizenship: The Civic Ideal in World History, Politics and Education* (1990), Longman.

Jesurun d'Oliveira, Hans-Ulrich, Note of Case C-369/90 Micheletti v Delegacion del Gobierno en Cantabria, (1993) 30 CML Rev 623.

Kapteyn, P.J.G. and Verloren van Themaat, P., *Introduction to the Law of the European Communities*, 2nd ed (1990), Kluwer Law and Taxation Publishers.

Lenz, Brigitte, "The Public Service in Article 48(4) EEC with Special Reference to the Law in England and in the Federal Republic of Germany", [1989] Legal Issues of European Integration 75.

Lionello Levi-Sandri, M., "Free Movement of Workers in the European Community", Bulletin of the Commission of the European Communities 11-1968 at pp 5-9.

Lord MacKenzie Stuart, "Recent Trends in the Decisions of the European Court: Towards the Creation of a Community Citizenship", [1976] Journal of the Law Society of Scotland 40.

Mancini, Federico, "The Making of a Constitution for Europe", (1989) 26 Common Market Law Review 595.

Massaro, Lorraine, "The Nationality of Married Women and the Principle of Gender Equality in the European Economic Communities: Airola v Commission of the European Communities", (1976) 15 Columbia Journal of Transnational Law 514.

Meehan, Elizabeth, *Citizenship and the European Community* (1993), Sage Publications.

O'Keeffe, David, "Union Citizenship", in O'Keeffe, David and Twomey, Patrick M. (eds); *Legal Issues of the Maastricht Treaty* (1994), Chancery.

O'Leary, Siofra, "Nationality Law and Community Citizenship: A Tale of Two Uneasy Bedfellows", (1992) 12 Yearbook of European Law 353.

Pescatore, Pierre, "The Doctrine of 'Direct Effect': An Infant Disease of Community Law", (1983) 8 European Law Review 155.

Plender, Richard, "An Incipient Form of European Citizenship", in Jacobs, F. (ed), *European Law and the Individual* (1976), North Holland.

Schermers, H.G., "The effect of the date 31 December 1992", (1991) 28 Common Market Law Review 275.

Simmonds, K.R., "The British Nationality Act 1981 and the definition of the term 'national' for Community purposes", (1984) 21 Common Market Law Review 675.

Timmermans, C.W.A., "Free Movement of Persons and the Division of Powers between the Community and its Member States: Why do it the intergovernmental way?", in Schermers, Henry G., Flinterman, Cees,Kellermann, Alfred E., van Haersolte, Johan C. and van de Meent, Gert-Wim A. (eds), *Free Movement of Persons in Europe: Legal Problems and Experiences* (1993), Martinus Nijhoff.

Toth, A.G., "The legal status of the declarations annexed to the Single European Act", (1986) 23 Common Market Law Review 803.

Van Den Berghe, Guido, *Political Rights for European Citizens* (1982), Gower.

van Panhuys, Haro Frederik, *The Role of Nationality in International Law* (1959), A.W. Sijthoff's Uitgevesmaatschappij.

Weatherill, Stephen and Beaumont, Paul, *EC Law* (1993), Penguin.

Weis, P., *Nationality and Statelessness in International Law*, 2nd ed (1979), Sijthoff & Noordhoff.

Weis, Paul, "The United Nations Convention on the Reduction of Statelessness", (1962) 11 International and Comparative Law Quarterly 1073.

Weiss, Friedl, "Greenland's Withdrawal from the European Communities", (1985) 10 European Law Review 173.

Wyatt, Derrick and Dashwood, Alan, *European Community Law*, 3rd ed (1993), Sweet and Maxwell.

PREFACE

This book is the result mainly of two years of research at the University of Oxford between 1991-1992 and 1993-1994.

Of the many persons to whom I owe a debt of gratitude in writing this book, first acknowledgement must undoubtedly go to Professor Bernard Rudden (Brasenose College, Oxford) who provided invaluable encouragement and guidance during my period of research at the University of Oxford. Thanks are also due to Mr Derrick Wyatt QC (St Edmund Hall, Oxford) who provided some useful insights during the very early stages of my work. Responsibility for any errors and inaccuracies is, however, mine alone.

It is less likely that I would ever have gone to Oxford in the first place without the support of Mr Richard Tur (Benn Law Fellow at Oriel College, Oxford) whom I first met on a visit to Oxford in 1989. An important role in impelling me towards Oxford by the provision of encouragement and good advice was played by Professor George Winterton (Faculty of Law, University of New South Wales). My keen interest in European Community law, perhaps unusual for an Australian, was kindled by Professor Gabriël Moens (Faculty of Law, University of Queensland).

The pleasure of living and working in the world's most beautiful and evocative university town was immensely augmented by the companionship of many friends in Oriel College, in the law school, and from other parts of the University.

I should also acknowledge the financial support provided by the Australian Attorney-General's Department whose Post-Graduate Study Award financed part of my research. Part of the period not covered by this award was financed by the Commonwealth Scholarship and Fellowship Plan under which I was awarded a Commonwealth Scholarship and by the United Kingdom's Committee of Vice-Chancellors and Principals who provided me with an Overseas Research Student's Award. To all these benefactors I am greatly indebted. I hope that this book is not too much of a disappointment to them.

I wish also to express my thanks to Mr Jim Lonergan who kindly proof-read the entire typescript and made a number of useful observations.

The text of this book was completed in November 1994.

Sydney, November 1994. Stephen Hall

CASES BEFORE THE COURT OF JUSTICE

175/78	*R v Saunders*	[1979] ECR 1129	79, 162
240/78	*Atalanta Amsterdam BV v Produktschap voor Vee en Vlees*	[1979] ECR 2137	64
251/78	*Firma Denkavit Futtermittel GmbH v Minister für Ernährung, Landwirtschaft und Forsten des Landes Nordrhein-Westfalen*	[1979] ECR 3369	138, 139
257/78	*Devred v Commission*	[1979] ECR 3767	51-54, 56, 77, 79
4/79	*Société Coopérative "Providence Agricole de la Champagne" v Office National Interprofessionel des Céréales (ONIC)*	[1980] ECR 2823	127, 128
9/79	*Wörsdorfer v Raad van Arbeid*	[1979] ECR 2717	196-197
32/79	*Commission v United Kingdom ("Re British Sea Fisheries")*	[1980] ECR 2403	64, 65, 66, 68, 70
34/79	*R v Henn and Darby*	[1979] ECR 3795	139
44/79	*Hauer v Land Rheinland-Pfalz*	[1979] ECR 3727	137
136/79	*National Panasonic (UK) Ltd v Commission*	[1980] ECR 2033	137
138/79	*SA Roquette Frères v Council*	[1980] ECR 3333	4, 101
139/79	*Maizena GmbH v Council*	[1980] ECR 3393	4, 101
149/79	*Commission v Belgium ("Re Belgian Public Service")*	[1980] ECR 3881, [1982] ECR 1845	37-38, 40
157/79	*R v Pieck*	[1980] ECR 2171	141, 179
1322/79	*Vutera v Commission*	[1981] ECR 127	54-55
22/80	*Boussac Saint-Frères SA v Gerstenmeier*	[1980] ECR 3427	168, 169
124/80	*Officier van Justitie v J van Dam & Zonen*	[1981] ECR 1447	71
150/80	*Elefanten Schuh GmbH v Jacqmain*	[1981] ECR 1671	192, 198
203/80	*Casati*	[1981] ECR 2595	190
270/80	*Polydor Limited v Harlequin Record Shops Limited*	[1982] ECR 329	160
272/80	*Frans-Nederlandse Maatschappij voor Biologische Producten BV*	[1981] ECR 3277	65
279/80	*Webb*	[1981] ECR 3305	174
15/81	*Gaston Schul Douane Expediteur BV v Inspecteur der Invoerrechten en Accijnzen, Roosendaal*	[1982] ECR 1409	30, 202
44/81	*Germany and Bundesanstalt für Arbeit v Commission*	[1982] ECR 1855	127
53/81	*Levin v Staatssecretaris van Justitie*	[1982] ECR 1035	33, 65, 160-161
95/81	*Commission v Italy ("Re Advance Payments for Imports")*	[1982] ECR 2187	71, 140, 180
115 and 116/81	*Adoui and Cornuaille v Belgian State*	[1982] ECR 1665	136, 140
124/81	*Commission v United Kingdom ("Re UHT Milk")*	[1983] ECR 203	139
230/81	*Luxembourg v European Parliament*	[1983] ECR 255	129-130
249/81	*Commission v Ireland ("Re 'Buy Irish' Campaign")*	[1982] ECR 4005	73, 130
283/81	*Srl CILFIT v Ministry of Health*	[1982] ECR 3415	192, 197
287/81	*Anklagemyndigheden v Kerr*	[1982] ECR 4053	167-168, 169
314-316/81 and 83/82	*Procureur de la République v Waterkeyn*	[1982] ECR 4337	69
13-28/82	*Arantzamendi-Osa v Procureur de la République*	[1982] ECR 3927	86
35 and 36/82	*Morson and Jhanjan v State of the Netherlands*	[1982] ECR 3723	159, 162
42/82	*Commission v France ("Re Italian Wine Imports")*	[1983] ECR 1013	65, 68-69, 71, 139

50-58/82	*Administrateur des Affaires Maritimes, Bayonne v Dorca Marina*	[1982] ECR 3949	91, 137, 162
152/82	*Forcheri v Belgian State*	[1983] ECR 2323	162, 163
238/82	*Duphar BV v Netherlands State*	[1984] ECR 523	140, 180
286/82 and 26/83	*Luisi and Carbone v Ministero del Tesoro*	[1984] ECR 377	11, 135
16/83	*Prantl*	[1984] ECR 1299	136
63/83	*R v Kirk*	[1984] ECR 2689	92, 93, 137, 166
72/83	*Campus Oil Limited v Minister for Industry and Energy*	[1984] ECR 2727	138, 140, 153-154, 156 180
108/83	*Luxembourg v European Parliament*	[1984] ECR 1945	129
112/83	*Société des Produits de Maïs SA v Administration des douanes et droits indirects*	[1985] ECR 719	127
180/83	*Moser v Land Baden-Württemberg*	[1984] ECR 2539	89, 162
188/83	*Witte v European Parliament*	[1984] ECR 3465	55
220/83	*Commission v France*	[1986] ECR 3663	174
229/83	*Association des Centres distributeurs Édouard Leclerc v Sàrl 'Au blé vert'*	[1985] ECR 1	65
231/83	*Cullet v Centre Leclerc Toulouse*	[1985] ECR 305	154
238/83	*Caisse d'Allocations Familiales de la Région Parisienne v Meade*	[1984] ECR 2631	162
246/83	*De Angelis v Commission*	[1985] ECR 1253	55
252/83	*Commission v Denmark*	[1986] ECR 3713	174
288/83	*Commission v Ireland ("Re Potato Imports")*	[1985] ECR 1761	140, 180
294/83	*Parti écologiste 'Les Verts' v European Parliament*	[1986] ECR 1339	22, 103, 129
41/84	*Pinna v Caisse d'allocations familiales de la Savoie*	[1986] ECR 1	127
44/84	*Hurd v Jones (Her Majesty's Inspector of Taxes)*	[1986] ECR 29	162
60, 61/84	*Cinéthèque SA v Fédération nationale des cinémas français*	[1985] ECR 2605	92, 93, 96, 137
131/84	*Commission v Italy ("Re Failure to Implement Judgment")*	[1985] ECR 3531	69
137/84	*Ministère public v Mutsch*	[1985] ECR 2681	152
205/84	*Commission v Germany ("Re Insurance Services")*	[1986] ECR 3755	33-34, 174
206/84	*Commission v Ireland*	[1986] ECR 3817	174
222/84	*Johnston v Chief Constable of the Royal Ulster Constabulary*	[1986] ECR 1651	81, 137, 142-149, 150, 151, 155, 156, 157, 177
298/84	*Iorio v Azienda autonoma delle ferrovie dello Stato*	[1986] ECR 247	162
61/85	*Urhausen v Commission*	[1987] ECR 2853	55
66/85	*Lawrie-Blum v Land Baden-Württemberg*	[1986] ECR 2121	33
121/85	*Conegate Limited v HM Customs and Excise*	[1986] ECR 1007	139
139/85	*Kempf v Staatssecretaris van Justitie*	[1986] ECR 1746	33
186/85	*Commission v Belgium ("Re Belgian Family Allowances")*	[1987] ECR 2029	68, 71
225/85	*Commission v Italy ("Re Employees of the Consiglio Nazionale delle Ricerche")*	[1987] ECR 2625	38
261/85	*Commission v United Kingdom ("Re Import Ban on Pasteurised Milk and Cream")*	[1988] ECR 547	139

281, 283, 285 and 287/85	*Germany, France, Netherlands, Denmark and United Kingdom v Commission ("Re Immigration Policy")*	[1987] ECR 3203	129, 133, 137
311/85	*VZW Vereniging van Vlaamse Reisbureaus v VZW Sociale Dienst van de Plaatselijke en Gewestelijke Overheidsdiensten*	[1987] ECR 3801	70
316/85	*Centre public d'aide sociale de Courcelles v Lebon*	[1987] ECR 2811	197, 207
330/85	*Richter v Commission*	[1986] ECR 3439	55
12/86	*Demirel v Stadt Schwäbisch Gmünd*	[1987] ECR 3719	9, 93, 95, 137
34/86	*Council v European Parliament*	[1986] ECR 2155	127
45/86	*Commission v Council ("Re Generalised Tariff Preferences")*	[1987] ECR 1493	123, 164
63/86	*Commission v Italy ("Re Access to Social Housing")*	[1988] ECR 29	179
197/86	*Brown v Secretary of State for Scotland*	[1988] ECR 3205	54
222/86	*Union nationale des entraîneurs et Cadres techniques professionnels du football (Unectef) v Heylens*	[1987] ECR 4097	137
229/86	*Brother Industries Limited v Commission*	[1987] ECR 3757	70
292/86	*Gullung v Conseils de l'ordre des avocats du barreau de Colmar et de Saverne*	[1988] ECR 111	171
300/86	*Van Landschoot v Mera NV*	[1988] ECR 3443	89
313/86	*Lenoir v Caisse d'allocations familiales des Alpes-Maritimes*	[1988] ECR 5391	168-169, 171
318/86	*Commission v France ("Re French Prison and Police Services")*	[1988] ECR 3559	148-149
105/87	*Morabito v European Parliament*	[1988] ECR 1707	55
196/87	*Steymann v Staatssecretaris van Justitie*	[1988] ECR 6159	116
211/87	*Nuñez v Commission*	[1988] ECR 2791	55
305/87	*Commission v Greece ("Re Immovable Property")*	[1989] ECR 1461	179
374/87	*Orkem v Commission*	[1989] ECR 3283	85
C-379/87	*Groener v Minister for Education*	[1989] ECR 3967	173
C-2/88 Imm	*Zwartveld*	[1990] ECR I-3365	22, 64, 103, 130
5/88	*Wachauf v Federal Republic of Germany*	[1989] ECR 2609	93-94, 95
C-35/88	*Commission v Greece ("Re Market in Feed Grain")*	[1990] ECR I-3125	64
C-70/88	*European Parliament v Council ("Chernobyl")*	[1990] ECR I-2041	123, 129, 164
201/88	*Palmerini v Commission*	[1989] ECR 3109	55
C-213/88, C-39/89	*Luxembourg v European Parliament*	[1991] ECR I-5643	129
C-217/88	*Commission v Germany ("Re Coercive Measures in Wine Market")*	[1990] ECR I-2879	64-65
C-262/88	*Barber v Guardian Royal Exchange Assurance Group*	[1990] ECR I-1889	88
C-265/88	*Messner*	[1989] ECR 4209	173, 179, 206-207
C-297/88, C-197/89	*Dzodzi v Belgian State*	[1990] ECR I-3763	85
C-23/89	*Quietlynn Ltd v Southend Borough Council*	[1990] ECR I-3059	139
C-68/89	*Commission v Netherlands ("Re Dutch Border Controls")*	[1991] ECR I-2637	131
C-100, C-101/89	*Kaefer and Procacci v French State*	[1990] ECR I-4647	26, 27
C-105/89	*Buhari v Institut national d'assurances sociales pour travailleurs indépendants*	[1990] ECR I-4211	162

C-106/89	*Marleasing SA v La Comercial Internacional de Alimentación SA*	[1990] ECR I-4135	64
C-154/89	*Commission v France ("French Tourist Guides")*	[1991] ECR I-659	174
C-158/89	*Dietz-Matti v Federal Republic of Germany*	[1990] ECR I-2013	65
C-180/89	*Commission v Italy ("Italian Tourist Guides")*	[1991] ECR I-709	174
C-192/89	*Sevince v Staatssecretaris van Justitie*	[1990] ECR I-3461	100
C-198/89	*Commission v Greece ("Greek Tourist Guides")*	[1991] ECR I-727	174
C-260/89	*Elliniki Radiophonia Tileorassi AE v Dimotiki Etairia Pliroforissis ("ERT")*	[1991] ECR I-2925	87, 94-95, 97, 131-132, 137, 198, 200
C-264/89	*Commission v United Kingdom ("Re Nationality of Fishermen")*	[1991] ECR I-4615	19
C-280/89	*Commission v Ireland ("Re British Fishing Boats")*	[1993] 1 CMLR 273	19
C-300/89	*Commission v Council ("Re Titanium Dioxide")*	[1991] ECR I-2867	4, 101
C-339/89	*Alsthom Atlantique SA v Compagnie de construction mécanique Sulzer SA*	[1991] ECR I-107	200
C-357/89	*Raulin v Minister van Onderwijs en Wetenschappen*	[1992] ECR I-1027	114, 119, 165
C-367/89	*Richardt*	[1991] ECR I-4621	154-155, 156
C-376/89	*Giagounidis v Stadt Reutlingen*	[1991] ECR I-1069	82
C-6 and C-9/90	*Francovich v Italian Republic*	[1991] ECR I-5357	130
C-38 and C-151/90	*R v Lomas*	[1992] ECR I-1781	127
C-41/90	*Höfner and Elser v Macrotron GmbH*	[1991] ECR I-1979	162
C-159/90	*Society for the Protection of Unborn Children Ireland Ltd v Grogan*	[1991] ECR I-4685	95, 134-136, 137
C-204/90	*Bachmann v Belgian State*	[1992] ECR I-249	171-172
C-286/90	*Anklagemyndigheden v Poulsen*	[1992] ECR I-6019	16, 19
C-295/90	*European Parliament v Council ("Re Students' Rights")*	[1992] 3 CMLR 281	9, 119, 122, 123, 124, 127, 164-167, 169, 173, 178, 181
C-332/90	*Steen v Deutsche Bundespost*	[1992] ECR I-341	162
C-369/90	*Micheletti v Delegación del Gobierno en Cantabria*	CJ CE 7 July 1992, Rec p I-4329	17, 57-60, 63, 66, 67, 81, 97, 98, 113
C-370/90	*R v Immigration Appeal Tribunal and Surinder Singh ex parte Secretary of State for the Home Department*	[1992] 3 CMLR 358	66, 78, 162
Opinion 1/91	*Re Draft EEA Treaty*	[1991] ECR I-6079	21-22, 103
C-153/91	*Petit v Office National des Pensions*	[1993] 1 CMLR 476	162
C-275/92	*Her Majesty's Customs and Excise v Schindler*	[1994] ECR I-1039	136
C-419/92	*Scholz v Opera Universitaria di Cagliari*	[1994] ECR I-505	54

CASES BEFORE THE COURT OF FIRST INSTANCE

T-113/89	*Nederlandse Associatie van de Farmaceutische Industrie 'Nefarma' v Commission*	[1990] ECR II-797	70
T-114/89	*Vereniging van Nederlandse Ziekenfondsen v Commission*	[1990] ECR II-827	70
T-116/89	*Vereniging Prodifarma v Commission*	[1990] ECR II-843	70
T-123/89	*Chomel v Commission*	[1990] ECR II-131	55

CASES BEFORE INTERNATIONAL COURTS AND TRIBUNALS

Flegenheimer Claim	Italian-United States Conciliation Commission	(1958) 25 ILR 91	18-19, 82
Flutie Cases	American-Venezuelan Commission	[1903] RIAA ix 148	82
Liechtenstein v Guatemala ("*Nottebohm*")	International Court of Justice	[1955] ICJR 4	17, 18, 19, 61-63, 66, 67, 74, 77-78, 81
National Union of Belgian Police Case	European Court of Human Rights	[1975] Series A, No 19	88
Nationality Decrees in Tunis and Morocco Case	Permanent Court of International Justice	[1923] PCIJ, Series B, No 4	17, 19-20, 61, 98
Open Door Counselling Ltd v Ireland	European Court of Human Rights	(1992) 14 EHRR 131	136-137
Paramanathan v Germany (Application 12068/86)	European Commission of Human Rights	(1986) 51 DR 237	100
X, Y and Z v United Kingdom (Application 9285/81)	European Commission of Human Rights	(1982) 29 DR 205	100

CASES BEFORE NATIONAL COURTS

Attorney-General v X	Irish High Court	[1992] 2 CMLR 277	134
Brunner v European Union Treaty	*Bundesverfassungsgericht* (German Federal Constitutional Court)	[1994] 1 CMLR 57	200
Crandall v Nevada	Supreme Court of the United States	6 Wall 35 (1868)	12-13
Edwards v California	Supreme Court of the United States	314 US 160 (1941)	13
Procureur du Roi a Bruges v De Quant	Belgian *Cour de Cassation*	[1981] 3 CMLR 609	31
R v Smithers ex parte Benson	High Court of Australia	(1912) 16 CLR 99	12
Society for the Protection of Unborn Children (SPUC) Ireland Ltd v Grogan	Irish High Court	[1993] 1 CMLR 197	134

CHAPTER 1

INTRODUCTION

Citizenship and the Union Treaty

Citizenship

> We Europeans are the children of Hellas. Our civilization, which has its roots in the brilliant city life of the eastern Aegean, has never lost traces of its origin, and stamps us with a character by which we are distinguished from the other great civilizations of the human family.[1]

These words, penned by H.A.L. Fisher sixty years ago, remind us that amidst the incredibly rich social, political and cultural diversity of the European continent there exist unifying themes. They are themes whose strains are all too easily forgotten amidst the frequently discordant, and often extremely violent, European clamour which fills the more than two and a half millennia separating Homer's age from our own.

The concerns of our distant cultural ancestors have been interpreted, reinterpreted, refined, defined, redefined and transmitted from one age to the next with greater or lesser degrees of consciousness and clarity. The great themes of Europe have in many ways also become the great themes of the modern world. This is most outstandingly so in the spheres of the natural sciences, philosophy, architecture, music, politics and law.

In the related fields of politics and law the Hellenic theme is particularly strong. Liberal democracy and the rule of law are the remote, though clearly identifiable, descendants of ideals which first flourished in the classical world. Nurtured, changing and sometimes hibernating in Europe, they have been transmitted to the rest of the world by settlement, conquest or example. Though born, nurtured and raised in Europe, they satisfy universal human needs.

Central to the liberal and democratic ideal is the concept of citizenship. Indeed, the birth of citizenship accompanies the birth in the city-states of ancient Greece of the earliest forms of democracy and ideas of freedom.

A single all-purpose definition of 'citizen' is not available. Even Aristotle quailed at formulating such a definition:

---

[1]H.A.L. Fisher, "*A History of Europe*" (1935), at p 13.

> Who is a citizen? and, Whom shall we call one? Here ... there is no unanimity, no agreement as to what constitutes a citizen.[1]

Such hesitation is at least equally justified in the modern world. There are countless legal definitions of 'citizen' and it is impossible to extract any useful generalisations from them. Yet the kernel of citizenship as a concept is reasonably clear. Although it is well beyond the scope of this book to embark on a comprehensive exegesis of citizenship in European thought we can with some justified hope of illumination return briefly to our Hellenic roots.

From its origin, the concept of citizenship was intimately linked with the performance of political powers and obligations. Plato wrote that "what we have in mind is education from childhood in *virtue*, a training which produces a keen desire to become a perfect citizen who knows how to rule and be ruled as justice demands".[2] Aristotle similarly commented that "[w]hat effectively distinguishes the citizen proper from all others is his participation in giving judgement and in holding office".[3] That this view of citizenship's essence was not confined to the Academy and the Lyceum is confirmed by Thucydides who reports Pericles, delivering a funeral oration for the Athenian dead in the Peloponnesian war, as saying:

> Here each individual is interested not only in his own affairs but in the affairs of state as well: even those who are mostly occupied with their own business are extremely well-informed on general politics - this is a peculiarity of ours: we do not say that a man who takes no interest in politics is a man who minds his own business; we say he has no business here at all.[4]

These formulations conceive of citizenship as involving not only a right to participate in the affairs of the community, but also a duty to do so. This conception of citizenship is a republican ideal which has enjoyed support by theorists such as Machiavelli and Rousseau. A modern manifestation of this ideal is the citizen's legal duty, and not merely his right, to vote in elections in such countries as Australia, Belgium, Chile, Ecuador, Greece and Israel. It can also be seen as one of several possible justifications for compulsory military service.

Europe's Christian heritage also provides a firm foundation for the citizenship ideal: "Man is rational and therefore like God; he is created with free will and is master of his own acts".[5] With its emphasis on the individual's fundamental physical, moral and spiritual dignity, and his freedom and responsibility to shape his own life according to God's will, Christianity proclaimed each individual person as a being with natural rights and responsibilities. An emperor and a slave are, in the eyes of God, of equal

[1] Aristotle, "*The Politics*", translated by T.A. Sinclair, Penguin, (1982) at p 168.
[2] Plato, "*Laws*", translated by T.J. Saunders, Penguin, (1970) at p 73.
[3] Aristotle, "*The Politics*", translated by T.A. Sinclair, Penguin, (1982) at p 169.
[4] Thucydides, "*The Peloponnesian War*", translated by R. Warner, Penguin, (1954) at pp 118-119.
[5] St Irenaeus, "*Adversus haereses*", 4, 4, 3.

intrinsic value. The emperor is, if anything, in the more difficult position, for his temporal power is accompanied by a heavy responsibility to recognise and promote the divine dignity of all his subjects. Christianity was vital in transposing the classical republican idea of political man, in a more richly textured form, to the mediaeval world. In so doing it inspired a civil order characterised, in spite of all its many faults, by a complex network of interlocking personal rights and attendant responsibilities informed by the supernatural equality of all believers.

There is also a competing liberal conception of citizenship, of more recent but related origin, which shifts the emphasis from the performance of duties to the enjoyment of rights. This view is exemplified by writers such as John Locke and John Stuart Mill. This competing conception is now the dominant one in contemporary liberal democratic theory and practice. The citizen is possessed of certain inalienable rights. Principal among these are the right to vote and seek election to public office, freely to impart and receive information and views about public affairs, and to enter and reside in the territory of the entity whose citizenship he possesses. His duties *qua* citizen are negligible and are effectively confined to refraining from treasonable acts. (Treason is generally the only crime which non-citizens are incapable of committing). Other duties such as the obligation to obey the law and to pay taxes are imposed on all people coming within the territorial jurisdiction and are not really citizenship duties as such.

But whether one favours the classical republican or the more modern liberal conceptions of citizenship, the core components of citizenship are essentially the same - participation in public affairs and the life of the political community (as either a right or duty) together with ancillary rights such as freedom of expression and association, and the right to enter, reside and move in the territory occupied by the political community. The essence of citizenship has been succinctly and usefully defined as "the constitutional arrangements made for participation by a defined category of individuals in the life of a state".[1]

The Member States of the European Community took up this important theme of European civilization, and in the *Treaty on European Union* ("*Union Treaty*") established a common *de jure* citizenship embracing not only the free inhabitants of Athens, but every national of each of the Member States - some 350 million people.

The first moves in this direction were initiated by the Court of Justice as long ago as 1963 when it decided that the nationals of Member States possessed not only obligations under Community law, but also rights which they could enforce at their own suit before national courts - even against their own Member States.[2] The Court has also elaborated a system of constitutional general principles which must be observed within the Community legal order. Among these is the "fundamental

[1]Andrew Evans, "*Nationality Law and European Integration*", (1992) 16 EL Rev 190 at pp 198-199.

[2]Case 26/62 *NV Algemene Transport- en Expeditie Onderneming van Gend & Loos v Nederlandse administratie der belastingen* [1963] ECR 1.

democratic principle that the peoples should take part in the exercise of power through the intermediary of a representative assembly",[1] ie the European Parliament.

These developments initiated by the Court of Justice were taken up by the Community's political institutions and the Member States. Although it is beyond the scope of this book to trace the development of citizenship within the European Community,[2] it is here worth noting that in 1977 the European Parliament, the Council and the Commission adopted a *Joint Declaration on Fundamental Rights*[3] pledging themselves to respect fundamental rights in the exercise of their powers.

The following year saw the adoption by the European Council meeting in Copenhagen of a *Declaration on Democracy*[4] in which the Member States associated themselves with the *Joint Declaration on Fundamental Rights* and in which they promised to safeguard the principles of representative democracy and the rule of law. "The application of these principles", the European Council said, "implies a political system of pluralist democracy which guarantees both the free expression of opinions within the constitutional organization of powers and the procedures necessary for the protection of human rights".

Neither of these political declarations created any legal effects within the Community legal order. It could not therefore be said that respect for the core components of citizenship was a legal condition for membership of the Community.[5] This situation has since changed.

The European Council meeting in Stuttgart in 1983 expressly reaffirmed its Copenhagen commitments in the *Solemn Declaration on European Union.*[6] This was followed in 1987 by the entry into force of the *Single European Act* which records[7] that the Member States were moved to transform their relations into a European Union in accordance with the *Solemn Declaration on European Union.* Thus the commitments made in the 1978 Copenhagen *Joint Declaration on Fundamental Rights* achieved the status of constitutional legal principles by incorporation into the *Single European Act* through the 1983 Stuttgart *Solemn Declaration on European Union.*

---

[1]Case 138/79 *SA Roquette Frères v Council* [1980] ECR 3333 at p 3360, paragraph 33 of the Court's judgment; Case 139/79 *Maizena GmbH v Council* [1980] ECR 3393 at p 3424, paragraph 34 of the Court's judgment; Case C-300/89 *Commission v Council* ("*Re Titanium Dioxide*") [1991] ECR I-2867 at p I-2900, paragraph 20 of the Court's judgment.

[2]For a brief survey of this development see David O'Keeffe, "*Union Citizenship*", in David O'Keeffe and Patrick M Twomey (eds), "*Legal Issues of the Maastricht Treaty*" (1994), p 87 at pp 87-89. See also Carlos Closa, "*The concept of citizenship in the Treaty on European Union*", (1992) 29 CML Rev 1137.

[3]OJ C103/27 of 27 April 1977.

[4]Bull EC 3-1978 p 5.

[5]Case 93/78 *Mattheus v Doego Fruchtimport und Tiefkühlkost eG* [1978] ECR 2203.

[6]Bull EC 6-1983 p 24, Article 1.2.

[7]First recital.

The consequence is that among the constitutional, and not merely political, conditions for membership of the Community is that a State must maintain the rule of law and a political system of pluralist democracy which guarantees both the free expression of opinions within the constitutional organisation of powers and the procedures necessary for the protection of human rights.[1] In other words, if a State wishes to join or to remain in the European Union, it must respect the core components of citizenship.

The Union Treaty

On 7 February 1992 in the Dutch town of Maastricht the twelve Member States of the European Community signed the *Union Treaty*, which was expressed to come into force, subject to ratification by all Member States in accordance with their own constitutional requirements, on 1 January 1993 at the earliest or on the first day of the month following the deposit of the instrument of ratification of the last Member State to ratify.[2] The ratification processes in several of the countries, notably Denmark, Germany and the United Kingdom, took longer than expected and it did not enter into force until 1 November 1993.

Article A of the *Union Treaty* established a "European Union" among the Twelve and declares that "[t]his Treaty marks a new stage in the process of creating an ever closer union among the peoples of Europe, in which decisions are taken as closely as possible to the citizen".

The Union is expressed to be founded on the European Communities and supplemented by the policies and forms of cooperation established by the *Union Treaty*. These policies and forms of cooperation established by the *Union Treaty*, and which are outside the structure of the European Communities, are contained in Title V[3] (Provisions on a Common Foreign and Security Policy) and Title VI[4] (Provisions on Cooperation in the Fields of Justice and Home Affairs). Titles V and VI of the *Union Treaty* provide mechanisms for intergovernmental cooperation among the Member States of the Union in the fields covered by their provisions. The European Union is thus founded on three pillars; (i) the European Communities, (ii) intergovernmental cooperation in the field of foreign and security policy, and (iii) intergovernmental cooperation in the field of justice and home affairs.

Among the objectives of the European Union are the "creation of an area without internal frontiers" as a means to balanced and sustainable economic and social

[1] Article F(1) of the *Treaty on European Union* provides that the Member States' systems of government "are founded on the principles of democracy". Having regard to Article M of the same Treaty, however, Article F(1) probably does not establish a criterion for Union membership which is enforceable by the Court of Justice.

[2] Article R of the *Union Treaty*.

[3] Articles J - J.11.

[4] Articles K - K.9.

progress, and the stronger "protection of the rights and interests of the nationals of its Member States through the introduction of a citizenship of the Union".[1]

The European Union is charged to respect the *acquis communautaire*.[2]

The *Union Treaty* changed the name of the *Treaty establishing the European Economic Community* ("*EEC Treaty*") to the *Treaty establishing the European Community* ("*EC Treaty*") and a new Part Two[3] entitled "Citizenship of the Union" was inserted.

Article 8(1) of the *EC Treaty* formally establishes citizenship of the Union and provides that "[e]very person holding the nationality of a Member State shall be a citizen of the Union". Union citizens are to enjoy the rights conferred and be subject to the duties imposed by the *EC Treaty*.[4]

Neither the *Union Treaty* nor the *EC Treaty*, nor any of the protocols attached to either Treaty, defines what is meant by "nationality of a Member State", although a *Declaration on Nationality of a Member State* adopted by the Intergovernmental Conferences on Political Union and on Economic and Monetary Union[5] states that wherever in the *EC Treaty*;

> ... reference is made to nationals of the Member States, the question whether an individual possesses the nationality of a Member State shall be settled solely by reference to the national law of the Member State concerned. Member States may declare, for information, who are to be considered their nationals for Community purposes by way of a declaration ... and may amend any such declaration when necessary.

The principal citizenship provisions in Part Two of the *EC Treaty* grant three types of rights; Articles 8b and 8d grant political rights; freedom of movement and residence is granted by Article 8a; certain rights to diplomatic and consular protection are dealt with by Article 8c.

Under Article 8b(1), every Union citizen living in a Member State of which he is not a national shall have the right to vote in and stand for elections at the municipal level under the same conditions applying to nationals of that Member State. The same Union citizens, pursuant to Article 8b(2), are to enjoy a similar right in respect of elections to the European Parliament. Both rights are to be exercised subject to detailed arrangements to be adopted unanimously by the Council on a proposal from

---

[1] Article B of the *Union Treaty*, first and third points.

[2] Article B (fifth point) and Article C (first paragraph) of the *Union Treaty*.

[3] Consisting of new Articles 8, 8a, 8b, 8c, 8d and 8e.

[4] Article 8(2) of the *EC Treaty*.

[5] Both conferences were convened on 15 December 1990 to adopt amendments to the *EEC Treaty*: see Article 1 of the Final Act of the conference.

the Commission after consulting the European Parliament.[1] In each case, the detailed arrangements may provide for derogations where warranted by problems specific to Member States.[2]

Article 8c of the *EC Treaty* entitles Union citizens, while in the territory of a third country where his own Member State lacks consular or diplomatic representation, to receive consular and diplomatic protection by the authorities of other Member States on the same conditions as nationals of those other Member States. The necessary rules for the implementation of this entitlement are to be established by and among the Member States before 31 December 1993. By the same date, the Member States (not the Commission) are to have started international negotiations with third countries to secure the protection of this provision.

Article 8d (first paragraph) of the *EC Treaty* guarantees every citizen of the Union the right to petition the European Parliament in accordance with Article 138d which in turn confers a right of parliamentary petition on every Union citizen and on every natural or legal person residing or having its registered office in a Member State. The second paragraph of Article 8d provides that every citizen of the Union may apply to the Ombudsman established in accordance with Article 138e. The Ombudsman is, by Article 138e, appointed by the European Parliament and is empowered to receive complaints from the same categories of persons as are entitled to petition the Parliament.

Article 8e of the *EC Treaty* obliges the Commission to make regular reports on the application of the provisions of Part Two and authorises the adoption of "provisions to strengthen or to add to the rights laid down" in Part Two.

The Union citizen's right of free movement and residence is contained in Article 8a of the *EC Treaty* which provides as follows:

> 1. Every citizen of the Union shall have the right to move and reside freely within the territory of the Member States, subject to the limitations and conditions laid down in this Treaty and by the measures adopted to give it effect.
>
> 2. The Council may adopt provisions with a view to facilitating the exercise of the rights referred to in paragraph 1; save as otherwise provided in this Treaty, the Council shall act unanimously on a

[1]In the case of municipal elections, the arrangements are to be completed by 31 December 1994: See Commission Proposal for a Council Directive COM(94) 38 final The equivalent arrangements for elections to the European Parliament were to be completed by 31 December 1993 and are contained in *Directive 93/109*.

[2]Certain derogations are permitted to Member States whose proportion of Union Citizens from other Member States exceeds 20% of the total number of Union Citizens resident and of voting age in that Member State; Article 12 of COM(94) 38 final and Article 14 of *Directive 93/109*. Only Luxembourg, 29% of whose population are nationals of another Member State, will be able to benefit from these derogations.

> proposal from the Commission and after obtaining the assent of the European Parliament.

The basic purpose of this book is to determine the impact upon Community law of Part Two of the *EC Treaty*, and especially Articles 8 and 8a.

On the whole, the *Union Treaty* embraces the liberal rights-based conception of citizenship. The rights of Union citizens are spelled out but citizens' duties, although a passing reference is made to them,[1] are nowhere specified as such in the treaties.

Impact of Union Citizenship

The entry into force on 1 November 1993 of the *Union Treaty* has not, however, significantly affected the material or personal scope of Community migration rights.

In purely practical terms, and notwithstanding the direct effect of Article 8a of the *EC Treaty*, nationals of Member States enjoyed no greater migration rights on 1 November 1993 than they enjoyed the previous day. In particular, the three EEC non-economic movement and residence directives (*Directives 90/364, 90/365* and *90/366*) are fully applicable to all the persons to which Article 8a is applicable, so that the limitations and conditions contained in those directives are effective to restrict the enjoyment of Article 8a migration rights. While this remains the case (as it will at least until the three directives are repealed or annulled or until Article 8a is modified) Member States may rely on the three directives to derogate from Article 8a migration rights on grounds of public policy, public security, public health and requirements as to financial self-sufficiency and health insurance.

Even without the three directives, the Member States would remain free to derogate from Article 8a migration rights on these same grounds to the extent that any such derogations can be objectively justified; ie to the extent that they are not a disguised form of nationality discrimination, that they are proportionate to their objective, that they serve a legitimate public interest, and that they are subject to judicial supervision. In making any such derogation Member States would need to observe the requirements of Articles 2(3) and 3 of *Directive 64/221* as manifestations of general principles of Community law[2] (although the appearance of one of the exceptional circumstances envisaged by Article 224 of the *EC Treaty* could in certain circumstances justify measures taken in disregard of some of these general principles).[3]

Nor has the entry into force of the *Union Treaty* in practical terms affected the range of persons entitled to benefit from Community movement rights. Those who were

---

[1] Article 8(2) of the *EC Treaty* inserted by Article G(9) of the *Union Treaty*.

[2] See Case 36/75 *Rutili v Minister for the Interior* [1975] ECR 1219 at p 1232, paragraph 32 of the Court's judgment and Chapter 4.

[3] See Chapter 4.

entitled to benefit from migration rights under Articles 48 (workers) and 52 (establishers) of the *EEC Treaty* and to movement rights under Article 59 (service providers/consumers) remain so entitled under the same provisions in the *EC Treaty*. They are now also entitled to enjoy those same rights as Union citizens, but no-one who was not entitled to benefit from economic migration rights under the *EEC Treaty* became so entitled because of the *Union Treaty*. Similarly, the *Union Treaty* did not extend non-economic migration rights to any person not already covered by *Directives 90/364*, *90/365* and *90/366*.

Furthermore, Article 8a does not of its own force extend migration rights to the families of Union citizens where such family members are not themselves Union citizens. Although the ability of a Community migrant to be accompanied by his family is an essential element of his freedom of movement,[1] no such right exists until a special provision on the matter has been adopted.[2] Such special provisions exist in *Directives 90/364*, *90/365* and *90/366*.

Community law will not apply a nationality imposed by a Member State on a person against his will if he is unable to renounce it, and if either the nationality was imposed in violation of human rights or if applying that nationality in the Community sphere would result in a breach of a general principle of law protected by the Court of Justice (*Airola v Commission*[3]). This principle, however, preceded the *Union Treaty* and remains unaffected by it. Also preceding the *Union Treaty* and remaining unaffected by it is the rule that, in in confering their nationality, Member States must have regard to their duty of co-operation and solidarity.

The *Union Treaty* may, however, have made a difference to the ability of Member States to effect a withdrawal of their nationality. Prior to 1 November 1993, Community law regarded questions of nationality as falling within the reserved domain of States. This meant that, although a conferral might be made in breach of the duty of co-operation and solidarity, its efficacy *vis-à-vis* the naturalised individual could generally not be called into question.[4]

There is now a *de jure* category of Union citizenship which is created by Community law and whose personal scope is referred by Community law to the nationality laws of the Member States. This act has removed nationality from the reserved domain of the Member States for it links nationality rules to the possession of a Union status. The *Union Treaty* thereby brings such rules within the framework of Community law and exposes them to supervision for conformity with the Community's general principles of law, and especially of fundamental freedoms. At the least, this means that a

---

[1]Case C-295/90 *European Parliament v Council* ("*Re Students' Rights*") [1992] 3 CMLR 281 at p 302, paragraph 19 of the Court's judgment

[2]See the opinion of Advocate General Darmon in Case 12/86 *Demirel v Städt Schwabisch Gmünd* [1987] ECR 3719 at p 3745, paragraph 27 of the opinion. The Court of Justice tacitly accepted this view in its judgment at p 3754, paragraph 28 of the judgment.

[3]Case 21/74 [1975] ECR 221.

[4]But see Case 21/74 *Airola v Commission* [1975] ECR 221.

withdrawal of nationality which violates the general principles cannot operate so as to deprive a person of his Union citizenship. The better view goes further and holds that such a withdrawal of nationality cannot be given any effect by national authorities, including national courts. This more radical view represents a significant erosion of national sovereignty.

The real importance of the *Union Treaty* in the area of migration rights, however, lies not in what it has effected, but in what it might presage. Citizenship is an essentially political concept rich with powerful and emotive symbolism, and whose ancestry can be traced back to near the beginnings of European civilisation. In the lead-up to the Intergovernmental Conference on Political Union which resulted in the *Union Treaty*, the Spanish government was a prime mover in establishing a European citizenship and expressly linked its view of European citizenship with an unfolding political union:

> As political union is a dynamic notion comprising the idea of a process of evolution towards a final objective, European citizenship is also a dynamic and evolving concept.[1]

This view of European citizenship, as an evolving rather than as a static phenomenon, and as being connected to the emergence of a political union, found expression in the *Union Treaty*. The right to vote in and stand for elections to municipal authorities and to the European Parliament is overtly political. The right of Union citizens enshrined in Article 8d to petition the European Parliament and to apply to the Union Ombudsman are also of a clearly political nature. These rights may be added to or strengthened (but not subtracted from or weakened) by provisions to be adopted under Article 8e.

Viewed through a political prism, the citizenship migration rights set out in Article 8a of the *EC Treaty* are but a staging post on the way to something more ambitious; ie they are political and dynamic. The political importance attached to such rights, and the political sensitivities likely to be aroused in elaborating them, are reflected in the uniquely rigorous legislative procedure set out in Article 8a(2) - unanimity on the Council and assent of the European Parliament.

Any Union citizen with adequate health insurance cover and the means to support himself can, even without pursuing an economic activity, migrate to another Member State and participate in political life at the municipal and European Parliamentary levels. If, however, the European Union is to evolve into a political union based on democracy, further development will need to occur. This development will principally involve two complementary strands, one involving movement rights and the other electoral rights.

---

[1] *Spanish Proposal on "European Citizenship"*, published in *Europe Documents* (Agence Internationale d'Information pour la Presse), No 1653, 2 October 1990, p 2.

At the moment, political power in the Union rests primarily in the hands of the Council of Ministers whose members are answerable to their elected national legislatures, and of the Commission which is nominated by Member State governments and, as from 1995, subject to approval as a body by the European Parliament.[1] The European Parliament may also cause the removal of the Commission as a body[2] and has had its function in the legislative process somewhat strengthened by the *Single European Act* and the *Union Treaty*. The Council, however, is not subject to confirmation or removal by the European Parliament and has the final word on most legislation. It is still fair to say that the Parliament's power in the Community's institutional structure is much weaker than that of either the Council or the Commission.

Thus the real *locus* of political power in the Community remains, as it has since the Community's foundations, with the governments of the Member States. This poses problems in terms of democratic participation by Union citizens. Frequently, decisions which are vital to interests which may be dispersed throughout the Community will be made by national governments in their national capitals, which governments are answerable only to their national legislatures and to their national electorates.

The government of Member State A might formulate a policy to be pursued in the Council of Ministers, which policy has a potentially adverse effect on Union citizens who are nationals of Member State B. These Union citizens, some of whom reside in Member State A and others of whom reside in their own Member State, desire to exert influence on the government of A in order to achieve a change in policy. Such a desire must be considered entirely reasonable in a political democracy possessed of a common citizenship. At the present stage of development of Community law, however, there are important legal obstacles to satisfying this desire.

The Union citizens who are nationals of Member State B and who reside in B will not have a Community right to travel to A's capital city unless they are covered by Articles 48-66 of the *EC Treaty* or by Article 8a of the *EC Treaty* as conditioned by *Directives 90/364, 90/365* and *90/366*. This means that Union citizens who are not workers, establishers or service providers/consumers in Member State A, or who are not endowed with the means to support themselves, or who are not insured against risks to their health, may be refused access to the capital city of A in order to exert influence on A's government. The same people would not even possess a right under Community law to enter the territory of a Member State where they were candidates in European Parliamentary elections. Union citizens who are economically marginalised, a considerable number in many Member States, are thus liable to be excluded from an important part of the democratic process. (Given that tourists are regarded as service consumers and therefore covered by Articles 59-66 of the *EC Treaty*,[3] and that such persons do not need to demonstrate financial self-sufficiency or health care status, it

[1] Article 158 of the *EC Treaty*.

[2] Article 144 of the *EC Treaty*.

[3] Joined Cases 286/82 and 26/83 *Luisi and Carbone* [1984] ECR 377 and Case 186/87 *Cowan v Le Trésor Public* [1989] ECR 195.

might be argued that the economically marginalised Union citizens of Member State B could demand entry into Member State A as tourists and then proceed to exert influence on A's government. It cannot nowadays be acceptable, whatever the practice in earlier ages, that the exercise of a right of democratic participation should be made dependent on the performance of an economic function or the possession of an economic status.[1])

The same problem will confront Union citizens if they seek to travel in order to exert influence even on the Community's own institutions when those institutions are located in another Member State.[2]

Furthermore, although the Union citizens who are nationals of B and who reside in A will be able to travel to A's capital city, they will not as of right under Community law be able to influence the policy of A's government by voting in A's national referendums or by voting in or standing for A's national elections. Yet, as we have seen, it is precisely at this national level that the main centres of Community power reside.

These legal difficulties in the way of democratic participation in the Union's affairs will not become pressing while it remains primarily a Union of nation States, a confederation rather than a federation. In such a Union, the citizens are likely to continue seeing their own national governments as the important object of political attention.

The establishment of common citizenship, however, reflects the existence of forces favouring a different and more ambitious vision of European unity. These forces see the future of Europe in unabashedly federal terms. Should the European Union take the federal road, citizenship of the Union will need to be strengthened so as to permit all Union citizens access on formally equal terms to the levers of political power in the federation. In such a Union it will be necessary to ensure that citizens can freely travel to the centres of political power. The connection between political democracy, a developed federal citizenship and the right of interstate movement was addressed by the Supreme Court of the United States shortly after the American civil war:

> [The Union citizen] has the right to come to the seat of government to assert any claim he may have upon that government, or to transact any business he may have with it. To seek its protection, to share its offices, to engage in administering its functions, he has a right to free access to its seaports, through which all the operations of foreign trade

---

[1]Even in 1912, the High Court of Australia refused to accept that a citizen's right to cross state borders could be made by the federal Constitution's interstate trade provision to depend on the performance of an economic activity. Were it otherwise, "the people of the Commonwealth would have to rest their right to cross a State line, not on their personality or their common citizenship, but on the sordid basis of some interstate business transaction"; *R v Smithers, ex parte Benson* (1912) 16 CLR 99 at p 113, per Isaacs J.

[2]It may, however, be possible to infer a limited political right of interstate movement for Union citizens from Articles 8d, 138d and 138e of the *EC Treaty* such that they may travel to the Ombudsman to make their application or to the relevant organs of the European Parliament to present their petition.

> and commerce are conducted, to the sub-treasuries, the land offices, the revenue offices, and the courts of justice in the several States, and this right is in its nature independent of the will of any State over whose soil he must pass in exercise of it.[1]

The same court, some seventy years later, also condemned as incompatible with possession of a federal citizenship in a democracy restrictions on interstate migration which discriminated against the economically marginalised:

> It would ... introduce a caste system utterly incompatible with the spirit of our system of government. It would permit those who were stigmatized by a State as indigents, paupers, or vagabonds to be relegated to an inferior class of citizenship. It would prevent a citizen, because he was poor, from seeking new horizons in other States. It might thus withhold from large segments of our people that mobility which is basic to any guarantee of freedom of opportunity. The result would be a substantial dilution of the rights of national citizenship, a serious impairment of the principles of equality.[2]

Any developments in the direction of a federal Europe must also be accompanied by a move in the direction of a federal citizenship, otherwise the gap between Community powers and democratic control (the so-called 'democratic deficit') will grow even wider than it is currently. Any such move will involve extending full electoral rights to Union citizens from other Member States who are resident in the host Member State on a basis of equality with the host Member State's own nationals. It will also involve removing the restrictions on movement rights which discriminate against Union citizens from other Member States on financial grounds. In the longer term the power of Member States to exclude or expel, on grounds of public policy, public security and public health, Union citizens who are nationals of other Member States will need to be further restricted, and perhaps abolished.

If and when a federal European Union arrives and a federal citizenship accompanies it, then it will be possible to think of Union citizenship less in terms of its symbolism, and more in terms of its *rôle* in securing and being secured by a European democracy. That day, if it comes at all, is still some way off.

---

[1] *Crandall v Nevada*, 6 Wall 35, 18 L Ed 745 (1868) at p 747, per Miller J delivering the opinion of the court.

[2] *Edwards v California*, 314 US 160 (1941) at p 181, per Douglas J concurring with the opinion of the court.

CHAPTER 2

NATIONALITY AND COMMUNITY LAW

Introduction

The purpose of this Chapter and the next is to determine the personal scope of the Union citizen's right of movement and residence under Article 8a of the *EC Treaty*. Who is a citizen of the Union?

The right contained in Article 8a is expressed to be conferred on "[e]very citizen of the Union".[1] Who are these 'citizens of the Union' to whom the new right of movement and residence is extended? Article 8(1) of the *EC Treaty* provides as follows:

> Citizenship of the Union is hereby established.
>
> Every person holding the nationality of a Member State shall be a citizen of the Union.

Articles 8 and 8a are both in Part Two of the *EC Treaty*, which Part is entitled "Citizenship of the Union". It is clear that the "citizen of the Union" referred to in Article 8a is subject to the definition of that term in Article 8(1) (second paragraph). Accordingly the persons entitled to benefit from the right contained in Article 8a are "[e]very citizen of the Union", that is to say, "[e]very person holding the nationality of a Member State".

The reference to "[e]very person" in Article 8(1) must be read as a reference to 'every natural person'. Citizenship, as opposed to nationality, is a concept ordinarily asscociated with the possession of civil and political rights and obligations by natural persons. Although it is possible to speak of legal persons having nationality, they are not generally regarded as possessing citizenship.

That citizenship of the Union is a status restricted to natural persons is confirmed by reference to two of the other provisions of Part Two of the *EC Treaty*.

Article 8a confers on Union citizens a right to "move and reside". The activities of corporations (as distinct from their personnel, capital and goods) are not ordinarily conceived of in terms of 'movement', even when they relocate their *siège social* or open a branch office. These activities are normally considered in terms of establishment, for which the Treaty makes special provision. Furthermore, although corporations might have a domicile for certain legal purposes, they are not commonly thought of as possessing a 'residence'. On the other hand although natural persons can

[1] Article 8a(1).

perform an act of establishment, movement and residence are activities which are ordinarily associated only with the activities of natural persons (contrast, for example, Article 48 of the *EC Treaty* with Article 52). Furthermore Article 8b, conferring certain electoral rights on Union citizens, could hardly have been intended to apply to corporations.

The result is that legal persons who do not fall within the definition of 'companies or firms' under Article 58 of the *EC Treaty*, and who therefore do not possess a right of establishment or a freedom to provide services under Articles 52-66 of the Treaty, do not acquire such rights as a result of the new Articles 8 and 8a.

We might therefore seem to have a complete answer to our enquiry. Either a natural person is or is not a national of a Member State, and this will automatically determine whether he is entitled to the rights contained in Article 8a as a Union citizen. On its face the question of who possesses citizenship of the Union depends on a simple reference to the law of the Member States, there being no alternative criteria provided by Community law for determining who is a Member State's national.

In order properly to understand the personal scope of Article 8a, however, we must determine whether Community law really does make a remission to national law for the purpose of determining the status of 'citizen of the Union' and, if it does, whether the remission is unqualified.

This Chapter will examine firstly whether, as a matter of general principle, States are solely competent to make dispositions of nationality and whether such dispositions are always effective to create obligations *vis-á-vis* other States. It will then examine whether Member State dispositions of nationality must, as a matter of principle, always be given effect to within the Community legal order. Chapter 3 will then go on to explore whether Community law in fact possesses its own rules or principles which affect the acquisition and loss of Member State nationality.

Disposition of Nationality: Exclusive Domestic Jurisdiction

We should first determine which authority is competent to make dispositions of nationality.

International law provides a useful source for Community law in areas concerning nationality. Thus in *van Duyn v Home Office*[1] the Court of Justice said:

> [I]t is a principle of international law, which the EEC Treaty cannot be assumed to disregard in the relations between Member States, that a

[1]Case 41/74 [1974] ECR 1337.

> State is precluded from refusing its own nationals the right of entry or residence.1

This same principle is reflected in the Fourth Protocol to the European *Convention for the Protection of Human Rights and Fundamental Freedoms*,[2] the *Universal Declaration of Human Rights*,[3] the *International Covenant on Civil and Political Rights*,[4] the *American Convention on Human Rights*,[5] and the *African Charter of Human Rights and Peoples' Rights*.[6]

Similarly, in *Anklagemyndigheden v Poulsen*[7] the Court of Justice acknowledged the force of the *Convention on the High Seas*[8] and the *United Nations Convention on the Law of the Sea*[9] in determining the nationality of fishing vessels for Community law purposes.[10]

The point of departure for international law in this area is that all States are free to decide for themselves who their nationals are to be. This principle finds expression in Article 1 of the *Convention on Certain Questions Relating to the Conflict of Nationality Laws* ("*Convention on Nationality*"):[11]

> It is for each State to determine under its own law who are its nationals. This law shall be recognised by other States in so far as it is consistent with international conventions, international custom, and the principles of law generally recognised with regard to nationality.

Article 1 consists of two limbs. The first limb lays down a general principle concerning the exclusive power of States to determine who are to be its nationals. In

[1]ibid at p 1351, paragraph 22 of the Court's judgment. Cf Case 10/61 *Commission v Italy* ("*Re Radio Tubes*") [1962] ECR 1 at p 10 (Article 234 of the *EEC Treaty* guarantees the rights held by third countries under agreements predating the *EEC Treaty*).

[2]Article 3(2): "No one shall be deprived of the right to enter the territory of the State of which he is a national".

[3]Article 13(2): "Everyone has the right to leave any country, including his own, and to return to his country".

[4]Article 12(4): "No one shall be arbitrarily deprived of the right to enter his own country".

[5]Article 22(5): "No one shall be expelled from the territory of the state of which he is a national or be deprived of the right to enter it".

[6]Article 12(2): "Every individual shall have the right to leave any country including his own, and to return to his country. This right may only be subject to restrictions, provided for by law for the protection of national security, law and order, public health or morality".

[7]CJ CE, 24 November 1992, (C-286/90 Rec p I-6019).

[8]450 UNTS 82.

[9]UN Doc A/CONF 62/122.

[10]CJ CE, *Anklagemyndigheden v Poulsen*, 24 November 1992, (C-286/90 Rec p I-6019, paragraph 13 of the Court's judgment).

[11]Signed at the Hague on 12 April 1930. 179 *League of Nations Treaty Series* 89; 5 *Hudson International Legislation* 359. The Convention entered into force on 1 July 1937 and is currently ratified by twenty States. The Community Member State parties are Belgium (4 April 1939), the Netherlands (2 April 1937) and the United Kingdom (6 April 1934). The other parties are Australia, Brazil, Canada, China, Cyprus, Fiji, India, Kiribati, Lesotho, Malta, Mauritius, Monaco, Norway, Pakistan, Poland, Swaziland and Sweden.

so far as States may exercise this power for domestic purposes, their authority is complete and final. The second limb of Article 1 is concerned with defining the extent to which other States are obliged, on the plane of international law, to recognise the effects of the power exercised under the first limb.

The general principle that States are competent, for domestic purposes, to confer nationality on, or to withdraw nationality from, whomever they please predated the *Convention on Nationality* and was articulated by the Permanent Court of International Justice in its advisory opinion in *Nationality Decrees Issued in Tunis and Morocco*:[1]

> The question whether a certain matter is or is not solely within the jurisdiction of a State is an essentially relative question; it depends upon the development of international relations. Thus, in the present state of international law, questions of nationality are, in the opinion of the Court, in principle within this reserved domain.[2]

That the rule in the first limb of Article 1 of the *Convention on Nationality* embodies a customary rule of international law[3] is evident from a consideration of the judgment of the International Court of Justice in *Liechtenstein v Guatemala (Second Phase)* ("*Re Nottebohm*"),[4] a case involving a demurrer by Guatemala to the standing of Liechtenstein to bring a claim for damages allegedly inflicted by Guatemala on an individual who was a naturalised Liechtenstein national. Neither Liechtenstein nor Guatemala had ever been parties to the *Convention on Nationality*. It is also evident from the views of publicists.[5]

[1] [1923] Permanent Court of International Justice, Series B, No 4.

[2] ibid at p 24.

[3] Article 18(2) of the *Convention on Nationality* provides as follows: "The inclusion of the above-mentioned principles and rules in the Convention shall in no way be deemed prejudicial to the question whether they do or do not already form part of international law".

[4] [1955] International Court of Justice Reports 4.

[5] In *Oppenheim's International Law*, 9th ed (1992) it is stated that "(i)n principle, and subject to any particular international obligations which might apply, it is not for international law but for the internal law of each state to determine who is, and who is not, to be considered its national" and "even where the effects in international law of a state's grant of nationality are limited, the individual will still be a national of that state for the purposes of its own laws" (Vol 1, at pp 852, 856). H. Lauterpacht has written that "(m)atters of nationality are, subject to the international obligations of the State, left to its municipal law" (*The Function of Law in the International Community* (1966), at p 300). According to P. Weis, "(n)ationality is one of the subjects which are considered as falling within the domestic jurisdiction, within the internal legislative competence, of the individual State" and "(t)hat rule is recognised by both customary and conventional international law" (*Nationality and Statelessness in International Law*, 2nd ed (1979), at p 65). Hans Ulrich Jessurun d'Oliveira regards Article 1 to be "at least binding as codification of customary law" (Note of Case C-369/90 *Micheletti v Delegación del Gobierno en Cantabria* (1993) 30 CML Rev 623 at p 629.

Community Acceptance of Member State Disposition

Some writers have suggested that domestic law is alone competent to define the nationality of the Member States for Community law purposes.[1]

Are there any good reasons for rejecting the idea that Member States are alone exclusively competent to define the personal scope of their nationalities for Community purposes? In other words, must the Community always be bound to accept the Member States' dispositions of their nationalities for the purposes of determining the personal scope of Community rights and obligations?

TRANSFER OF SOVEREIGNTY

The rule that States are free to make dispositions of their nationalities for domestic purposes is concomitant with their sovereign independence in international law. In *Re Nottebohm* the International Court of Justice said:

> It is for Liechtenstein, as it is for every sovereign State, to settle by its own legislation the rules relating to the acquisition of its nationality, and to confer that nationality by naturalization granted by its own organs in accordance with that legislation. ... Furthermore, nationality has its most immediate, its most far-reaching and, for most people, its only effects within the legal system of the State conferring it. Nationality serves above all to determine that the person upon whom it is conferred enjoys the rights and is bound by the obligations which the law of the State in question grants to or imposes upon its nationals. This is implied in the wider concept that nationality is within the domestic jurisdiction of the State.[2]

The Italian-United States Conciliation Commission, in the *Flegenheimer Claim*,[3] referred similarly to "an unquestionable principle of international law according to which every State is sovereign in establishing the legal conditions which must be

[1] Eg., P.J.G. Kapteyn and P. Verloren van Themaat, "*Introduction to the Law of the European Communities*", 2nd Ed., (1990), pp 441-442; N. Green, T.C. Hartley and J.A. Usher, "*The Legal Foundations of the Single European Market*", (1992), at pp 102-103; Francesco Capotorti et al, "*The European Union Treaty*", (1986), at pp 36-37; "*Halsbury's Laws of England*", 4th Ed, (1986), Vol 52, para 15.09. For a different view, see: Christopher Greenwood, "*Nationality and the Limits of the Free Movement of Persons in Community Law*", (1987) 7 Yearbook of European Law 185, especially at pp 187-193; W.R. Boehning, *The Scope of the EEC System of Free Movement of Workers: a Rejoinder*, (1972) 9 CML Rev 81; Albert Bleckman, "*The Personal Jurisdiction of the European Community*", (1980) 17 CML Rev 467 at pp 477-478. Burrows says that "(i)t is *primarily* for each member state to define who are its nationals", F. Burrows, "*Free Movement in European Community Law*", (1987), p 124 (emphasis added).

[2] *Liechtenstein v Guatemala (Second Phase)* ("*Re Nottebohm*") [1955] International Court of Justice Reports 4 at p 20.

[3] (1958) 25 ILR 91.

fulfilled by an individual in order that he may be considered to be vested with its nationality".[1]

The connection between the sovereignty of States and the power of States exclusively to determine who shall be their nationals, made by the International Court of Justice in *Re Nottebohm* and by the Italian-United States Conciliation Commission in the *Flegenheimer Claim*, is echoed by Andrew Evans who has remarked that "[w]ithin the conceptual framework of the modern state, sovereignty and nationality are inseparable".[2] P. Weis has described the relationship thus:

> There cannot be any doubt that this right [of States to determine the incidents of acquisition and loss of their nationality] is a concomitant of State sovereignty. ... The right to delimit this group of individuals termed nationals, and to determine their status in the sense of their rights and duties, is, indeed - unless personal supremacy were to become co-extensive with territorial supremacy - a prerequisite of personal supremacy and, therefore, of sovereignty. The right of a State to determine who are, and who are not, its nationals is an essential element of its sovereignty.[3]

The Court of Justice has also expressly linked the sovereignty of States with their power to determine the conditions for holding their nationalities. In *Anklagemyndigheden v Poulsen*[4] the Court of Justice held that a State, *in casu* Panama, was entitled in the exercise of its sovereign powers to determine the conditions for permitting a vessel to be registered in that State thereby attaching its nationality to that vessel.[5] The same principle and reasoning was applied by the Court of Justice in respect of vessels registered in the United Kingdom in *Commission v Ireland* ("*Re British Fishing Boats*").[6]

It will be recalled that in *Nationality Decrees Issued in Tunis and Morocco* the Permanent Court of International Justice said that "whether a certain matter is or is

[1] ibid at p 97.

[2] Andrew Evans, "*Nationality Law and European Integration*", (1991) 16 EL Rev 190.

[3] P. Weis, *Nationality and Statelessness in International Law*, 2nd ed (1979), at p 65.

[4] CJ CE, 24 November 1992, (C-286/90 Rec p I-6019) paragraph 15 of the Court's judgment.

[5] While a Member State remains free, in the exercise of its sovereign power, to determine the conditions under which a vessel may acquire its nationality by registering under its laws, it is not free to impose requirements which discriminate against nationals of other Member States who own a vessel for which registration is sought if the vessel is to be used for an economic purpose. In Case C-246/89 *Commission v United Kingdom* ("*Re Nationality of Fishermen*") [1991] ECR I-4585 the Court of Justice said that "the concept of 'nationality' of ships, which are not persons, is different from that of the 'nationality' of natural persons" (at p I-4615, paragraph 28 of the Court's judgment). The Treaty does not prohibit discrimination against ships as such, but it does prohibit discrimination against natural and legal persons on the basis of their nationality where they seek to establish themselves for an economic purpose by seeking to have a vessel registered in a Member State. While tacitly accepting the United Kingdom's submission that a Member State is free to determine the conditions for the conferral of its nationality, the Court of Justice said that "in exercising its power for the purpose of defining the conditions for the grant of its 'nationality' to a ship, each member-State must comply with the prohibition of discrimination against nationals of member-States on grounds of their nationality" (at p I-4615, paragraph 30 of the Court's judgment).

[6] Case C-280/89 [1993] 1 CMLR 273 at p 286, paragraph 24 of the Court's judgment.

not solely within the jurisdiction of a State is an essentially relative question; it depends upon the development of international relations" and that "in the present state of international law, questions of nationality are ... in principle within this reserved domain".[1]

Thus although the power to make dispositions of nationality is in principle within the reserved domain of States as an adjunct of their sovereignty in international law, the scope of this reserved domain is contingent upon developments in the sphere of international relations. The traditional view of State sovereignty in international law poses an obstacle to developments which restrict that sovereignty.

The judgment in *Nationality Decrees Issued in Tunis and Morocco* was, of course, delivered well before the European Community came into existence. Can it be said that the establishment and evolution of the Community represents a development in international relations such as to warrant a modification of the rule that questions of nationality are within the reserved domain of States?

In this connection it is instructive to consider the preamble to the *ECSC Treaty* which records, *inter alia*, the Member States' resolve "to lay the foundations for institutions which will give direction to a destiny henceforward shared" and to create "a broader and deeper community among peoples long divided by bloody conflicts". The preamble to the *EEC Treaty* similarly recorded (and the preamble to the *EC Treaty* still records) the Member States' determination "to lay the foundations for an ever closer union among the peoples of Europe", while the preambles to the *Treaty of Accession 1972*, the *Treaty of Accession 1979* and the *Treaty of Accession 1985* state a determination "to construct an ever closer union among the peoples of Europe on the foundations already laid". In the preamble to the *Single European Act* the Member States expressed their will to "transform relations as a whole among their States into a European Union". Furthermore the *Union Treaty*, in its preamble, records the Member States' resolve "to mark a new stage in the process of European integration", their desire "to deepen the solidarity between their peoples" and their resolution "to continue the process of creating an ever closer union among the peoples of Europe".

Moreover, if questions of nationality are within the reserved domain of States, so too is the power to issue passports and other documentation attesting to an individual's possession of the issuing State's nationality.[2] Yet the Member States have already lost the legal power to refuse to issue such documentation in respect of their nationals who seek to exercise their Community economic migration rights.[3]

We should also recall the views expressed by the Court of Justice over thirty years ago on the impact of the Community's establishment on the development of international

[1] *Nationality Decrees Issued in Tunis and Morocco* [1923] Permanent Court of International Justice, Series B, No 4 at p 24.

[2] See the discussion by Siofra O'Leary, "*Nationality Law and Community Citizenship: A Tale of Two Uneasy Bedfellows*" (1992) 12 Yearbook of European Law 353 at pp 372-373.

[3] Article 2 of *Directive 68/360*.

law and on the sovereignty of the Member States. In *NV Algemene Transport- en Expeditie Onderneming van Gend & Loos v Nederlandse administratie der belastingen*[1] the Court said:

> [T]he Community constitutes a new legal order of international law for the benefit of which the states have limited their sovereign rights, albeit within limited fields, and the subjects of which comprise not only Member States but also their nationals. Independently of the legislation of Member States, Community law therefore not only imposes obligations on individuals but is also intended to confer upon them rights which become part of their legal heritage.[2]

The Court's decision in *van Gend & Loos* established the Community as a revolutionary phenomenon in international relations, thereby qualifying the decision as probably the most significant in the Community's legal history. About eighteen months later, in *Costa v ENEL*,[3] the Court of Justice elaborated:

> By contrast with ordinary international treaties, the EEC Treaty has created its own legal system which, on the entry into force of the Treaty, became an integral part of the legal systems of the Member States and which their courts are bound to apply.
>
> By creating a Community of unlimited duration, having its own institutions, its own personality, its own legal capacity and capacity of representation on the international plane and, more particularly, real powers stemming from a limitation of sovereignty or a transfer of powers from the States to the Community, the Member States have limited their sovereign rights, albeit within limited fields, and have thus created a body of law which binds both their nationals and themselves. ...
>
> The transfer by the States from their domestic legal system to the Community legal system of the rights and obligations arising under the Treaty carries with it a permanent limitation of their sovereign rights, against which a subsequent unilateral act incompatible with the concept of the Community cannot prevail.[4]

The dynamic aspect of the Community's impact on the development of international relations has been lately underlined by the Court of Justice in its opinion given under Article 228(1) of the *EEC Treaty* on the legality of the draft Treaty on a European Economic Area ("*Re Draft EEA Treaty*")[5] in which it said that "the Community

[1]Case 26/62 [1963] ECR 1.
[2]ibid at p 12.
[3]Case 6/64 [1964] ECR 585.
[4]ibid at pp 593, 594.
[5]Opinion 1/91 [1991] ECR I-6079.

treaties established a new legal order for the benefit of which the States have limited their sovereign rights, *in ever wider fields*, and the subjects of which comprise not only Member States but also their nationals".[1]

The Court of Justice has also recently referred to the *EEC Treaty* as the Community's "constitutional charter"[2] thereby further emphasising the novel development which the Community represents in relations among States. Indeed, Federico Mancini (a judge of the Court) has argued that the "main endeavour" of the Court of Justice has been to seek to "constitutionalise" the Treaty by fashioning "a constitutional framework for a federal-type structure in Europe".[3]

The Community is much more than a traditional international organisation of the type usually established and regulated by international law. Rather, the Member States have transferred part of their sovereignty to the Community. This has implications in deciding whether the Member States' dispositions of their nationalities, being a concomitant of State sovereignty, are solely within their jurisdiction to the extent that such dispositions have effects on the plane of Community law. Christopher Greenwood thinks that the Community has affected the scope of the Member States' power in this area:

> The European Communities are the product of a development of international relations, between the Member States, in the direction of a greater degree of integration than any hitherto seen. While the Member States remain free to decide who are, or are not, their nationals, it is not unreasonable to suppose, therefore, that it is for Community law to determine what consequences under Community law follow from that decision.[4]

The qualitative advance in international relations which the Community represents justifies the conclusion that the Member States have entered into obligations with each other of such a nature as to limit, even more severely than in international law, their entitlement to have their dispositions of nationality unquestioningly recognised for Community law purposes.

Consequently, the Member States cannot in principle be regarded as free conclusively to determine the beneficiaries of Community rights by the exercise of their power to make dispositions of nationality with full effect for domestic purposes. Rather, the transfer of sovereignty which membership of the Community involves subjects the

[1] ibid at p I-6102, paragraph 21 of the Court's judgment (emphasis added).

[2] Case 294/83 *Parti écologiste 'Les Verts' v European Parliament* [1986] ECR 1339 at p 1365, paragraph 23 of the Court's judgment, Case C-2/88 Imm *Zwartveld* [1990] ECR I-3365 at p I-3372, paragraph 16 of the Court's judgment, Opinion 1/91 *Re Draft EEA Treaty* [1991] ECR I-6079 at p I-6102, paragraph 21 of the Court's judgment.

[3] Federico Mancini, "*The Making of a Constitution for Europe*", (1989) 26 CML Rev 595 at p 596.

[4] Christopher Greenwood, "*Nationality and the Limits of the Free Movement of Persons in Community Law*", (1987) 7 YEL 185 at p 188.

exercise of the Member States' power to Community supervision at least to the extent that the exercise of the power produces effects on the level of Community law.

TREATY PROVISIONS

Authority for rejecting the idea that Member States are alone exclusively competent to define the personal scope of their nationalities for all Community purposes is, moreover, to be found even in the text of the treaties themselves.

There are provisions establishing a special *régime* for some non-metropolitan territories of the Member States which render certain of their nationals unentitled to benefit from the Community's rules on free movement. In this connection we shall examine the legal position of Faroe Islanders, of Channel Islanders and Manxmen and of the inhabitants of the Overseas Countries and Territories.

Faroe Islanders

Certain Danish nationals are affected by Article 4 of Protocol 2 to the *Treaty of Accession 1972* which provides that "Danish nationals resident in the Faroe Islands shall be considered to be nationals of a Member State" only from the date on which a declaration extending the Community treaties to the islands is made by the Danish government. Denmark has never made such a declaration,[1] with the consequence that certain persons who are Danish nationals, with all rights as such under Danish domestic law, are not "nationals of a Member State" and therefore not citizens of the Union within the meaning of Article 8 of the *EC Treaty*. This is so notwithstanding that the Faroe Islands are a part of the Kingdom of Denmark.

Channel Islanders and Manxmen

Some British nationals are similarly affected by Article 2 of Protocol 3 to the Treaty of Accession 1972 which provides that certain rights enjoyed by Channel Islanders and Manxmen in the United Kingdom are not affected by the Act of Accession, but that they "shall not benefit from Community provisions relating to the free movement of persons and services". Thus, notwithstanding their status as British citizens,[2] Channel Islanders and Manxmen are not entitled to the enjoyment of the rights contained in Article 8a of the EC Treaty. Unlike the Faroe Islanders, Channel Islanders and Manxmen are not deprived entirely of their status as 'nationals of a Member State' under Community law. They are therefore citizens of the Union who are nevertheless unable to benefit from the Union citizen's right to move and reside freely within the territory of the Member States.[3]

[1]After Denmark's accession to the Community, Article 227(5)(a) of the *EEC Treaty* provided that the Treaty did not apply to the Faroe Islands but that Denmark had until the end of 1975 to declare that the Treaty did apply to the Faroe Islands. No such declaration ever having been made, the *Union Treaty* (Article G(79)(b)) amended the provision so that Article 227(5)(a) of the *EC Treaty* now merely declares the non-application of the Treaty to the Faroe Islands.

[2]*British Nationality Act 1981* sections 1, 11 and 50(1).

[3]Channel Islanders and Manxmen, because they are citizens of the Union and notwithstanding their exclusion from the Community's migration rights, are entitled to benefit from the provisions of Articles 8b-8e of the *EC Treaty*. Faroe Islanders, on the other hand, are not citizens of the Union and are therefore not entitled to benefit from any of the Treaty's citizenship provisions.

Overseas Countries and Territories

Like the Faroe Islands, Greenland is a part of the Kingdom of Denmark.[1] Unlike the Faroe Islands, however, Greenland accompanied metropolitan Denmark into the Community in 1973.[2] In the 1972 referendum on Denmark's membership of the Community, the Danish populations of both the Faroe Islands and Greenland voted against accession. The Faroe Islands' special status as a non-Community part of Denmark owed much to the fact that it was already a largely self-governing part of the Kingdom at the time of the referendum.[3] Greenland, on the other hand, did not achieve a comparable status until 1979.[4] In the first elections to the *Landsting* (Greenland's home rule legislature) in 1979, candidates committed to Greenland's withdrawal from the Community won a majority of the seats. A referendum of Greenlanders in 1982 produced a small majority in favour of Greenland's withdrawal.

Subsequently, the Member States concluded the *Treaty amending, with regard to Greenland, the Treaties establishing the European Communities*[5] (the "*Greenland Treaty*"). The *Greenland Treaty* effected as from 1 February 1985 the first and, so far, only withdrawal from the Community.

The *Greenland Treaty* amended the *EEC Treaty* so as to bring Greenland within the terms of Part Four of the *EEC Treaty* ("Association of the Overseas Countries and Territories").[6] Part Four establishes a special legal relationship between certain countries and territories and the Community. In order to qualify for this special relationship, the countries and territories must be "non-European", have "special

[1]Until 1953, when Greenland was incorporated into the Kingdom of Denmark, it was a Danish possession. The Faroe Islands and Greenland are guaranteed two seats each in the *Folketing* (the Danish parliament); Article 28 of the Constitution of the Kingdom of Denmark.

[2]See generally: Frederik Harhoff, "*Greenland's Withdrawal from the European Communities*", (1983) 20 CML Rev 13; Friedl Weiss, "*Greenland's Withdrawal from the European Communities*", (1985) 10 EL Rev 173.

[3]Until 1948 the Faroe Islands were a Danish possession. A Home Rule law in 1948 (Act No 137 of 23 March 1948) formally made the islands a part of Denmark with special status as a self-governing community. The Faroe Islands legislature (the *Lagting*), and a local administration appointed by it (the *Landsstyre*), exercises control over local affairs. Certain matters such as foreign affairs, defence, the monetary system and the judiciary remain within the legislative and administrative competence of Copenhagen. Since 1972 the Danish government has permitted the Faroe Islanders to negotiate directly with foreign countries on matters of special local interest, while Copenhagen retains authority on most foreign policy matters. (See Roxann E Henry's and Kenneth E Miller's Faroe Islands supplement to the Constitution of the Kingdom of Denmark in Albert P Blaustein and Gisbert H Flanz, "*Constitutions of the Countries of the World*".

[4]Act No 577 of 29 November 1978.

[5]OJ 1985 L29/1, 1 February 1985.

[6]Article 3 of the *Greenland Treaty* inserted a new Article 136a into the *EEC Treaty* which expressly applied the provisions of Part Four to Greenland, subject to the terms of a Protocol to the *Greenland Treaty* which Protocol was to be annexed to the *EEC Treaty*. Article 4 of the *Greenland Treaty* added Greenland to the list of places in Annex IV of the *EEC Treaty*, which Annex prescribes the countries and territories having "special relations" with one of the Member States, and which are associated with the Community.

relations with Belgium, Denmark, France, Italy, the Netherlands and the United Kingdom" and be listed in Annex IV to the *EC Treaty*.[1]

The purpose of association under Part Four is "to promote economic and social development of the countries and territories and to establish close economic relations between them and the Community as a whole"[2] and "to further the interests and prosperity of the inhabitants of those countries and territories in order to lead them to the economic, social and cultural development to which they aspire".[3] Association status under Part Four for the overseas countries and territories carries with it a range of rights and duties.

The Member States are under an obligation to "contribute to the investments required for the progressive development" of the overseas countries and territories.[4] The overseas countries and territories enjoy the same advantages of the Community customs union as the Member States.[5] Thus their goods enjoy access to the Community's common market free from customs duties, quantitative restrictions and all measures having equivalent effect. The overseas countries and territories must extend to each other and to all Member States the same treatment in trade as they apply to the Member State with which they have special relations,[6] and they are under an in-principle obligation progressively to abolish customs duties on imports from Member States.[7] Notwithstanding this obligation the overseas countries and territories may nevertheless preserve, and even impose, "customs duties which meet the needs of their development and industrialisation or produce revenue for their budgets".[8] Any customs duties maintained on these grounds must be reduced so as not to exceed the level imposed on the Member State possessing the special relationship,[9] and any new or existing customs duty must not discriminate between Member States.[10]

The advantages enjoyed by the overseas countries and territories under Part Four of the *EC Treaty* do not, however, extend to the free movement of persons.

As far as workers are concerned, Article 135 of the *EC Treaty* provides as follows:

> Subject to the provisions relating to public health, public security or public policy, freedom of movement within Member States for

[1]Article 131 (first paragraph) of the *EC Treaty*. Inclusion in Annex IV is not sufficient, the other two conditions must also be met. In particular, a territory which achieves independence will not fall within the scope of Part IV of the *EC Treaty* notwithstanding that it remains listed in Annex IV: Case 147/73 *Carlheinz Lensing Kaffee-Tee-Import KG v Hauptzollamt Berlin-Packhof* [1973] ECR 1543.

[2]Article 131 (second paragraph) of the *EC Treaty*.

[3]Article 131 (third paragraph) of the *EC Treaty*.

[4]Article Article 132(3) of the *EC Treaty*. Financial aid is given through the European Development Fund and the European Investment Bank.

[5]Articles 132(1) and 133(1) of the *EC Treaty*.

[6]Article 132(2) of the *EC Treaty*.

[7]Article 133(2) of the *EC Treaty*.

[8]Article 133(3) (first paragraph) of the *EC Treaty*.

[9]Article 133(3) (second paragraph) of the *EC Treaty*.

[10]Article 133(5) of the *EC Treaty*.

> workers from the countries and territories, and within the countries and territories for workers from Member States, shall be governed by agreements to be concluded subsequently with the unanimous approval of Member States.

No agreements of the sort foreshadowed by Article 135 have been concluded. In the absence of any such agreements "nationals of Member States may not rely on Community law to claim the right to enter and reside in an overseas country or territory in order to obtain and pursue salaried employment there".[1] The same disability applies, *a fortiori* the language of Article 135, to "workers from the countries and territories" seeking to move and reside within the Member States.[2]

The right of establishment and the freedom to provide or consume services are separately provided for. Article 132(5) of the *EC Treaty* applies, in relations between Member States and the overseas countries and territories, "the provisions and procedures laid down in the Chapter relating to the right of establishment" subject to any special provisions laid down pursuant to Article 136. The Council may, acting unanimously under Article 136, lay down provisions for the details of and procedure for the association of the overseas countries and territories.

The current Council act made pursuant to Article 136 of the *EC Treaty* is *Decision 86/283*,[3] Article 176 of which deals with the right of establishment and the provision of services. Article 176 provides that, in making arrangements for establishment and the provision of services, the overseas countries and territories may not discriminate between nationals and companies or firms of Member States. Thus, whatever treatment is extended to nationals of the Member State possessing the special relationship with the host overseas country or territory must likewise be extended to nationals of the other Member States.[4] No corresponding obligation, however, is placed upon Member States to admit into their territory individuals or companies from the overseas countries and territories. In accordance with the principle of reciprocity, however, an overseas country or territory is under no obligation to grant a right of establishment or a right to provide services to nationals or companies of a Member State where that Member State does not grant similar rights to nationals or companies or firms of Denmark, France, the Netherlands or the United Kingdom established in that overseas country or territory.[5]

The language employed in Article 176 of *Decision 86/283* presupposes that the Member States are free to refuse migration rights, for establishment and services purposes, to nationals of Member States established in an overseas country or

[1]Joined Cases C-100 and C-101/89 *Kaefer and Procacci v French State* [1990] ECR I-4647 at p I-4671, paragraph 13 of the Court's judgment.

[2]"*Halsbury's Laws of England*", 4th Ed, (1986), Vol 52, para 15.35; Hans Smit and Peter E. Herzog, "*The Law of the European Economic Community: a Commentary*", Vol 3, p 4-27.

[3]OJ 1986 L175/1 of 30 June 1986.

[4]Joined Cases C-100 and C-101/89 *Kaefer and Procacci v French State* [1990] ECR I-4647 at p I-4672, paragraph 17 of the Court's judgment.

[5]ibid at pp I-4671 - I-4672, paragraph 16 of the Court's judgment.

territory. The provision also presupposes that a Member State ('the parent State') may, in regulating the right to enter and reside in an overseas country or territory with which it possesses a special relationship, impose different requirements as between those of its nationals who are from that overseas country or territory and those who are not. Indeed, the Court of Justice has expressly indicated that such a difference in treatment is presupposed by Article 176.[1] Nationals of other Member States, to the extent that they have a right of migration to the overseas country or territory at all, need only be treated equally with those nationals of the parent State who are not from the overseas country or territory.

Thus, persons who are "workers from the countries and territories" (Article 135 of the *EC Treaty*) currently enjoy no Community law right to move and reside in the territory of the Member States for the purpose of obtaining or pursuing salaried employment there. Similarly, persons who are from an overseas country or territory do not enjoy Community privileges in the territory of Member States as regards establishment and services. Any privileges they enjoy as 'nationals of a Member State from an overseas country or territory' will arise solely from the operation of the host Member State's domestic law, and then only to the extent that other Member States reciprocate with respect to nationals and companies or firms of Denmark, France, the Netherlands and the United Kingdom established in the overseas country or territory.

The law concerning the association of the overseas countries and territories suggests that for Community purposes there is something akin to a separate nationality for nationals of Member States who are from an overseas country or territory. Indeed, in a different but related context, it has been suggested that the régime for Channel Islanders and Manxmen "comes close to establishing a separate nationality" for them,[2] and we have already seen that Faroe Islanders are not 'nationals of a Member State' notwithstanding their Danish nationality and their residence within part of the European territory of the Kingdom of Denmark.[3]

In some instances the inhabitants of the overseas countries and territories will not ordinarily hold the nationality of the Member State with which they possess a special relationship. This will be particularly true of those overseas countries and territories possessing a special relationship with the United Kingdom.[4] In the case, however, of

[1]ibid at p I-4672, paragraph 17 of the Court's judgment.

[2]T.C. Hartley, "*EEC Immigration Law*", (1976), n 36 at p 85.

[3]The Faroe Islands are not among the countries and territories to which Part Four of the *EC Treaty* may be made to apply. Such countries and territories must, according to Article 131 (first paragraph) of the *EC Treaty*, be "non-European". This is also a reason for not making Part Four applicable to the Channel Islands and the Isle of Man. Greenland, on the other hand, is part of North America - at one point its coastline is only 30 kilometers from the coastline of Canada.

[4]The overseas countries and territories having a special relationship with Britain are not constitutionally part of the United Kingdom. The *British Nationality Act 1981* does not operate so as to confer British citizenship on persons by virtue simply of having been born in one of the overseas countries or territories. Indeed even a person born of British parents in one of the British overseas countries and territories will not ordinarily be a British citizen if neither of his parents were born, adopted or naturalised in the United Kingdom. According to the latest legislative list of the overseas countries and territories (Annex I to *Decision 86/283*, updating the list in Annex IV of the *EC Treaty*) the overseas countries and territories possessing a special relationship with the United Kingdom are; Anguilla, Cayman Islands, Falkland

the overseas countries and territories possessing a special relationship with Denmark,[1] France[2] and the Netherlands,[3] the inhabitants will ordinarily hold the nationality of their overseas country's or territory's parent State. We have already seen that this will be true of Greenland, which actually forms part of the Kingdom of Denmark. Similarly, all the French overseas countries and territories are, by various pieces of French legislation, declared to be integral parts of the French Republic and the Dutch overseas countries and territories have been legally integrated into the Kingdom of the Netherlands. The Danish and all but one of the French overseas countries and territories are, moreover, directly represented in their parent States' national legislatures.[4]

The Treaties do not expressly provide criteria for determining when a national of a Member State is connected with an overseas country in such a way as to preclude him from access to the Community migration rights conferred by Articles 48, 52 and 59 of the *EC Treaty*. Yet as Christopher Greenwood has observed, "those criteria must be found in Community law not least because, with the exception of United Kingdom law, the nationality laws of the Member States do not make sufficient distinction between nationals who are connected with the overseas countries and territories and those connected with the metropolitan territory".[5] What might those criteria be?

The answer appears to be that residence is a sufficient connection with the overseas country or territory so as to preclude a person possessing the nationality of a Member State from access to the Community's economic migration rights. According to T.C. Hartley, if a person connected with an overseas country or territory is excluded from the Community's migration rights it is the fact that he is an inhabitant of one of those places which produces the effect.[6]

Islands, South Georgia and South Sandwich Islands (this entry was corrected by corrigendum (OJ 1987, L66/20), Montserrat, Pitcairn, Saint Helena and Dependencies, British Antarctic Territory, British Indian Ocean Territory, Turks and Caicos Islands, and British Virgin Islands. Article 227(3) of the *EC Treaty* provides specifically that the Treaty shall not apply to those overseas countries and territories having special relations with the United Kingdom which are not included in the list set out in Annex IV to the Treaty.

[1] According to the latest legislative list of the overseas countries and territories (Annex I to *Decision 86/283*) the only overseas country or territory possessing a special relationship with Denmark is Greenland.

[2] According to the latest legislative list of the overseas countries and territories (Annex I to *Decision 86/283*) the overseas countries and territories possessing a special relationship with France are; New Caledonia and Dependencies, French Polynesia, French Southern and Antarctic Territories, Wallis and Futuna Islands, Mayotte, and Saint Pierre and Miquelon.

[3] According to the latest legislative list of the overseas countries and territories (Annex I to *Decision 86/283*) the overseas countries and territories possessing a special relationship with the Netherlands are; Aruba, and Netherlands Antilles (specifically Bonaire, Curacao, Saba, Saint Eustatius, and Saint Martin).

[4] The exception is the French Southern and Antarctic Territories, which possess no permanent population.

[5] Christopher Greenwood, "*Nationality and the Limits of the Free Movement of Persons in Community Law*", (1987) 7 YEL 185 at p 189.

[6] T.C. Hartley, "*EEC Immigration Law*" (1976) at p 60: "It seems possible ... that the inhabitants of the overseas countries and territories are outside the personal scope of the Treaties for all purposes concerning immigration". Cf D.F. Edens and S. Patijn, "*The Scope of the EEC System of Free Movement of Workers*", (1972) 9 CML Rev 322 where it is argued that there are simply no criteria that lay down a precise distinction between workers 'from' the Member States and workers 'from' the overseas countries

It will be recalled that Article 135 of the *EC Treaty* extends freedom of movement within the Member States to workers "from the countries and territories" in accordance with agreements to be concluded. This expression suggests that the worker must have some established attachment, by way of residence or domicile, in the overseas country or territory. The corresponding expressions in the German,[1] French[2] and Italian[3] versions of Article 135 are similarly, and perhaps even more, redolent of such an attachment on the part of the worker.

The criterion of residence is also in harmony with the approach taken with respect to Faroe Islanders. The Treaty provides, it will be recalled, that "Danish nationals *resident* in the Faroe Islands"[4] would have been considered nationals of a Member State only if Denmark had made the prescribed declaration.

Residence plays a similar, albeit not an identical, *rôle* in determining the status of Channel Islanders and Manxmen. In Article 6 of Protocol 3 to the *Treaty of Accession 1972* Channel Islanders and Manxmen are defined as persons who hold citizenship of the United Kingdom and Colonies[5] by virtue of having been born, adopted naturalised or registered in one of the islands (or by virtue of one of their parents or grandparents having been born, adopted naturalised or registered in one of the islands). A Channel Islander or Manxman loses his exceptional status, however, "if he has at any time been resident in the United Kingdom for five years".[6]

Conclusion

An examination of the constitutional position of the Faroe Islands, the Channel Islands, the Isle of Man and the overseas countries and territories demonstrates that the Treaty itself does not always allow Member States to make dispositions of their nationality such as conclusively to determine the personal scope of movement rights under Community law.

The conferral or possession of British citizenship does not permit Channel Islanders or Manxmen to exercise migration rights under Community law, just as Member State nationals who are residents of the overseas countries and territories enjoy no automatic

---

and territories in so far as they are nationals of Member States. It is submitted that this view is untenable, tending as it does to render a provision of Community law ineffective or meaningless.

[1] "*aus den Ländern und Hoheitsgebieten*" - ie 'out of the countries and territories'.

[2] "*des pays et territoires*" - ie 'of, or belonging to, the countries and territories'.

[3] "*dei paesi e territori*" - ie to identical effect as the French version in the previous footnote.

[4] Article 4 of Protocol 2 to the *Treaty of Accession 1972* (emphasis added).

[5] The *Treaty of Accession 1972* was done before the *British Nationality Act 1981*. The reference to citizens of the United Kingdom and Colonies is now to be read as a reference to British citizens; see Appendix, § 2.

[6] Being British citizens, and lacking the right under Community law to move freely in the Member States, Channel Islanders and Manxmen have a legal right to move and reside only in their own island and in the United Kingdom. It is reasonable to suppose, therefore, that most Channel Islanders and Manxmen who leave their island take up residence in the United Kingdom. It is anomalous that a Channel Islander or Manxman who leaves his island and manages to live in any place other than the United Kingdom for more than five years, especially if that place is another Member State, does not lose his exceptional status and its attendant disability from access to the Treaty's economic migration rights.

entitlement to the Community's migration rights. The conferral or possession of Danish citizenship on or by a resident of the Faroe Islands does not cause the Faroe Islander to be a 'national of a Member State' for the purposes of the Treaty.

The Treaty cannot, therefore, be said to establish a principle that a Member State's disposition of its nationality must always determine whether a person is entitled to the Community's migration rights.

OBSTACLE TO FULL REALISATION OF THE COMMON MARKET

That the Member States are not free finally to determine the personal scope of Community rights and obligations by making dispositions of their nationality which are always to be given effect in Community law is also possibly to be deduced from the logic of the common market project.

Article 2 of the *EC Treaty* provides that the Community shall achieve its task by establishing, *inter alia*, a common market, which expression "refers to the whole of the economic activities of the Community"[1] and involves "the elimination of all obstacles to intra-Community trade in order to merge the national markets into a single market bringing about conditions as close as possible to those of a genuine internal market".[2] Article 7a gives the Community the task of establishing an internal market which is defined as comprising "an area without internal frontiers in which the free movement of goods, persons, services and capital is ensured in accordance with the provisions of this Treaty". Article 3(c) provides that the Community's activities shall include "an internal market characterized by the abolition, as between Member States, of obstacles to the free movement of goods, persons, services and capital".

The logic of the Community's mission of economic integration can impose fatal pressures on national measures which preserve or create obstacles to the realisation of a single market among the Member States. These national measures include not only ones which directly regulate areas of economic life and which fall directly within the legislative competence of the Community, but also those which indirectly affect the enjoyment of the benefits which Community law confers on its subjects and in relation to which the Community either has not legislated or does not possess legislative competence.

An illustration of this feature of the common market's logic is to be found in the decision of the Court of Justice in *Choquet*.[3] Mr Choquet was a French national living and working in Germany as an employed electrician. Following his involvement in a motor vehicle accident, the German authorities prosecuted him for driving in Germany without a German driver's licence. The prosecution was brought

[1]Case 167/73 *Commission v France* ("*Re French Sailors*") [1974] ECR 359 at p 369, paragraph 19 of the Court's judgment.
[2]Case 15/81 *Gaston Schul Douane Expediteur BV v Inspecteur der Invoerrechten en Accijnzen, Roosendaal* [1982] ECR 1409 at pp 1431-1432, paragraph 33 of the Court's judgment.
[3]Case 16/78 [1978] ECR 2293.

notwithstanding that Mr Choquet was at all relevant times in possession of a valid French driver's licence. A reference was made to the Court of Justice by the German trial court which sought to establish whether Community law permitted Member States to require those taking advantage of the *EEC Treaty*'s freedom of movement provisions and who wished to drive a car to be in possession of a local driver's licence even when they possess a valid licence from their own Member State.

The United Kingdom government (intervening) argued that the national law could not be called into question because there was no Community legislation specifically relating to the issue of driver's licences. The Court rejected this proposition:

> It must ... be appreciated that national rules relating to the issue and mutual recognition of driving licences by the Member States exert an influence, both direct and indirect on the exercise of the rights guaranteed by the provisions of the Treaty relating to freedom of movement for workers, to establishment and ... to the provision of services in general.[1]

The Court went on to observe that the power to make rules regarding the issue and recognition of driver's licences "fall primarily within the scope of the responsibilities devolving upon the Member States ... concerning the safety of highway traffic".[2] Because the conditions for the grant of licences varied widely as among the Member States, it was not possible to require them simply to recognise each other's licences until the conditions had been harmonised. Until such harmonisation occurred, the national measure requiring foreign nationals to possess local licences could not be regarded as an obstacle to the freedoms guaranteed by the Treaty.

Nevertheless, the host Member State's authorities were not free to impose whatever conditions they chose for the issue of a driver's licence to a person exercising his migration rights under the Treaty. Certain restrictions on the Member States' discretion must be observed. Legislative provisions imposing requirements for the possession of a local licence and for its issue;

> ... could be considered to contravene Community law only if their application were to cause persons in one Member State who had obtained a driving licence in another Member State such difficulties that those persons would in fact be hindered in the free exercise of the rights which Articles 48, 52 and 59 of the Treaty guarantee them ... .[3]

It is conceivable that nationality laws could operate so as to deter the exercise of migration rights conferred by the Treaty. British law, for example, does not provide for the automatic acquisition of British citizenship by a child born in the territory of

[1]ibid at p 2301, paragraph 4 of the Court's judgment.

[2]ibid at p 2302, paragraph 6 of the Court's judgment.

[3]ibid at p 2302, paragraph 8 of the Court's judgment. *Choquet* was applied by the Belgian Cour de Cassation in *Procureur du Roi a Bruges v De Quant* [1981] 3 CMLR 609.

another Member State to British parents neither of whom were themselves born in the United Kingdom, unless one of the parents is, at the time of the birth, in the service of the British government or of a Community institution.[1] Provisions exist enabling, in certain limited circumstances,[2] a child born abroad of British parents who were not themselves born in the United Kingdom to be registered as a British citizen.[3]

The fact nevertheless remains that persons who are British nationals by descent run the risk, in giving birth to a child in another Member State, of not enabling that child to be born British and not being able subsequently to register the child as British. Such a child would not have a right under British domestic law to enter the United Kingdom and would not subsequently be entitled to exercise a range of other rights not presently open to Union citizens possessing the nationality of other Member States (eg voting in and nomination for elections to the Parliament at Westminster). Depending on the laws of the Member State in whose territory the child was born, it might automatically acquire and be unable to renounce that Member State's nationality (at least until the child can acquire a different nationality), thereby becoming eventually exposed to the obligation to perform military service in that Member State. Even if the parents are British citizens otherwise than by descent, the child itself would be born British only by descent and its children would be born British only if they were born in the United Kingdom or if the other parent were British otherwise than by descent.

The prospect of their future children or grandchildren being subject to such disabilities could conceivably amount to an indirect hindrance to the free exercise of the migration rights granted by the Treaty.

The power to make dispositions of nationality falls, as currently does the power to issue and recognise driver's licences, within the scope of the responsibilities remaining to the Member States. As in the field of rules relating to the issue and recognition of driver's licences, there is no Community legislation specifying the manner in which the power is to be exercised. Nevertheless, as with the exercise of powers in connection with driver's licences, an exercise by a Member State of its power to make dispositions of nationality exerts an influence on the exercise of the rights guaranteed by the provisions of the Treaty relating to freedom of movement.

[1] *British Nationality Act 1981*, section 2. The qualifications to the general rule have been summarised for the sake of brevity, albeit at the expense of some exactitude.

[2] Application must be made within twelve months of birth (*British Nationality Act 1981*, section 3(2)). Except in the case where the child would be otherwise stateless, either parent must be a British citizen by descent, that parent's parent must have (or would have been had he/she lived until the commencement of the Act) been a British citizen otherwise than by descent, and the parent must have spent three years in the United Kingdom at some time prior to the birth without being absent from the United Kingdom for more than 270 days during that period (*British Nationality Act 1981*, section 3(3)). The provisions have been summarised for the sake of brevity, albeit at the expense of some exactitude.

[3] For a more detailed consideration of some of the problems presented to Community law by the *British Nationality Act 1981* see David Bonner, "*British citizenship: implications for United Kingdom nationals in the European Communities*", (1982) 7 EL Rev 69.

Accordingly, it is conceivable that the Member States may not be able to exercise their power to make dispositions of nationality in such a way as to impose on persons seeking to exercise their Community migration rights difficulties such that those persons would in fact be hindered, either directly or indirectly, in the free exercise of their rights.

Some interesting possibilities could flow from such a view were the Court of Justice to embrace it. A result could be that, in making dispositions of nationality which had the effect of hindering the exercise of Community migration rights, the Member State concerned would have failed to fulfil its obligations under the *EC Treaty*, thereby exposing the Member State to proceedings brought under Articles 169 or 170 of the Treaty. Furthermore, an administrative decision based on such a delinquent disposition, such as a decision not to allow our hypothetical child into the territory of the United Kingdom, or to prevent him from seeking election to a political office reserved to British citizens, or even perhaps a decision by the Member State whose nationality the child was born with that the child must serve in that Member State's armed forces,[1] could constitute an infringement of Community law to which national courts should not give effect.

'WORKERS' AND 'NATIONALITY': COMMON POLICY CONSIDERATIONS?

Moreover, some of the policy considerations adopted by the Court of Justice for giving the term "workers" an autonomous Community meaning can be applied to the way in which Community law approaches the concept of Member State nationality.

A principal reason for shielding the concept of "workers" from definition by domestic law was the Court of Justice's view that the free movement of workers is a fundamental principle of Community law. The personal scope of such a fundamental principle of the Community legal order should not, according to the Court of Justice, be vulnerable to destruction or restriction through the expedient of redefinition by domestic legal acts.[2]

[1] That the performance of compulsory military service must not operate as a barrier to the completion and maintenance of the common market finds expression in Article 6(2) of *Directive 68/360* which states that the validity of a residence permit issued to a worker or establishee from another Member State shall not be affected by the holder's absence on military service. The provision does not on its face apply only to absence in the military service of the person's own Member State. Rather, its language is wide enough to suggest that absence in the military service of any State, including that of the host Member State, is covered. Furthermore in Case 15/69 *Württembergische Milchverwertung Südmilch AG v Ugliola* [1969] ECR 363 the Court of Justice held that the right of a Community migrant worker to equal treatment in respect of his conditions of work and employment contained in Article 7(1) of *Regulation 1612/68* extends to forbid unfavourable treatment resulting from a migrant worker's absence in the compulsory military service of his own Member State where such treament is not imposed on native workers who are absent in the compulsory military service of the host Member State.

[2] Case 75/63 *Hoekstra v Bestuur der Bedrijfsvereniging voor Detailhandel en Ambachten* [1964] ECR 177; Case 53/81 *Levin v Staatssecretaris van Justitie* [1982] ECR 1035; Case 139/85 *Kempf v Staatssecretaris van Justitie* [1986] ECR 1746; Case 66/85 *Lawrie-Blum v Land Baden-Württemberg* [1986] ECR 2121. The meaning of "establishment" in Articles 52-58 of the *EEC Treaty* is also probably the subject of an autonomous Community meaning and immune from redefinition by a Member State. Thus in Case 205/84 *Commission v Germany* ("*Re Insurance Services*") [1986] ECR 3755 at p 3801, paragraph 21 of the Court's judgment, the Court of Justice suggested that in order for a company to take advantage of the right of establishment it is sufficient that it establish an office managed by the company's

The same consideration can be said to apply to the notion of Member State nationality, at least in the context of the freedom of personal movement. If a person is entitled to exercise that freedom he could just as easily be arbitrarily deprived of his rights by domestic redefinition of Member State nationality as by a similar redefinition of the three functional categories (workers, services, establishment).

Secondly in *Hoekstra v Bestuur der Bedrijfsvereniging voor Detailhandel en Ambachten*[1] the Court of Justice said that "by the very fact of establishing freedom of movement for 'workers'", Articles 48 to 51 of the *EEC Treaty* had given a "Community scope" to the term.[2]

But it is not to all workers that the *EC Treaty* grants the Community right of free personal movement. The Treaty itself established freedom of movement only for those workers who are 'workers of the Member States'.[3] Thus, it can be argued, by the very fact of establishing freedom of movement for 'workers who are nationals of Member States' the *EEC Treaty* gave a Community scope not only to 'worker', but also to the expression "nationals of a Member State" and its cognates. The fact that this terminology is deployed in the Community treaties can, by the same reasoning, be said to give it a Community scope for the purposes of matters falling within the jurisdiction of Community law. A similar point is made by T.C. Hartley:

> [T]he identification of the persons within the personal scope of the Community provisions is basically a question of Community law. It is true that, in adopting the criterion of nationality, Community law has conferred a certain competence on national law - it is for the national law of each Member State to determine who the nationals of that State are - but since the criterion of nationality was adopted by a rule of Community law, it is open to Community law to make exceptions to it.[4]

It follows that there are good reasons for at least hypothesising that the concept of Member State nationality, to the extent that it helps determine the personal scope of Community migration rights, is subject to Community supervision.

---

own employees or by some other person authorised to act on the company's behalf, even if domestic law were to require a more formal arrangement. Moreover, the general principles applicable to the right of establishment are the same as those applicable to the free movement of workers and services (In Case 48/75 *Royer* [1976] ECR 497 at p 509, paragraph 12 of the judgment, the Court of Justice said that the *EEC Treaty* provisions dealing with the free movement of workers and services and the right of establishment "are based on the same principles both in so far as they concern the entry into and residence within the territory of Member States of persons covered by Community law and the prohibition of all discrimination between them on grounds of nationality").

[1]Case 75/63 [1964] ECR 177.

[2]ibid at p 184.

[3]See Article 48(2).

[4]T.C. Hartley, "*EEC Immigration Law*" (1978), p 76.

The comparison of the concepts of 'worker' and 'Member State nationality', however, suggests a consequence going radically beyond our initial purpose, which was to establish whether there are good reasons for rejecting the idea that Member States are exclusively competent to define the personal scope of their nationalities for Community purposes. As we have seen, Community law is not content merely with supervising the exercise of a Member State discretion in defining the meaning of 'worker'. Rather, Community law itself exhaustively defines the category of 'worker' for Community purposes. Could the real position possibly, and radically, be that Community law approaches the concept of 'Member State nationality' such that there is, for Community purposes, an autonomous Community meaning for it completely independent of the prescriptions of domestic law?

Two Grounds of Objection

It is possible to attack both propositions - ie the analogy between 'worker' and 'Member State nationality' indicates that Community law *supervises* domestic dispositions of nationality for Community purposes and that Community law prescribes an *autonomous meaning* to 'Member State nationality' - from the same direction. However this will not, as we shall see, guarantee equally efficacious results as against both propositions.

The attack is constituted by an objection that the concepts of 'worker' and 'Member State nationality' are fundamentally different, that the analogy is a false one, and that there are therefore no reasons supporting either proposition. The success of this objection would lead to a conclusion that the analogy with the concept of 'worker' can provide no support for a proposition abolishing or circumscribing the power of domestic law to make dispositions of nationality in whatever ways the Member States please, with corresponding full effect in Community law.

Such an attack might consist of two prongs.

Firstly the Community treaties, including the *Union Treaty* and the *EC Treaty*, do not expressly define nationality of a Member State. In *Hoekstra*, on the other hand, the Court of Justice was able to refer to the terms of Article 48(2), enumerating some of the entailments of free movement for workers, in support of articulating an autonomous Community meaning for "workers":

> [N]othing in Articles 48 to 51 of the Treaty leads to the conclusion that these provisions have left the definition of the term 'worker' to national legislation.
>
> On the contrary, the fact that Article 48(2) mentions certain elements of the concept of 'workers', such as employment and remuneration, shows that the Treaty attributes a Community meaning to that concept.[1]

[1]Case 75/63 *Hoekstra v Bestuur der Bedrijfsvereniging voor Detailhandel en Ambachten* [1964] ECR 177 at p 184.

By contrast, such an argument might run, the Community treaties do not mention any "elements" of the concept of Member State nationality. It could be said to follow that the treaties were not intended independently to regulate that concept for Community law purposes.

The second prong of the attack is an argument that Member State nationality, by its very nature, is so intimately associated with State sovereignty that it cannot be subject to requirements of Community law, even when it helps determine the personal scope of Community rights and obligations. Such an invasion into the heartland of State sovereignty, it might be argued, is all the more impossible because of the lack of any clear textual authority in the treaties supporting it.

Do either of these lines of attack invalidate the propositions (moderately) qualifying or (radically) abrogating the power of Member States conclusively to make dispositions of their nationalities for Community purposes?

Failure of Treaties to Define Nationality
The force of the first line of attack must be conceded. Although the *EC Treaty* provides explicit criteria by which a person can be considered to fall within the Community law concept of 'worker', no similar guidelines are expressed in connection with nationality. The analogy between the concepts of 'worker' and 'nationality' cannot therefore be employed to advance the proposition that there is an autonomous Community law concept of Member State nationality.

The absence of such guidelines in Community law does not, however, disprove the proposition that Community law may supervise the Member States in making dispositions of nationality such as to produce Community effects. The Member States' discretion in the field of public policy, for example, is subject to Community supervision notwithstanding the absence of any guidelines on the content of public policy spelled out in the treaties.

Much more damaging to the proposition that Community law may supervise the Member States in making dispositions of nationality such as to produce Community effects is the second line of attack which argues that nationality, by its very nature, is so intimately associated with State sovereignty that it cannot be subject to requirements of Community law.

State Sovereignty, the Public Service and Official Authority
An attempt to refute this line of attack can best be made by reference to the way in which the Court of Justice has dealt with the public service exception in Article 48(4) and the official authority exception in Article 55 of the *EC Treaty*.

Articles 48(4) and 55. Article 48(4) provides that the free movement of workers does not apply to "employment in the public service", while Article 55 provides that the right of establishment does not extend to activities which are "connected, even occasionally, with the exercise of official authority". Article 66 applies the exception in Article 55 to the free movement of services. The rationale for the exceptions under Articles 48(4) and 55 appears to be the preservation of the political identity of each Member State. Article 8 of Regulation 1612/68 also provides that a worker who is a national of a Member State and who is employed in another Member State "may be excluded from taking part in the management of bodies governed by public law and from holding an office governed by public law".

Public Service. From its first encounter with a problem under Article 48(4), however, the Court of Justice has acted to limit the potential scope of the provision.

In *Sotgiu v Deutsche Bundespost*[1] the Court of Justice said that the provision permits the Member States to restrict "admission of foreign nationals to *certain* activities in the public service".[2]

The Court declared that a Member State could not rely on the exception in Article 48(4) by the expedient of classifying a public service worker according to criteria, such as "workman", "clerk", or "official", which possessed some special significance in domestic labour law, or even by indicating that he is employed under the public law of the State:

> These legal designations can be varied at the whim of national legislatures and cannot therefore provide a criterion for interpretation appropriate to the requirements of Community law.[3]

The concept of 'public service', therefore, was to be subject to Community supervision notwithstanding the centrality of the public service concept to State sovereignty.

In *Commission v Belgium* ("*Re Belgian Public Service*")[4] the Commission brought an Article 169 action against Belgium for requiring, or permitting to be required, the possession of Belgian nationality for employment in a range of occupations such as gardeners, plumbers, carpenters, electricians, teachers, supervisors, architects, security guards, stock controllers and nurses with the City of Brussels, and a variety of locomotive jobs with the publicly owned railways.

The Court referred to the fact that the constitutions of certain Member States require holders of civil posts to possess the nationality of that Member State, and acknowledged national sensitivities on the issue of non-national access to the public service by stating that such national requirements are to be taken into account in applying Article 48(4). Nevertheless "the demarcation of the concept of 'public service'

[1] Case 152/73 [1974] ECR 153.

[2] ibid at p 162, paragraph 4 of the Court's judgment (emphasis added).

[3] ibid at p 163, paragraph 5 of the Court's judgment.

[4] Case 149/79 [1980] ECR 3881 (preliminary decision), [1982] ECR 1845 (final judgment).

cannot be left to the total discretion of the Member States".[1] The domestic laws of Member States are relevant only to the extent that they do not limit the personal and material scope of rights conferred under Community law:

> [R]ecourse to provisions of the domestic legal systems to restrict the scope of the provisions of Community law would have the effect of impairing the unity and efficacy of that law and consequently cannot be accepted. That rule, which is fundamental to the existence of the Community, must also apply in determining the scope and bounds of Article 48(4) of the Treaty. ... [I]t is necessary to ensure that the effectiveness and scope of the provisions of the Treaty on freedom of movement of workers and equality of treatment of nationals of all Member States shall not be restricted by interpretations of the concept of public service which are based on domestic law alone and which would obstruct the application of Community rules.2

Some of the disputed posts were held to fall within the public service exception (eg security guards, supervisors, architects and stock controllers) while others did not (eg nurses, teachers, gardeners and locomotive personnel).

Stressing that the Article 48(4) concept of the public service "requires uniform interpretation and application throughout the Community",[3] the Court said that the exception excluded from Article 48(1) to (3);

> ... posts which involve direct or indirect participation in the exercise of powers conferred by public law and duties designed to safeguard the general interests of the State or other public authorities. Such posts in fact presume on the part of those occupying them the existence of a special relationship of allegiance to the State and reciprocity of rights and duties which form the foundation of the bond of nationality.[4]

Article 8 of *Regulation 1612/68* was assigned a similar meaning.

When Italian law restricted permanent appointment to the position of research scientist at the *Consiglio Nazionale delle Ricerche* (National Research Council) to those possessing Italian nationality, the Court of Justice ruled that Italy had failed to fulfil its obligations under Article 48.[5] According to the Court, "[o]nly the duties of management or of advising the State on scientific and technical questions could be described as employment in the public service within the meaning of Article 48(4)".[6]

[1] [1980] ECR 3881 at p 3903, paragraph 18 of the Court's judgment.

[2] ibid, paragraph 19 of the Court's judgment.

[3] ibid at p 3901, paragraph 12 of the Court's judgment.

[4] ibid at p 3900, paragraph 10 of the Court's judgment.

[5] Case 225/85 *Commission v Italy ("Re Employees of the Consiglio Nazionale delle Ricerche")* [1987] ECR 2625.

[6] ibid at p 2639, paragraph 9 of the Court's judgment.

After these and similar judgments, the Commission issued a statement outlining an action programme in respect of access to public sector employment by Community migrant workers.[1] In the Commission's view, the judgments of the Court of Justice showed that the Article 48(4) exception "covers specific functions of the State and similar bodies such as the armed forces, the police and other forces for the maintenance of order, the judiciary, the tax authorities and the diplomatic corps" and also "posts in State Ministries, regional government authorities, local authorities and other similar bodies, central banks and other public bodies, where the duties of the post involve the exercise of State authority, such as the preparation of legal acts, monitoring of their application and supervision of subordinate bodies".[2]

Official Authority. The Court's approach to the corresponding exception in Article 55 is similar. In *Reyners v Belgian State*,[3] a Dutch national who was born, educated and resided in Belgium obtained the qualifications which permitted Belgian nationals to be admitted to the bar as an *avocat*. When he applied for admission, however, he was refused on the basis that Belgian law required him to be of Belgian nationality.

On an Article 177 reference to the Court of Justice, the Luxembourg government[4] argued that the whole profession of *avocat* must be excluded from the right of establishment because it was organically connected with the functioning of the public service and the administration of justice, and therefore within the Article 55 exception. The Court, however, felt no compulsion to accept such a unilateral definition by a Member State of the scope of 'official authority'.

Rather, the Court said that the right of establishment possessed a "fundamental character" in the Community system and that Article 55 had to be construed in that context.[5] Although the possible restrictions on the right of establishment allowed by Article 55 must be considered separately in connection with each Member State's organisation of the legal profession, such consideration must;

> ... take into account the Community character of the limits imposed by Article 55 on the exceptions permitted to the principle of the freedom of establishment in order to avoid the effectiveness of the Treaty being defeated by unilateral provisions of Member States.[6]

The Court held that only certain activities associated with the practice of an *avocat*, ie those which "constitute a direct and specific connection with the exercise of official

[1]*Freedom of movement of workers and access to employment in the public service of the Member States - Commission action in respect of the application of Article 48(4) of the EEC Treaty*, OJ C 72/2 of 18.3.1988.
[2]ibid at p 3.
[3]Case 2/74 [1974] ECR 631.
[4]In this submission, Luxembourg was supported by the *Ordre national des avocats de Belgique*.
[5]Case 2/74 *Reyners v Belgian State* [1974] ECR 631 at p 654, paragraph 43 of the Court's judgment.
[6]ibid at p 655, paragraph 50 of the Court's judgment.

authority" fell within the Article 55 exception.[1] The Court indicated that activities directly involving the exercise of judicial power and discretion were clearly covered by the exception. But the most typical activities performed by an *avocat*, such as the giving of advice and legal assistance and the representation of parties in court were not covered by Article 55. Consequently, only those activities caught by the exception could be reserved to Belgian nationals, and the possibility that Community migrants with the requisite qualifications could be prevented from admission as an *avocat* altogether was excluded.

Community Law, Public Service and Official Authority. The Court of Justice has therefore shown itself ready to restrict the scope of national action in areas as intimately bound up with the notion of State sovereignty as the public service and the exercise of official authority. In neither case are Member States permitted unilaterally to set the limits of their sovereignty to the extent that such exercise adversely affects the uniform application of Community law and the achievement of the Community's goals. In both cases the States' determination as to the limits of their sovereign jurisdiction are subject to Community supervision so as to harmonise them with a Community protection for the fundamental right of free movement for persons.

It is important to note, however, that there is no autonomous Community law category by which a person can be definitively categorised as a member of the public service or engaged in the exercise of official authority. Rather as *Re Belgian Public Service* demonstrates, domestic legal requirements are to be taken into account in applying Article 48(4). Community law begins with the domestic concept of what constitutes the public service, and intervenes only to protect the enjoyment of the fundamental Community right contained in Article 48 when the application of domestic law standards threatens the uniform enjoyment of that right. Community law provides the bounds of the exception contained in Article 48(4), but it is domestic law which provides the content.[2]

The same considerations apply to the concept of official authority. In *Reyners* it was said that the possible restrictions on the right of establishment allowed by Article 55 must be considered separately in connection with each Member State's organisation of the legal profession. Thus domestic law provides the point of departure for ascertaining whether a particular function falls within the rubric of official authority, Community law intervening to avoid the effectiveness of the Treaty being defeated by unilateral provisions of Member States.

This approach to the meaning of 'public service' and 'official authority' contrasts with the Court's approach to the meaning of 'worker'. This is not surprising, however, having regard to the different purposes which these two sets of legal categories serve. The category of 'worker' contributes to defining the personal scope of a fundamental right of Community law, whereas the categories of 'public service' and 'official

[1]ibid at p 654, paragraph 45 of the Court's judgment.

[2]See Brigitte Lenz, "*The Public Service in Article 48(4) EEC with Special Reference to the Law in England and in the Federal Republic of Germany*", [1989] LIEI 75 especially at pp 90-93.

authority' operate so as to provide exceptions to the enjoyment of fundamental rights of Community law which a State may invoke. It is a Member State's duty to extend certain migration rights to workers, but it is a Member State's right to invoke the public service and official authority exceptions in appropriate circumstances.

It is entirely apt that a Member State should retain an area of discretion, as it does in the realm of public policy and public security,[1] in deciding when an activity touches upon a subject as sensitive and as vital to the political identity of the State as non-national access to the public service and the exercise of official authority.[2] Just as there is no single Community-wide standard of public morality, so there is no single Community-wide concept of public service and official authority. Both are, however, subject to Community supervision for the purpose of ensuring that the Member States' area of discretion is not abused for purposes inconsistent with the objectives of the Community. But it is also entirely apt that Member States should not retain any discretion in defining the economically functional criteria, such as that of 'worker', upon which depends the very existence of a fundamental Community right in the first place.

Nationality Compared to Public Service and Official Authority. While it is true that, in the context of the migration rights governed by Articles 48-66 of the *EC Treaty*, the concept of Member State nationality operates as an element in defining the personal scope of fundamental Community rights, it is also true that the concept is not an economically functional one and that it does touch upon matters which go to the very heart of the political identity of all the Member States.

Were Community law conclusively to define, without reference to the domestic law of the Member States, the meaning of 'Member State nationality' and thus also of citizenship of the Union, the Member States would no longer have any influence over the range of people *potentially* entitled to the benefit of Community rights. The Community would thus be possessed of an attribute which could profoundly threaten the national identities of the Member States contrary to the requirements of the *Union Treaty*.[3] Such a result does not, however, flow from the existence of an autonomous Community definition of merely functional criteria such as 'worker'.

The second line of attack for equating the concept of 'worker' with that of 'Member State nationality' therefore fails to the extent that it is sought to argue that Community law provides an autonomous definition of 'Member State nationality'.

[1]See Stephen Hall, "*The European Convention on Human Rights and Public Policy Exceptions to the Free Movement of Workers under the EEC Treaty*", (1991) 16 EL Rev 466.

[2]Article F(1) of the *Union Treaty* provides as follows: "The Union shall respect the national identities of its Member States, whose systems of government are founded on the principles of democracy". It is also to be noted that under Article 8b of the *EC Treaty* the political identities of the Member States are further protected by extending the electoral franchise to Union citizens not residing in their own Member States only in respect of municipal and European Parliamentary elections - elections to public office at the national (and probably regional and *Land*) level are not included.

[3]See previous footnote.

Nevertheless the two concepts cannot be treated differently on the grounds that nationality is too intimately associated with the notion of State sovereignty to be subject to Community control for Community purposes. We have seen that the Court of Justice has been robust in curtailing the attempts of Member States unilaterally to restrict the personal scope of Community free personal movement in areas just as intimately associated with State sovereignty as the national 'public service' and the exercise of 'official authority'. This is done, however, not by substituting a Community category of 'public service' and 'official authority' for that provide by the Member States' domestic laws, but by placing limits on the application, for Community purposes, of domestic categories.

In other words, the Community category of 'public service' and 'official authority' must be based on a State law in order to exist and be productive of effects at Community level. This is, as we have seen, the way nationality works at the level of international law - it is *based* on State law, but its international effects are not *determined* by State law.

The result, therefore, is that the centrality of the 'public service' and 'official authority' concepts in the *EC Treaty* to the political identity of the Member States does prevent those terms from possessing an autonomous Community meaning. In this way 'public service' and 'official authority' are different from the concept of 'worker', which concept is not vital to a Member State's political identity and is subject to an autonomous Community meaning. On the other hand the *rôle* played by 'public service' and 'official authority' in potentially limiting the enjoyment of fundamental Community migration rights means that they are subject to Community supervision so that they cannot be manipulated by Member States for purposes inconsistent with the objectives of the Community.

The objection that there is no valid analogy between 'worker' and 'Member State nationality' for our present purposes is therefore only partly successful. It defeats the radical assertion that, because there is an autonomous Community meaning of 'worker', there must also be one of 'Member State national'.

It does not however defeat the more moderate proposition that 'Member State nationality', while being based on domestic law, is not solely determined by domestic law. This suggests that the exercise by the Member States of their power to make dispositions of nationality is subject to Community supervision so that it cannot be manipulated for purposes inconsistent with the objectives of the Community. This result roughly corresponds to the effect given by international law to domestic dispositions of nationality on the plane of inter-State relations.

Summary and Conclusion

In order to ascertain the personal scope of Article 8a of the *EC Treaty* it is necessary to determine who is possessed of the status of citizen of the Union. Citizenship of the Union is dependent upon holding the nationality of a Member State.

International law, which provides a useful source for Community law in areas concerning nationality, tells us that in principle States are competent to confer nationality on, or to withdraw nationality from, whomever they please. Yet on the plane of Community law there are good reasons for believing that this principle is not necessarily applicable.

The power of States to make dispositions of nationality is an expression of their sovereignty in international law. Membership of the Community, however, involves the transfer of part of their sovereignty to the Community. To the extent that the exercise of State power to make dispositions of nationality impacts upon the rights and obligations arising under Community law, there is reason to believe that in principle State sovereignty in this area is subject to limits.

The treaties themselves seem tacitly to reflect the general principle that the disposition by a Member State of its nationality need not automatically be given effect in Community law.

An examination of the constitutional position of the Faroe Islands, the Channel Islands, the Isle of Man and the overseas countries and territories demonstrates that the Treaty itself does not always allow Member States to make dispositions of their nationality such as conclusively to determine the personal scope of movement rights under Community law.

The conferral or possession of British citizenship does not permit Channel Islanders or Manxmen to exercise migration rights under Community law, just as Member State nationals who are residents of the overseas countries and territories enjoy no automatic entitlement to the Community's migration rights. The conferral or possession of Danish citizenship on or by a resident of the Faroe Islands does not cause the Faroe Islander to be a 'national of a Member State' for the purposes of the Treaty.

Were Member States to possess a power to make dispositions of their nationality without the encumbrance of any limits imposed by Community law it is possible that the common market could be prejudiced. It is conceivable that certain nationality laws could operate so as to deter the exercise of migration rights conferred by the Treaty.

Finally, the reasons that impel Community law to subject the functional criteria for economic migration rights (such as 'worker') to Community control are equally applicable to making the concept of nationality subject to Community supervision. An unfettered Member State power to make dispositions of nationality could expose the enjoyment of fundamental Community rights to the same jeopardy as would a similar Member State power to define the concept of 'worker'. Because the Treaties do not, in contrast to their treatment of 'worker', contain criteria by which nationality can be tested it cannot be said that a person acquires or loses his Member State nationality as the result of the operation of Community law. However it remains in principle likely that, as with the concept of public policy, Community law possesses a power of supervision over the way in which Member States exercise their discretion.

We will now turn to consider whether Community law in fact possesses its own rules or principles which affect the acquisition and loss of Member State nationality.

CHAPTER 3

NATIONALITY AND UNION SUPERVISION

In the previous Chapter we saw that there are good reasons for thinking that, in principle, Community law circumscribes the power of Member States to make dispositions of their nationality. This Chapter will explore whether Community law actually possesses its own rules or principles which affect the acquisition and loss of Member State nationality. This topic is important not least because the vast majority of complaints about discrimination brought before or referred to the Court of Justice are about nationality discrimination.

We will first examine whether Community law always gives effect to a Member State's conferral of its nationality on persons who do not request the conferral and who already possess another State's nationality. We shall see that the Court of Justice will, in certain circumstances, refuse to give effect to such an unrequested naturalisation. This will firmly establish the principle that Community law need not always accept a Member State's disposition of its nationality.

We will then turn to consider whether the Member States' duty of co-operation and solidarity places any restrictions on a Member State's power to make conferrals of nationality in other circumstances.

We shall see that Community law supervises conferrals of nationality such that, in certain unusual circumstances, Member States may be required to revoke them. Such conferrals, however, will remain effective in Community law until they are revoked by the delinquent Member State.

Of more significance are the restrictions Community law places on the power of Member States to withdraw their nationality from individuals. In this connection we shall see that a Member State's act of denationalisation (a term here used to denote an act withdrawing a State's nationality from a person), done in violation of the fundamental rights protected by the Court of Justice, must not be given effect by national authorities, including national courts. Even if such an act of denationalisation remains valid within the national legal order, the denationalised individual retains his citizenship of the Union and all the rights attaching thereto.

Finally, we shall see that none of the various declarations on nationality made by the Member States affect this Chapter's findings.

Unrequested Conferral of Nationality

FOUR STAFF CASES

The issue of whether Community law must always accept a Member State's conferral of its nationality when the conferral affects the application of Community rights and obligations arose squarely in four staff cases involving the expatriation allowance paid by the Community to certain of its officers.

Gunnella

The first of these cases is *Gunnella v Commission.*[1] Miss Gunnella was born in France in 1925 of an Italian father and a French mother. She automatically acquired French nationality, French law conferring it on any legitimate child born in France of a French mother. She also automatically acquired Italian nationality, Italian law conferring it on any child of an Italian father wherever the place of birth. She resided in Italy from 1930 to 1945. When Miss Gunnella reached her age of majority in 1946 she took advantage of a provision of Italian law permitting her to renounce her Italian nationality, thereby becoming exclusively French. In 1949 she returned to live and work in Italy where she remained until 1961 when she took a job with the Commission of the European Atomic Energy Community in Belgium. She took special leave from the service of the Community in 1962, returned once more to Italy where she took other employment and where, in 1965, she was taken back into the service of the Commission.

The *Staff Regulations* provided for the payment of an expatriation allowance to officers in one of two circumstances. Under Article 4(1)(a) of Annex VII, the allowance was payable to officers who both (i) were not and had never been nationals of the State in whose European territory the place where they were employed was situated, and (ii) during the five years ending six months before they entered into the Commission's service had not habitually resided or carried on their main occupation within the European territory of that State. Alternatively, under Article 4(1)(b) the allowance was payable to officials who were or had been nationals of the State in whose territory the place where they were employed was situated but who during the ten years preceding the date of their entering the service habitually resided outside the European territory of that State for reasons other than the performance of duties in the service of that State or of an international organisation.[2]

Upon being taken back into the Commission's service in 1965, a decision was made fixing the several components of Miss Gunnella's remuneration. By that decision it was determined that she was not to be paid the expatriation allowance, and she was subsequently paid in accordance with that decision. In 1971 Miss Gunnella formally requested the Commission that she be paid the expatriation allowance. The

[1]Case 33/72 [1973] ECR 475.
[2]Article 69 read together with Article 4(1)(a) of Annex VII.

Commission formally rejected her request in 1972 and Miss Gunnella commenced proceedings in the Court of Justice seeking annulment of the Commission's 1972 decision and a ruling that she was entitled to be paid the expatriation allowance from 1965.

The Commission argued that Miss Gunnella was not entitled to be paid the expatriation allowance. Miss Gunnella had been an Italian national up until 1946 and was thus ineligible to receive the allowance under Article 4(1)(a). She was also said to be ineligible under Article 4(1)(b) because she had resided in Italy from 1949 to 1961, ie for twelve years before entering the service of the Commission. Her history of residence in Italy also disqualified her under Article 4(1)(a), according to the Commission, even if she were to be considered a person who had never been an Italian national.

For present purposes, it is only Miss Gunnella's claim to entitlement under Article 4(1)(a) which concerns us. Her case for entitlement under this provision rested on three propositions.[1]

Firstly, it was argued, the *ratio legis* of the nationality rule in Article 4(1)(a) was not to disqualify an officer who involuntarily held more than one Community nationality, but to prevent an officer from becoming entitled to an expatriation allowance by the device of voluntarily changing his previous nationality. This interpretation of Article 4(1)(a) was said to apply *a fortiori* when the officer renounces his dual nationality as soon as the law permits him to do so. It followed, according to Miss Gunnella, that the rule as to nationality in Article 4(1)(a) should not have been applied literally and that she should have been treated as never having possessed Italian nationality for the purposes of the provision.

Secondly, Miss Gunnella argued that her dominant nationality had always been French and that it was her French nationality alone which should have been taken into account for the purposes of Article 4(1)(a).

Finally, it was submitted that the application of Article 4(1)(b) to Miss Gunnella's case was unjust and infringed general principles of law. In particular, it was alleged that the Community principle of equality of treatment had been infringed, and that there were general principles supporting the right of individuals to change their nationality and the giving of full effect to nationality which had been infringed.

The Court of Justice found it unnecessary to decide the case on its merits. Because Miss Gunnella did not appeal to the Court within the prescribed three months of the contested decision being made (in 1965), her application was ruled inadmissible.

Advocate General Mayras also regarded Miss Gunnella's application as inadmissible for the same reasons. He nevertheless gave his opinion on the merits. In his view it is

[1]See Case 33/72 *Gunnella v Commission* [1973] ECR 475 at p 478.

appropriate to consider the objective and spirit of the provisions of a Community enactment in the light of the general arrangement of the legislation in which they are contained only where there is an ambiguity in the text. He argued that no such ambiguity existed in Article 4(1). In determining whether Miss Gunnella had ever possessed Italian nationality for the purposes of Article 4(1), the Advocate General was blunt:

> [T]he present or previous nationality of the official is taken *as a fact* determined solely by the domestic legislation applicable. It excludes any distinction as to the method of acquisition or loss of that nationality.
>
> The Community legislature rightly refrained from granting the institutions any discretionary powers in this connection. Whilst the concept of habitual residence might possibly give rise to interpretation, the condition of nationality must be derived from a pure and simple finding, proof regarding which is governed exclusively by the law of each state. Therefore it is not possible to retain here the concept of dominant or effective nationality.[1]

It followed, according to the Advocate General, that Miss Gunnella must be regarded as having possessed Italian nationality until her majority. As the place where she was re-engaged was in Italian territory, it followed that her situation could not be governed by Article 4(1)(a), but by Article 4(1)(b). Her history of residence in Italy prior to 1961 was said to disqualify her under the latter provision.

On Miss Gunnella's plea that to regard her as having possessed Italian nationality was unlawful for infringement of general principles of law, the Advocate General contented himself with the opinion that the principle of equal treatment had not been infringed in her case. This was so because the "criterion of nationality adopted is in fact the same for all staff; in law, it does not introduce any discrimination between them".[2]

Interestingly, however, the Advocate General did not go so far as in principle to rule out the option of rejecting, for Community law purposes, Italy's attribution of its nationality had such an attribution actually involved or resulted in an infringement of a fundamental principle of Community law.

[1] ibid at p 486 (emphasis in original).

[2] ibid at p 487. The Advocate General effectively dealt with Miss Gunnella's plea concerning the alleged general principles supporting the right of individuals to change their nationality and the giving of full effect to nationality in discussing the full effect to be given by Community law to the "condition of nationality" under the domestic law of the Member States.

Airola

The question left open by Advocate General Mayras in *Gunnella* was answered by the Court of Justice in *Airola v Commission.*[1]

Mrs Airola was a Belgian national when she commenced employment with the Commission in Italy. Soon afterwards she married an Italian national. In accordance with Italian law[2] she automatically acquired, and was unable to renounce, her husband's Italian nationality upon her marriage. Italian law did not similarly impose Italian nationality on alien men who married Italian women. Mrs Airola also retained her Belgian nationality by making a special declaration under Belgian law.

Mrs Airola satisfied the residence requirement but was refused the expatriation allowance because she was said by the Commission to be a national of the State to which she had been posted. She sought from the Court of Justice annulment of a Commission decision discontinuing payment to her of the expatriation allowance and an order directing the Commission to resume payment of the allowance. In her view, the Commission's decision was *ultra vires* in that it violated a fundamental general principle of Community law by treating women less favourably than men to the extent that, if the Applicant had been a non-Italian man marrying an Italian women, she would not have been deprived of her expatriation allowance.

Advocate General Trabucchi urged the Court to dismiss the application. In his opinion the fact that Italian domestic law produced the discriminatory result when applied through Community law did not invalidate the Commission's decision:

> [I]t is always necessary to act in terms of nationality being an overall symbol which Community legislation has adopted, not because of its actual legal content but as a point of reference for a rational application of the expatriation allowance.3

He accepted that, in the present case, the application by the Commission of domestic law criteria might actually have resulted in Mrs Airola receiving less favourable treatment than if she had been a man in a similar situation, and that a Community law which violated the principle of sex equality would be invalid. Nevertheless, there were argued to be good reasons why the Court should not grant the application:

> Community law cannot remould from its own point of view the whole world of social and human relationships. Where the national legislation provides for a method of acquiring nationality and links it with the normal consequences of a status which takes the form of various rights and obligations, those responsible for drafting the

[1]Case 21/74 [1975] ECR 221. Discussed by Lorraine Massaro, "*The Nationality of Married Women and the Principle of Gender Equality in the European Economic Communities: Airola v Commission of the European Communities*", (1976) 15 Columbia Journal of Transnational Law 514.

[2]*Legge 13 giugno 1912, n. 555.*, Article 10.

[3]Case 21/74 *Airola v Commission* [1975] ECR 221 at p 233.

> Community legislation rightly accept the situation as they find it as a point of reference, and they will do so so long as it is not in itself repugnant to a fundamental human right, as discrimination based on sex alone would be. Community law cannot object to the fact that, in the management of its internal relationships, each State pays regard to the principle of family unit in accordance with its own conception of it and without in social terms conflicting with the public policy of the Community.[1]

The Advocate General did not accept the view, therefore, that a reference by Community law to Member State nationality must always result in a servile application of domestic law rules. In his view, the question of whether an individual possesses the nationality of a Member State will be settled by reference to the national law of that Member State unless that national law is itself violative of fundamental human rights or in conflict with the Community's public policy. As the present case did not involve the application of a domestic law standard which was *per se* repugnant to human rights or other fundamental principles of Community law, the Commission's decision was said to be unassailable.

Notwithstanding Advocate General Trabucchi's submissions, the Court of Justice granted the application. In so doing it seemed nevertheless to accept the Advocate General's view that domestic law could not be applied to determine whether a person possesses the nationality of a Member State if that domestic law directly infringes human rights or other fundamental principals of Community law.

The Court, however, was prepared to go further. It said that the concept of 'nationals' in the relevant provision of the *Staff Regulations* must "be interpreted in such a way as to avoid any unwarranted difference of treatment as between male and female officials who are, in fact, placed in comparable situations".[2] Such an unwarranted difference of treatment would result, in the context of expatriation allowances, "from an interpretation of the concept of 'nationals' ... as also embracing the nationality which was imposed by law on an official of the female sex by virtue of her marriage, and which she was unable to renounce".[3]

According to the Court of Justice it was therefore necessary to "define the concept of an official's present or past nationality" under the relevant provision of the *Staff Regulations* "as excluding nationality imposed by law on a female official upon her marriage with a national of another State, when she has no possibility of renouncing it".[4]

[1] ibid.
[2] ibid at p 228, paragraph 10 of the Court's judgment.
[3] ibid at p 229, paragraph 11 of the Court's judgment.
[4] ibid at p 229, paragraph 12 of the Court's judgment.

In adopting this approach, the Court definitively broke with any dogmatic view that Community law must always and in all circumstances apply the dispositions of nationality made by the Member States.

Van den Broeck

In *Van den Broeck v Commission*,[1] decided on the same day as *Airola*, Mrs Van den Broeck was born in France thereby acquiring French nationality. At the age of 24 she moved to Belgium and, about one month later, married a Belgian national. Belgian law conferred Belgian nationality on her by virtue of her marriage to a Belgian male. Alien men marrying Belgian women did not similarly acquire Belgian nationality. In this respect, then, the Belgian nationality law was identical to the Italian nationality law at issue in *Airola*.

In accordance with the terms of an international agreement between Belgium and France, Mrs Van den Broeck had the option of making, within six months of acquiring her Belgian nationality, a declaration under Belgian law renouncing her Belgian nationality thereby enabling her to retain her French nationality which she would otherwise have lost as a consequence of acquiring Belgian nationality. She did not avail herself of this opportunity and consequently lost her French nationality. About 3 years later she entered the service of the Commission in Belgium, but was denied the same expatriation allowance that was in issue in *Gunnella* and *Airola*.

Mrs Van den Broeck's application for an order against the Commission to pay the expatriation allowance was dismissed. The Court took the view that Mrs Van den Broeck's failure to take advantage of the procedure which allowed her to renounce her Belgian nationality and would have allowed her to retain her French nationality deprived her of "reasons associated with equal treatment why her Belgian nationality should not be taken into account in applying the provision concerned".[2] If Mrs Van den Broeck had made the declaration which was available to her under Belgian law, she would have been in no worse position than a French man marrying a Belgian woman in like circumstances.

Devred

The last of our four expatriation cases is *Devred v Commission*.[3] Mrs Devred was a British national when she married a Belgian man thereby acquiring Belgian nationality. She failed to exercise the option, available to her under Belgian law, of renouncing her Belgian nationality within six months of acquiring it. Thus far, *Devred* is materially identical to *Van den Broeck*. Unlike Mrs Van den Broeck, however, Mrs Devred did not lose her original nationality. Thus, Mrs Devred became a dual British and Belgian national. In this *Devred* resembles *Airola*, inasmuch as Mrs Airola became a dual Belgian and Italian national.

[1]Case 37/74 [1975] ECR 235.
[2]ibid at p 245, paragraph 14 of the Court's judgment.
[3]Case 257/78 [1979] ECR 3767.

At the time of her marriage, Mrs Devred was employed by the Commission in Brussels and was receiving the same expatriation allowance that was in issue in *Gunnella*, *Airola* and *Van den Broeck*. She continued receiving the allowance until she resigned from the service of the Commission. Some years later she joined the service of the Council in Brussels but was very soon transferred to the service of the Commission. The Commission for a while paid Mrs Devred the expatriation allowance, but terminated it after deciding that she was not eligible to receive it because she was a national of the State in whose European territory she was employed.

Mrs Devred sought from the Court of Justice, *inter alia*, a declaration annulling the decision to terminate her expatriation allowance.[1] This application rested, relevantly for present purposes, on two grounds.

Firstly Mrs Devred argued that as she had retained her British nationality she should be treated as a British national for the purposes of the expatriation allowance. This was said to be necessary in order to comply with Article 119 of the *EEC Treaty* and the Community principle of equality. Had Mrs Devred been a British man marrying a Belgian woman she would not have acquired Belgian nationality and could not therefore have been denied the expatriation allowance on the basis of her Belgian nationality.

In this connection, *Van den Broeck* was submitted to be distinguishable because Mrs Van den Broeck was forced to choose between her French and her Belgian nationalities. To have ignored Mrs Van den Broeck's Belgian nationality would have been to treat her as stateless. Mrs Devred, by contrast, could retain both her British and her Belgian nationalities by simply declining to make the declaration provided for by Belgian law within the stipulated six month period after acquiring Belgian nationality by marriage. Viewed from this angle, it was argued, *Airola* was of more assistance - especially as Mrs Airola needed to perform the positive act of making a declaration under Belgian law in order to retain her original Belgian nationality.

The Court rejected this argument, albeit somewhat peremptorily:

> [W]here the person concerned is able to renounce the nationality which causes her to lose the benefit of the expatriation allowance, there is no reason associated with the purposes for which that allowance was granted for disregarding the fact that, by an act of her own volition subsequent to, but distinct from, her marriage, the official decided to assume the nationality of the place in which she is employed.[2]

[1] After Mrs Devred rejoined the service of the Commission, but shortly before she commenced her action in the Court of Justice, the *Staff Regulations* were amended retroactively so as expressly to provide that any official who has by marriage automatically acquired and cannot renounce the nationality of the State in whose territory he is employed shall be treated in the same way as an official who has never been a national of that State. This amendment gave express legislative effect to the Court of Justice's decision in *Airola*.

[2] Case 257/78 *Devred v Commission* [1979] ECR 3767 at p 3782, paragraph 12 of the Court's judgment.

By employing these reasons, the Court decided merely to apply *Van den Broeck* to Mrs Devred's situation without addressing the reasons advanced by her as to the inappropriateness of so doing. Advocate General Warner, whose opinion the Court accepted, dealt with Mrs Devred's first argument in more detail:

> Mrs Devred, like Mrs Van den Broeck, had an option. True it was not quite the same option. It was in fact a less daunting option. Mrs Van den Broeck had to choose between the nationality to which she was entitled by birth and the nationality to which she was entitled by marriage. Mrs Devred had only to choose whether or not to accept permanently the nationality to which she was entitled by marriage. She would retain the nationality to which she was entitled by birth in any event. It is true also that to have ignored Mrs Van den Broeck's Belgian nationality would have amounted to treating her as a stateless person. But the decision of the Court in her case did not turn on that. It turned on the fact that, because she had the option, she was in no worse a position than a male official would have been: neither of them could have the nationality of his or her spouse foisted on him or her. Indeed, it seems to me, a female official in Mrs Devred's position is, in a way, better off than a male official who marries a national of another Member State. He is, in general, given no right to acquire his wife's nationality, even if he would like to do so.[1]

Thus the fact that Mrs Van den Broeck was forced to choose between her French and Belgian nationalities was not regarded by the *Devred* court as the decisive factor in *Van den Broeck*. It was not germane that Mrs Van den Broeck was forced to choose between her two nationalities, but that she had a choice the exercise of which would have removed the unlawfully discriminatory effect of applying domestic nationality definitions in the determination of rights under Community law.

Mrs Devred secondly argued that, although she possessed Belgian nationality, her 'preponderant' nationality was British, either because that was her nationality before acquiring her Belgian nationality by marriage or because it was her 'effective' nationality. In either case, she argued, she was entitled to be treated as British for the purposes of the relevant provisions of the *Staff Regulations*.

The Court rejected this argument on the basis that:

> The concept of effective nationality is used mainly in private international law in order to resolve positive conflicts of nationality. The concept cannot be transferred to a quite different sphere from that for which it was developed, specifically the scope of the Staff Regulations for Officials of the Communities, in order to determine

[1] ibid at p 3789.

> entitlement to receive the expatriation allowance, when ... an official who has the nationality of the place in which he is employed is not entitled to that allowance.[1]

In so reasoning, the Court of Justice was asserting a view that, at least as far as the *Staff Regulations* are concerned, the possession by an individual of the nationality of more than one Member State does not involve the resolution of conflicts in the realm of private international law. Both nationalities will be relevant in determining an individual's rights or liabilities under the *Staff Regulations*.[2]

STAFF CASES NOT HELPFUL?

Yet it may be argued that none of our four staff cases are really helpful in deciding whether and to what extent the concept of 'Member State nationality' is subject to Community supervision. Such an objection would be based on the peculiar *ratio legis* of the provisions regulating payment of the expatriation allowance. We shall consider this objection before proceeding to draw conclusions from our examination of the staff cases.

The Court of Justice in *Airola* observed that the "object of the expatriation allowance is to compensate officials for the extra expense and inconvenience of taking up employment with the Communities and being thereby obliged to change their residence".[3]

In *Vutera v Commission*[4] an Italian officer of the Commission employed in Belgium claimed entitlement to the expatriation allowance. Although Mr Vutera possessed only Italian nationality he had lived in Belgium for almost his entire life before being

[1] ibid at p 3782, paragraph 14 of the Court's judgment.

[2] There is no reason in principle why this approach should not prevail when other Community rights and obligations, not covered by the *Staff Regulations*, are in issue. Consequently, it can be inferred, a person possessing the nationality both of a host Member State and of another Member State would be entitled to exercise, for example, the movement and residence rights under Articles 8a and 48-66 notwithstanding that his effective nationality was that of the host Member State. In Case C-419/92 *Scholz v Opera Universitaria di Cagliari* [1994] ECR I-505 (at p I-521, paragraph 8 of the judgment) the Court of Justice held that a German national was not disqualified in Italy from relying on Article 48 movement rights simply because she had also acquired Italian nationality. Cf Case 197/86 *Brown v Secretary of State for Scotland* [1988] ECR 3205 in which Advocate General Sir Gordon Slynn considered an argument advanced by the Danish government that a dual British and French national could not rely on any Treaty provision dealing with discrimination against the United Kingdom. Rejecting the Danish submission, the Advocate General said, "on the basis that as a French national he can claim rights as such, France being the country in which he has resided and with which, apart from the fact that he is the son of a British national, he has the closest connection" (at p 3227). The Advocate General therefore resolved the problem raised by the Danish government by making a choice between the individual's British and French nationalities based on determining the individual's effective or preponderant nationality, the very course rejected by the Court of Justice in *Devred*. The Court, however, made no reference whatever to the individual's dual nationality, treating him simply as French and therefore entitled to the protection of the Treaty's anti-discrimination provisions while in the United Kingdom. It is not clear whether he was treated as French because he had a closer connection with France than with the United Kingdom, as argued by the Advocate General, or simply because he held French nationality, consistently with *Devred*.

[3] Case 21/74 *Airola v Commission* [1975] ECR 221 at p 228, paragraph 8 of the Court's judgment.

[4] Case 1322/79 [1981] ECR 127.

recruited. The Commission refused him the allowance on the basis that he failed the residence condition contained in Article 4(1)(a) of Annex VII of the *Staff Regulations* in that he had habitually resided in Belgium during the five years ending six months before entering the service.

Mr Vutera argued that the residence requirement in Article 4(1)(a) infringed the principle of equality and non-discrimination because it created an unwarranted difference of treatment between officials who are in comparable situations (ie persons employed by the Community in a Member State of which they are not a national). The Court rejected the assertion that the residence requirement was discriminatory and said:

> The provisions of Article 4 considered as a whole indicate that, whilst the Community legislature made the fact of foreign origin the sole basis for the grant of the foreign residence allowance [Article 4(2) provided for this less generous allowance - SJH], for the purposes of the grant of the expatriation allowance it adopted actual change of residence as the primary criterion and regarded nationality as merely of secondary importance.[1]

On the basis of these and similar passages in other staff expatriation cases[2] it might be tempting to argue that the use of the nationality concept in the legislation dealing with the expatriation allowance is distinguishable from its use in the contexts with which we are here concerned.

In particular, it might be suggested, the concept of nationality in the expatriation allowance legislation plays only an ancillary *rôle* in determining the identity of the persons entitled to a right under Community law. Moreover, given that the object of the expatriation allowance is to compensate officials for the extra expense and inconvenience of taking up employment with the Communities and being thereby obliged to change their residence, there is a powerful reason to disregard dispositions of nationality which would otherwise have the effect of frustrating that object. By contrast, in the context of the migration rights under Articles 8a and 48-66 of the *EC Treaty*, such an argument might continue, the concept of nationality is critical in determining the identity of the beneficiaries and there is no overriding reason to disregard dispositions by Member States of their nationalities.

[1] ibid at p 138, paragraph 6 of the Court's judgment.

[2] eg, Case 188/83 *Witte v European Parliament* [1984] ECR 3465 at p 3473, paragraph 8 of the Court's judgment, Case 246/83 *De Angelis v Commission* [1985] ECR 1253 at p 1263, paragraph 13 of the Court's judgment, Case 330/85 *Richter v Commission* [1986] ECR 3439 at p 3447, paragraph 6 of the Court's judgment, Case 61/85 *Urhausen v Commission* [1987] ECR 2853 at p 2863, paragraph 7 of the Court's judgment, Case 105/87 *Morabito v European Parliament* [1988] ECR 1707 at p 1718, paragraph 10 of the Court's judgment, Case 211/87 *Nuñez v Commission* [1988] ECR 2791 at pp 2802-2803, paragraph 9 of the Court's judgment, Case 201/88 *Palmerini v Commission* [1989] ECR 3109 at pp 3121-3122, paragraph 9 of the Court's judgment, Case T-123/89 *Chomel v Commission* [1990] ECR II-131 at p II-137, paragraph 14 of the Court's judgment.

This objection to our use of *Airola* and the other three staff cases is, however, not well founded. It is certainly true that nationality in the expatriation allowance legislation plays only an ancillary *rôle* in determining the identity of the persons entitled to a right under Community law. Nevertheless in the four staff cases the issue of whether to recognise an unrequested conferral of an additional Member State nationality was (or, in the case of *Gunnella*, was potentially) central, and not merely ancillary, to their resolution. The fact that the criterion of nationality is merely of secondary importance in expatriation allowance cases does not deprive it of all importance, for, as the Court's jurisprudence demonstrates, cases can turn on questions of nationality. Furthermore, although as a matter of policy there might be better reasons for disregarding an unrequested conferral of a second nationality in an expatriation allowance case than in cases involving Community migration rights, neither the Court of Justice nor the Advocates General have sought to rely on any such reasons in approaching problems of nationality in expatriation allowance cases. They have rather invoked considerations of general legal principle in resolving the problems before them.

The four staff cases are therefore useful in helping us to understand whether and to what extent Community law must always accept and apply Member State dispositions of nationality in the context of Community migration rights.

FORCED CONFERRAL NOT ALWAYS APPLIED IN COMMUNITY LAW

What, then, are we to make of *Gunnella*, *Airola*, *Van den Broeck* and *Devred* in the context of determining the extent to which the Community must always accept a Member State's disposition of its nationality when it affects the application of Community rights and obligations?

The starting point for deciding whether a person is a national of a Member State for the purposes of determining the personal scope of rights under Community law is the domestic law of the Member States. Community law must give full effect to a domestic law conferral of nationality unless to do so results in a violation of the Community law principle of sex equality. It does not matter that the domestic conferral of nationality is not *per se* violative of the principle,[1] provided that in its application through the operation of Community law such a result is achieved. If the asserted violation of the principle of sex equality stems from the application of a domestic law imposing an additional nationality, the individual affected must take advantage of any reasonable opportunity to renounce his imposed additional nationality before being allowed to argue that he should not be regarded as a national of that Member State for Community law purposes.

Before any of these expatriation cases, the principle of sex equality had been established as a general principle of Community law against which inconsistent

[1]A *per se* violation of the principle of sex equality in the conferral by a Member State of its nationality would, on the basis of Advocate General Trabucchi's opinion in *Airola*, be sufficient to entitle the Court of Justice not to apply it in interpreting Community law.

Community legislation could not stand.[1] It would be discrepant if sex equality were to be the only general principle of Community law which must be respected in deciding whether, for Community purposes, to give effect to a Member State's forced conferral of its nationality on a person who already holds a nationality. The better view is that such a forced conferral by a Member State of its nationality cannot be applied in Community law in such a way as to violate any of the Community's general principles of law, including the protection of fundamental freedoms. This analysis is entirely consistent with Advocate General Trabucchi's opinion in *Airola* which, so far as it went, the Court of Justice accepted.

The principle that an individual who does not take an available opportunity to renounce his involuntarily acquired additional nationality is unable to deny the effect of that nationality in Community law would apply *a fortiori* where he acquires the nationality voluntarily, eg by a naturalisation which he requested.

Duty of Solidarity and Fundamental Rights

That the disposition by Member States of their nationality need not result in effects at the level of Community law was most recently adumbrated by the Court of Justice in *Micheletti v Delegación del Gobierno en Cantabria.*[2]

MICHELETTI

Mr Micheletti was an Argentine national who obtained professional qualification as a dentist in Argentina. Pursuant to a bilateral agreement between Argentina and Spain, Mr Micheletti applied for and, in January 1989, received Spanish recognition of his dental qualifications.

Mr Micheletti arrived in Spain from Argentina shortly afterwards. Before leaving Argentina, he had been issued with an Italian passport by the Italian consulate in Rosario. The passport was issued in accordance with Italian law on the basis of Mr Micheletti's Italian parentage. Argentine law did not deprive Mr Micheletti of his Argentine nationality.

Upon arriving in Spain, Mr Micheletti applied for, and was granted, a provisional Community residence document valid for six months on the basis of his Italian passport. Before the expiry of the provisional period he applied for a permanent Community residence document, with a view to establishing himself in a dental practice. His application was refused and, after unsuccessfully pursuing an administrative appeal he commenced proceedings before the *Tribunal Superior de Justicia de Cantabria.*

[1] Case 20/71 *Sabbatini v European Parliament* [1972] ECR 345, Case 32/71 *Chollet v Commission* [1972] ECR 363.

[2] CJ CE 7 July 1992, (C-369/90, Rec. p I-4239). Noted by Hans Ulrich Jessurun d'Oliveira at (1993) 30 CML Rev 623.

The Spanish authorities had refused Mr Micheletti's application because, according to Spanish legislation, he was regarded as possessing only Argentine nationality. Article 9 of the Spanish Civil Code provided in part that where it is necessary to ascertain a person's nationality, where he possesses more than one nationality, and where neither or none of those nationalities is Spanish, the person shall be regarded as the national of only that country where he habitually resided before his arrival in Spain. The Spanish authorities contended that Mr Micheletti habitually resided in Argentina before his arrival in Spain, and was therefore to be regarded as possessing only Argentine nationality.

The Spanish court asked the Court of Justice whether a national law which refused to recognise the Community rights inherent in the quality of nationality of another Member State, solely by virtue of the Member State national also possessing the nationality of a third State and having been resident in that third State before arriving in the host Member State, is compatible with Community law. In essence, the Spanish court wanted to know whether the relevant provisions contained within Article 9 of the Civil Code were compatible with Article 52 of the *EEC Treaty* and *Directive 73/148* on the abolition of restrictions on movement and residence within the Community for nationals of Member States with regard to establishment and the provision of services.

The full Court of Justice noted that Article 52 of the *EEC Treaty* expressly grants the right of establishment to persons having the quality of a "nationals of a Member State". Who are these persons? The Court answered in the following terms:

> *La définition des conditions d'acquisition et de perte de la nationalité relève, conformément au droit international, de la competence de chaque Etat membre, compétence qui doit être exercée dans le respect du droit communautaire.*[1]

In so saying the Court was advancing a proposition consisting of two parts. Firstly the legal conditions concerning disposition of nationality are, in accordance with the rules of public international law, within the competence of each Member State. This is consistent with the rule of customary international law embodied in the first limb of Article 1 of the *Convention on Nationality* that it is for each State to determine under its own law who are its nationals, and with the principle expressed in *Nationality Decrees in Tunis and Morocco* that questions of nationality are within the reserved domain of States. Secondly the Member States are, in exercising their reserved domain power, under an obligation to have due regard to the requirements of Community law.

[1]'The definition of the conditions of acquisition and loss of nationality is, in conformity with international law, within the competence of each Member State, which competence must be exercised with due regard to Community law' (author's translation). CJ CE 7 July 1992, *Micheletti / Delegación del Gobierno en Cantabria* (C-369/90, Rec. p I-4239) at paragraph 10 of the Court's judgment.

The Court went on to state that the exercise of the fundamental right guaranteed by the Treaty cannot be made subject to national legislation demanding a 'supplementary condition' ("*condition supplémentaire*") for the recognition of another Member State's nationality.[1] Consequently Article 52 cannot be interpreted as permitting national legislation to subject a Community national, who also holds the nationality of a third State, to a residence test as a precondition for giving effect to his nationality of a Member State.[2] Were it otherwise, the application of the right of establishment could vary from one Member State to another.[3]

The same result followed from a consideration of the relevant provisions of *Directive 73/148*. The Member States must admit into their territory the persons covered by the directive "merely upon production of a valid identity card or passport".[4] Similarly, a Member State must grant a right of residence to any person covered by the directive upon production of "the identity card or passport with which he or she entered its territory".[5] Taking a literal approach to these provisions the Court of Justice said that once a person covered by the directive produces one of the documents prescribed for the purposes of establishing his nationality of a Member State, another Member State may not contest his nationality on the basis that its domestic legislation regards him as being the national of a non-member country.[6]

Accordingly, Mr Micheletti was entitled to be issued with his residence permit by showing that he intended to establish himself in Spain and upon production of his Italian passport. The Spanish law which regarded him as possessing only Argentine nationality conflicted with Article 52 of the *EEC Treaty* and could not be applied.

This approach by the *Micheletti* Court to the treatment to be accorded persons endowed with the nationality of another Member State coheres with the view it expressed some thirteen years earlier in *Ministère public v Auer*:[7]

> There is no provision in the Treaty which, within the field of application of the Treaty, makes it possible to treat nationals of a Member State differently according to the time at which, or the manner in which, they acquired the nationality of that State, as long as, at the time at which they rely on the benefits of Community law, they possess the nationality of one of the Member States and that, in addition, the other conditions for the application of the rule on which they rely are fulfilled.[8]

[1]ibid.
[2]ibid at paragraph 11 of the Court's judgment.
[3]ibid at paragraph 12 of the Court's judgment.
[4]Article 3(1).
[5]Article 6(a).
[6]CJ CE 7 July 1992, *Micheletti / Delegación del Gobierno en Cantabria* (C-369/90, Rec. p I-4239) at paragraph 15 of the Court's judgment.
[7]Case 136/78 [1979] ECR 437.
[8]ibid at p 450, paragraph 28 of the Court's judgment.

The decision of the Court of Justice in *Micheletti* is of signal, albeit somewhat enigmatic, importance in determining the extent to which Member States may make dispositions of their nationality such as to produce effects at the level of Community law.

As we have seen, the power of Member States to make dispositions of their nationality is a "*compétence qui doit être exercée dans le respect du droit communautaire*". The Court did not elaborate on what this implies for the scope of the Member States' reserved domain power to make dispositions of their nationality. That it implies some limitation on the scope of the power is, however, certain.

What then are we to make of the qualification put by the *Micheletti* Court on the Member States' reserved domain power, ie that in exercising their power they must show due regard to Community law?

The Court expressly stated that the conditions for both acquisition and loss of nationality are, in conformity with international law, within the competence of the Member States. The constraints which Community law places upon the exercise of power by Member States within their reserved domain differ according to whether the Member States are prescribing conditions for the acquisition or for the loss of their nationality.

CONDITIONS FOR ACQUISITION OF NATIONALITY

Position in international law

When the exercise by a State of its domestic jurisdiction over the status of nationality affects the interests of other States, a question might arise as to whether international law will operate so as to limit the international effect of the domestic rules. In other words, are States ever entitled in international law to disregard another State's disposition of nationality in so far as the disposition impinges on relations between States? According to Oppenheim;

> ... a state's own determination that an individual possesses its nationality as a matter of its internal law is not lightly to be questioned. It creates a very strong presumption both that the individual possesses that state's nationality as a matter of its internal law and that that nationality is to be acknowledged for international purposes.[1]

Nevertheless, there will be occasions when a State will be entitled in international law not to acknowledge another State's conferral of its nationality. After referring to the general international rule that the disposition of nationality is within the "reserved

[1] *Oppenheim's International Law*, 9th ed (1992), at p 856.

domain" of States, the Permanent Court of International Justice in *Nationality Decrees Issued in Tunis and Morocco* said;

> ... it may well happen that, in a matter which, like that of nationality, is not, in principle, regulated by international law, the right of a State to use its discretion is nevertheless restricted by obligations which it may have undertaken towards other States. In such a case, jurisdiction which, in principle, belongs solely to the State, is limited by rules of international law.[1]

It will be recalled that while in Article 1 of the *Convention on Nationality* it is provided that it is for each State to determine under its own law who are its nationals, there are qualifications on the extent to which this principle must be given effect on the plane of international law. A domestic disposition need only be "recognised by other States in so far as it is consistent with international conventions, international custom, and the principles of law generally recognised with regard to nationality". According to the *British Digest of International Law*:

> Although international law does not in general attempt to prescribe who is a national of a particular State, or what particular nationality is to be attributed to any particular person or class of persons, so that the question whether a person possesses the nationality of a particular State falls primarily to be determined by the law of that State, it does not follow that a person's nationality, however good and valid under the law of the State concerned, will necessarily be accorded recognition for international purposes. This is because, in certain classes of cases, international law denies the right of a State to confer its nationality on particular persons. It cannot prevent the State doing so for internal purposes, but it can deny *international* effect to the status thus claimed.[2]

Thus a State need not always accord international effect to an attribution by another State of the latter's nationality.

Nottebohm

That international law regards a State's power to make attributions of its nationality as only contingently creating effects in relations among States is classically exemplified in the well known decision of the International Court of Justice in *Liechtenstein v Guatemala (Second Phase)* ("*Re Nottebohm*").[3]

The mere fact that Liechtenstein had validly conferred nationality on an individual according to its own laws did not automatically create a corresponding obligation on

[1] *Nationality Decrees Issued in Tunis and Morocco* [1923] Permanent Court of International Justice, Series B, No 4 at p 24.

[2] *British Digest of International Law*, Vol 5, pp 5-6 (emphasis in original).

[3] [1955] International Court of Justice Reports 4.

Guatemala to recognise that conferral for the purposes of interstate protection. What additional factors needed to exist before such an obligation on the part of States in Guatemala's position could be said to arise?:

> According to the practice of States, to arbitral and judicial decisions and to the opinions of writers, nationality is a legal bond having as its basis a social fact of attachment, a genuine connection of existence, interests and sentiments, together with the existence of reciprocal rights and duties. It may be said to constitute the juridical expression of the fact that the individual upon whom it is conferred, either directly by the law or as a result of an act of the authorities, is in fact more closely connected with the population of the State conferring nationality than with that of any other State. Conferred by a State, it only entitles that State to exercise protection vis-à-vis another State, if it constitutes a translation into juridical terms of the individual's connection with the State which has made him its national.[1]

One of the grounds for the court's decision was its expressed concern that Mr Nottebohm's acquisition of Liechtenstein nationality appeared to be a mere sham or a device to avoid any potential adverse consequences associated with being a German national in Guatemala while Guatemala and Germany were at war:

> His country had been at war for more than a month, and there is nothing to indicate that the application for naturalization then made by Nottebohm was motivated by any desire to dissociate himself from the Government of his country. ...
>
> Naturalization was asked for not so much for the purpose of obtaining a legal recognition of Nottebohm's membership in fact in the population of Liechtenstein, as it was to enable him to substitute for his status as a national of a belligerent State that of a national of a neutral State with the sole aim of thus coming within the protection of Liechtenstein but not of becoming wedded to its traditions, its interests, its way of life or of assuming the obligations - other than fiscal obligations - and exercising the rights to the status thus acquired.
>
> Guatemala is under no obligation to recognize a nationality granted in such circumstances.[2]

Thus, Mr Nottebohm's lack of effective links with Liechtenstein was tightly bound up with the issue of the disingenuity of his Liechtenstein naturalisation. His acquired Liechtenstein nationality was not internationally questionable as against Guatemala

[1] ibid, at p 23.
[2] ibid, at pp 25, 26.

because of his lack of effective links *per se* with Liechtenstein. Rather, the lack of such effective links confirmed, in all the circumstances, the suspicion that his Liechtenstein naturalisation was nothing more than a merely technical device intended to prevent Guatemala from taking measures against a person who in reality gave his allegiance to an enemy State.

In the words of Ian Brownlie, "the *Nottebohm* principle is essentially the assertion that in reference to institutions of municipal law, international law has a reserve power to guard against giving effect to ephemeral, abusive, and simulated creations".[1]

International law imposes a merely *prima facie* obligation on States to recognise the disposition of another State's nationality. A disposition made in violation of international norms need not always be accorded international effect by other States. In particular, a nationality conferred pursuant to an application for naturalisation need not be recognised if, in all the circumstances, the conferral was to effect an abusive purpose. What this might mean in the context of Community law will be considered later.

Duty of solidarity and co-operation
The *Micheletti* judgment makes it clear that in Community law a host Member State cannot refuse to recognise a conferral of nationality made by another Member State. No "*condition supplémentaire*" may be imposed before recognition is extended to a person's nationality of another Member State.

Once a Member State confers its citizenship on an individual a host Member State must, as a matter of obligation under Community law, unreservedly treat the individual as a 'national of a Member State'. The danger thus to be avoided is the variable application, as between Member States, of the right of establishment. The only permissible conditions for recognition are those laid down by Community law and are confined to the production of a valid identity card or passport.[2]

The Source of the Obligation: Article 5. The caveat placed by the Court of Justice on the exercise by Member States of their reserved domain power to lay down the conditions for the acquisition of their nationality must, nevertheless, have some meaning. If the Member States have an obligation to exercise their reserve domain power with due regard to Community law, to whom do they owe that obligation? Who has the right to ensure that the obligation is observed? These questions can adequately be answered only after ascertaining the source of the obligation. Assuming the obligation is not an invention of the Court's, it must lie in Article 5 of the *EC*

[1]Ian Brownlie, "*Principles of Public International Law*", 4th edition (1990) at p 489. Professor Brownlie also discusses the nationality of legal persons and, after remarking that certain tribunals prefer to determine the question by reference to criteria such as the *siège social* rather than the place of incorporation, says that "by demanding the existence of *siège social*, control, domicile, and so on, they would seem to require a guarantee that the grant of personality is reasonable and not a device for limiting the proper sphere of protection of other governments" (p 487).

[2]Articles 2(1) and 6(a) of *Directive 73/148* (establishment and services), and Articles 3(1) and 4(3)(a) of *Directive 68/360* (workers).

Treaty which imposes several general obligations on Member States by providing as follows:

> Member States shall take all appropriate measures, whether general or particular, to ensure fulfilment of the obligations arising out of this Treaty or resulting from action taken by the institutions of the Community. They shall facilitate the achievement of the Community's tasks.
>
> They shall abstain from any measure which could jeopardise the attainment of the objectives of this Treaty.

Being in Part One ("Principles") of the Treaty, Article 5 is one of the fundamental provisions of the Community legal order.[1] The provision refers to the exercise of power by any organ or institution exercising the power of the State.[2] It lays down, in the first paragraph, two positive obligations and, in the second paragraph, one negative obligation. As we are here concerned with an obligation on the Member States not to exercise their reserved domain power in a particular way, we must focus on the negative obligation contained in Article 5 (second paragraph).[3]

In a striking passage the Court of Justice has held that Article 5 of the Treaty provides for a duty of "solidarity which is at the basis of ... the whole of the Community system"[4] and that the "exercise of reserved powers cannot ... permit the unilateral adoption of measures prohibited by the Treaty".[5] Furthermore, where the Member states are exercising their powers in an area where the Community has power to act, but has not done so, the Member States may exercise State powers only subject to the "obligation to co-operate" imposed by Article 5 of the Treaty.[6] This duty of solidarity or to co-operate applies not only as between the Community institutions and the Member States,[7] but also as among the Member States themselves.[8]

[1]Case 43/75 *Defrenne v Société Anonyme Belge de Navigation Aérienne Sabena* [1976] ECR 455 at p 474, paragraph 28 of the Court's judgment, referring specifically to Article 7 of the *EEC Treaty* (Article 6 of the *EC Treaty*) which is also in Part One.

[2]Joined Cases 51-54/71 *International Fruit Company NV v Produktschap voor Groenten en Fruit* [1971] ECR 1107 at pp 1115-1116, paragraphs 3-4 of the Court's judgment; Case 240/78 *Atalanta Amsterdam BV v Produktschap voor Vee en Vlees* [1979] ECR 2137 at p 2148, paragraph 5 of the Court's judgment (Article 5 was not expressly invoked in the Court's judgment, but Advocate General Reischl referred in his opinion (ibid at p 2156) to *International Fruit*); Case C-106/89 *Marleasing SA v La Comercial Internacional de Alimentación SA* [1990] ECR I-4135 at p I-4159, paragraph 8 of the Court's judgment.

[3]For a much more comprehensive discussion of Article 5 see John Temple Lang, "*Community Constitutional Law: Article 5 EEC Treaty*", (1990) 27 CML Rev 645.

[4]Joined Cases 6 and 11/69 *Commission v France* ("*Re Preferential Rediscount Rate*") [1969] ECR 523 at p 540, paragraph 16 of the Court's judgment.

[5]ibid at paragraph 17 of the Court's judgment.

[6]Case 61/77 *Commission v Ireland* ("*Re Irish Sea Fisheries*") [1978] ECR 417 at p 449, paragraph 65 of the Court's judgment; Case 32/79 *Commission v United Kingdom* ("*Re British Sea Fisheries*") [1980] ECR 2403 at p 2432, paragraph 10 of the Court's judgment.

[7]eg Case C-2/88 Imm *Zwartveld* [1990] ECR I-3365 (obligation of the Commission to co-operate with a Member State); Case C-35/88 *Commission v Greece* ("*Re Market in Feed Grain*") [1990] ECR I-3125 (obligation of a Member State to co-operate with the Commission); Case C-217/88 *Commission v*

The way in which Member States exercise their reserved domain power to make dispositions of their nationality could, in certain circumstances, jeopardise the attainment of the Treaty's objectives.

Economic Dislocation. If for example one of the Member States with an imperial past were, in the face of opposition from the other Member States or the Community institutions, to extend its nationality *en masse* to all the inhabitants of non-European countries which had formerly been part of its empire, could it really be contested that such an act would jeopardise the basic task laid down in Article 2 of the *EC Treaty*[1] of promoting "throughout the Community a harmonious and balanced development of economic activities, ... a high level of employment and of social protection, the raising of the standard of living and quality of life, and ... solidarity among Member States"?[2] Having regard to the probable consequences of such an act by a Member State on several of the Community's basic tasks,[3] it seems highly likely that it would, in terms of Article 5 (second paragraph), "jeopardise the attainment of the objectives" of the *EC Treaty.* A Member State pursuing such a course would be indulging where the Treaty expressly demands abstinence.

Would the jeopardy to the Treaty's basic objectives be removed if the Member State adopted a law permitting the inhabitants of former imperial territories to receive its

---

Germany ("*Re Coercive Measures in Wine Market*") [1990] ECR I-2879 (mutual obligation of the Commission and a Member State to co-operate).

[8] eg Case 61/77 *Commission v Ireland* ("*Re Irish Sea Fisheries*") [1978] ECR 417; Case 32/79 *Commission v United Kingdom* ("*Re British Sea Fisheries*") [1980] ECR 2403; Case 272/80 *Frans-Nederlandse Maatschappij voor Biologische Producten BV* [1981] ECR 3277; Case 42/82 *Commission v France* ("*Re Italian Wine Imports*") [1983] ECR 1013; Case C-158/89 *Dietz-Matti v Federal Republic of Germany* [1990] ECR I-2013.

[1] That Articles 2 and 3 of the Treaty set out the basic objectives of the Community has been accepted by the Court of Justice; eg Case 53/81 *Levin v Staatssecretaris van Justitie* [1982] ECR 1035 at p 1050, paragraph 15 of the Court's judgment.

[2] In Case 229/83 *Association des Centres distributeurs Édouard Leclerc v Sàrl 'Au blé vert'* [1985] ECR 1 at pp 10-11 Advocate General Darmon opined that a threat to the Member States' "reciprocal duties of solidarity" would become a potential source of economic disintegration. Albert Bleckman has taken the view that the Community might "refuse to recognize the wide definitions of British and French nationals, subjects or citizens which partly include the inhabitants of former colonies, protectorates, dominions and so on, on the basis that this wide definition does not refer to nationality in the strict sense of public international law or that Articles 131 to 136 and 227 exclude these nationals from the application of the EEC Treaty": "*The Personal Jurisdiction of the European Communities*", (1980) 17 CML Rev at pp 477-478.

[3] When the less developed southern Member States acceded to the Community in 1981 (Greece) and 1986 (Portugal and Spain) their nationals were not immediately endowed with the complete range of personal movement rights. Free movement for Greek, Portuguese and Spanish workers was instead phased in by transitional provisions (see Articles 44-48 of the *Act of Accession 1979* and Articles 55-60 and 215-220 of the *Act of Accession 1985*). No equivalent restrictions were placed upon British, Danish or Irish workers when their countries acceded in 1973. Denmark and the United Kingdom enjoyed levels of development comparable to those of the existing Member States. Ireland, with a much smaller population than Greece, Portugal or Spain, but comparably less developed, already had in place with the United Kingdom liberal arrangements for the free movement of persons between the two countries. There is, however, the *Joint declaration on the free movement of workers*, attached to the *Final Act of Accession 1972*, in which the Member States expressly reserve a right to bring before the Community institutions any difficulties which might arise in the social situation as a result of the 1973 accessions and the free movement of workers.

nationality merely upon application and proof of residence? (In this connection it should perhaps also be recalled that the process of European decolonisation is still on-going.)[1]

Would the jeopardy to the Treaty's basic objectives be removed if the Member State cast its net even further than its past or present imperial possessions and, following Liechtenstein's example in *Re Nottebohm*, adopted a law or administrative practice conferring nationality on virtually any person who applied and paid a fee?

Any of the above mentioned hypothetical national measures could, having regard to *Micheletti*, expose the Community's labour market, its markets for services and any markets affected by the right of establishment to serious disruption possibly to the point of jeopardising the Treaty's objectives.

In this connection it is important to note that the Court of Justice has held a Member State to be in breach of its Treaty obligations by acting unilaterally and without consulting its partners thereby "having adversely affected the interests for [*sic*] another Member State".[2] All of these hypothetical national measures would place the responsible Member State in breach of its duty of solidarity under Article 5 (second paragraph) of the *EC Treaty*.

Solidarity. The reality or potential of economic dislocation is not, however, a necessary precondition for establishing a breach of a Member State's duty of co-operation. One of the basic objectives of the *EC Treaty*, as embodied in Article 2, is the promotion of solidarity among the Member States. Thus, the Treaty's objectives are jeopardised if a Member State adopts or maintains in force a measure which undermines that solidarity in an area falling within the scope of the Treaty. The movement of persons is within the Treaty's scope (Articles 3(c), 3(d), 8a, 48, 52, 59 and 100c).

A duty of solidarity must include refraining from acts, within the scope of that duty, which are deceptive or misleading towards those to whom the duty is owed.[3] Any

[1]In particular, the the Portuguese territory of Macau (population 452,300 - official estimate as at 31 December 1989) and the United Kingdom Crown Colony of Hong Kong (population 5,800,600 - official estimate as at mid-year 1990) are destined to come under China's sovereignty in 1999 and 1997 respectively. As at May 1989, 135,220 of the residents of Macau were Portuguese nationals. Source: "*The Far East and Australasia 1992*", 23rd edition. As the dates for transfer of sovereignty to China approach, and particularly in the event of supervening political or economic turmoil in China, it is not unreasonable to suppose that there will be increased political pressure on Portugal and the United Kingdom from the populations of the affected territories, from the international community and perhaps from within Portugal and the United Kingdom themselves, to adopt a liberal approach to conferring Portuguese and British citizenship on the inhabitants of the two territories.

[2]Case 32/79 *Commission v United Kingdom* ("*Re British Sea Fisheries*") [1980] ECR 2403 at p 2450, paragraph 58 of the Court's judgment.

[3]In Case C-370/90 *R v Immigration Appeal Tribunal and Surinder Singh ex parte Secretary of State for the Home Department* [1992] 3 CMLR 358 at p 375, paragraph 24 of the Court's judgment, the Court of Justice said in connection with the free movement of persons that "the facilities created by the Treaty cannot have the effect of allowing the persons who benefit from them to evade the application of national legislation and of prohibiting member-States from taking the measures necessary to prevent such abuse". If individuals, who possess no duty of solidarity to the Community and its Member States, cannot use the

deceptive or misleading act by a Member State towards other Member States or the Community institutions can be categorised as a breach of the duty of solidarity even without the element of real or potential economic disruption of the sort occasioned by the hypothetical situations discussed above. Thus the conferral by a Member State of its nationality on a person who possesses no genuine link with that State, but who thereby becomes clothed with the status of 'national of a Member State', constitutes a violation of the duty of solidarity contained in Article 5 of the *EC Treaty* even if the impugned act does not seriously jeopardise "a harmonious and balanced development of economic activities, ... a high level of employment and of social protection, (and) the raising of the standard of living and quality of life".

In this connection it is useful to recall Professor Brownlie's characterisation of the decision of the International Court of Justice in *Re Nottebohm*; "the *Nottebohm* principle is essentially the assertion that in reference to institutions of municipal law, international law has a reserve power to guard against giving effect to ephemeral, abusive, and simulated creations".[1] Not only does international law possess such a power, so too does Community law. Indeed the case for Community law possessing this power is, if anything, even stronger than that for international law. The Community does, after all, constitute "a new legal order of international law for the benefit of which the states have limited their sovereign rights"[2] and it embodies a level of co-operation, integration and mutual trust never before seen in international relations.

This clearly raises an issue about the requirement for a genuine link between the Member State conferring its nationality and the person on whom it is conferred.

Commenting on the *Micheletti* judgment, Professor Jessurun d'Oliveira has suggested that the decision "rejects all restrictions to the exercise of the fundamental freedoms expressed in *Nottebohm* that, in order to function properly on the international level the nationality has to be the expression of a genuine link as indicated by habitual residence, effective residence, social ties, etc".[3] To the extent that *Micheletti* means only that the *Re Nottebohm* restrictions are rejected at the level of a host Member State's dealings with an individual endowed with the status of a 'national of a Member State', Professor Jessurun d'Oliveira is undoubtedly right. Thus a host Member State is not permitted to refuse an individual who is a 'national of a Member State' access to the rights guaranteed him by Community law even if the host Member State has good reasons for regarding the individual as lacking a genuine link with the other State whose nationality he possesses.

Treaty rules on free movement evasively or abusively then neither can the Member States who are under such a duty.

[1]Ian Brownlie, "*Principles of Public International Law*", 4th edition (1990) at p 489.

[2]Case 26/62 *NV Algemene Transport- en Expeditie Onderneming van Gend & Loos v Nederlandse administratie der belastingen* [1963] ECR 1 at p 12.

[3]Hans Ulrich Jessurun d'Oliveira, note of Case C-369/90 *Micheletti v Delegación del Gobierno en Cantabria*, (1993) 30 CML Rev 623 at p 625 (footnote omitted).

It would not be correct, however, to say that the requirement for a genuine link between the Member State conferring its nationality and the person on whom it is conferred is without any significance in Community law. The Member States owe each other and the Community a duty of solidarity derived from Article 5 of the *EC Treaty*. This duty includes an obligation not to engage in acts within the scope of the Treaty which are deceptive or misleading to other Member States or to the Community institutions. It is precisely to avoid giving efficacy to such acts in the realm of nationality that international law demands a genuine link between the individual and the State whose nationality he possesses.

The crux of any proceedings to enforce the duty would be the breach of solidarity occasioned by the deceptive or misleading act of bestowing nationality on a person lacking a genuine link to the conferring State. The basis of the complaint would disappear if, notwithstanding the absence of a genuine link, there was no deception involved. In this connection it is instructive to note that part of the duty of co-operation shared by the Member States is a duty to consult or inform. This duty has usually manifested itself when the Council has agreed a specific consultation procedure before Member States may enact national measures within the unexercised legislative competence of the Community.[1]

The duty to inform and consult does, however, possesses an existence deriving from Article 5 of the *EC Treaty* which is independent of any more specific procedures prescribed by secondary legislation, resolution, agreement or otherwise. Thus in *Commission v Belgium* ("*Re Belgian Family Allowances*"),[2] Belgium was held to be in breach of Article 5 when it amended its laws regarding payment of family allowances so that such allowances paid to persons receiving similar benefits under the Community's *Staff Regulations* would be reduced by an amount proportionate to those Community benefits. The failure to fulfil its obligations under Article 5 occurred because Belgium had not consulted the Commission prior to adopting its amendments.[3] It should be noted that this breach occurred in the absence of any mandated consultation procedure specified by secondary legislation, resolution or similar act, and in a field where Belgium had an undoubted right to legislate.

In *Commission v France* ("*Re Italian Wine Imports*")[4] the Court of Justice said that France was in breach of its duty of co-operation in changing an established administrative procedure in processing imports of Italian wine without first giving notice of the change to the Italian authorities affected by the change.[5] Again, there was

[1]For example, in Case 61/77 *Commission v Ireland* ("*Re Irish Sea Fisheries*") [1978] ECR 417, Case 141/78 *France v United Kingdom* [1979] ECR 2923 and Case 32/79 *Commission v United Kingdom* ("*Re British Sea Fisheries*") [1980] ECR 2403, Annex VI of the Council Resolution of 3 November 1976 was regarded as laying down a binding procedure for prior consultations pending the adoption of Community legislation pursuant to Article 102 of the *Act of Accession 1972*.

[2]Case 186/85 [1987] ECR 2029.

[3]ibid at p 2057, paragraph 40 of the Court's judgment.

[4]Case 42/82 [1983] ECR 1013.

[5]ibid at p 1044, paragraph 36 of the Court's judgment.

no mandated consultation procedure specified by secondary legislation, resolution or similar act and France was acting within its sphere of competence.

If a Member State proposes to confer its nationality in circumstances where no genuine link of the sort commonly recognised exists between it and the recipient, the violation of Article 5 which would otherwise occur can be avoided by informing or consulting about the proposal. Given that it is the Commission's duty to ensure that the provisions of the Treaty are applied,[1] the duty to inform or consult will be discharged if the information is directed to, or if the consultation involves, the Commission.

Proceedings to Enforce Article 5 Duties. The duties imposed by Article 5 of the *EC Treaty* may be enforced by the Member States in proceedings brought under Article 170 or by the Commission under Article 169. If the Court of Justice were to find that a Member State had failed to fulfil its Article 5 obligations by bestowing its nationality in a particular way, Article 171(1) would oblige the Member State to "take the necessary measures to comply with the judgment".

In this connection it is important to bear in mind that a judgment against a Member State under Articles 169 or 170 does not have executory effect; it does not operate to annul the national measure. Rather, the Member State is placed under an obligation to repeal or amend the national measures which violated its Treaty obligation.[2] If the Court's judgment was that a particular national law or practice in conferring nationality was inconsistent with the Treaty, the law would need to be amended or repealed and the practice would need to be modified or discontinued. If the Court's judgment was that the conferral of nationality on a particular person or persons was inconsistent with the Treaty, the conferral would need to be revoked.

Until the Member State complied with any obligation to revoke a conferral of nationality, the recipient would continue to be a 'national of a Member State' and a citizen of the Union. Failure by a Member State to take immediate steps to implement the Court's judgment, and to complete those steps within a reasonable time, itself amounts to a failure to fulfil its obligations under the Treaty.[3] Article 171(2) of the *EC Treaty*, inserted by the *Union Treaty*, provides a procedure by which Member States may be fined by the Court of Justice for failure to comply with a judgment given under Articles 169 or 170.

No New Obligation on Member States. It might be objected that Article 5 cannot be employed to create obligations on Member States in the absence of a legally binding

[1] Article 155 of the *EC Treaty*.

[2] Joined Cases 314-316/81 and 83/82 *Procureur de la République v Waterkeyn* [1982] ECR 4337.

[3] Case 131/84 *Commission v Italy* ("*Re Failure to Implement Judgment*") [1985] ECR 3531 at p 3536, paragraph 7 of the Court's judgment.

Community act or Treaty provision.[1] There is no Community act or Treaty provision regulating or harmonising legal conditions for conferring nationality.

This limitation on Article 5 is, however, associated with the positive obligations contained within its first paragraph and it is not here suggested that Member States are required to adopt any new measures. Rather Article 5 (second paragraph) operates as a restraint on the adoption or maintenance in force of certain national measures, specifically those which could jeopardise the attainment of the Treaty's objectives.

Nationality Outside Community's Competence? It might also be objected that Article 5 does not create obligations binding on the Member States unless the impugned State measure falls within a field of Community legislative competence specifically granted by the Treaty. Because nationality is not a matter the Treaty specifically deals with, such an argument might run, Article 5 cannot be the basis of any duty by the Member States in the field of their nationality laws and practices. This objection is unsustainable.

The requirement that a specific Treaty manifestation of the legislative competence of the Community be involved before Article 5 can be said to impose any obligations on the Member States arises from an incorrect interpretation of the jurisprudence of the Court of Justice. In *Deutsche Grammophon Gesellschaft mbH v Metro-SB-Großmärkte GmbH*[2] the Court of Justice said of Article 5 (second paragraph) that "[t]his provision lays down a general duty for the Member States, the actual tenor of which depends in each individual case on the provisions of the Treaty or on the rules derived from its general scheme".[3] This might appear to indicate that Article 5 (second paragraph) cannot create an obligation unless the impugned State measure falls within a field of Community legislative competence specifically granted by the Treaty.[4]

[1]eg Case 229/86 *Brother Industries Limited v Commission* [1987] ECR 3757 at p 3763; Case T-113/89 *Nederlandse Associatie van de Farmaceutische Industrie 'Nefarma' v Commission* [1990] ECR II-797 at pp II-816 - II-817, paragraphs 68-69 of the Court's judgment; Case T-114/89 *Vereniging van Nederlandse Ziekenfondsen v Commission* [1990] ECR II-827; Case T-116/89 *Vereniging Prodifarma v Commission* [1990] ECR II-843 at p II-865, paragraph 79 of the Court's judgment.

[2]Case 78/70 [1971] ECR 487.

[3]ibid at p 499, paragraph 5 of the Court's judgment.

[4]Two of the Court's decisions provide further useful illustrations. In Case 61/77 *Commission v Ireland* ("*Re Irish Sea Fisheries*") [1978] ECR 417 the Court of Justice appeared to link Ireland's obligation not to take unilateral measures in the field of fisheries conservation to Article 102 of the *Act of Accession 1972*, which required the Council to adopt such measures within a prescribed period (at p 449, paragraph 65 of the Court's judgment - see also Case 32/79 *Commission v United Kingdom* ("*Re British Sea Fisheries*") [1980] ECR 2403 at p 2432, paragraph 10 of the Court's judgment). The prescribed period not having expired and the required measures not having been adopted, Ireland was permitted to adopt unilateral measures only after it had complied with a consultation procedure involving a veto power by the Commission, which procedure had previously been unanimaously agreed to by resolution of the Council. Similarly in Case 311/85 *VZW Vereniging van Vlaamse Reisbureaus v VZW Sociale Dienst van de Plaatselijke en Gewestelijke Overheidsdiensten* [1987] ECR 3801 the Court of Justice appeared to link the Member States' Article 5 obligation not to adopt or maintain in force certain national measures with the existence of a legally binding Treaty provision (*in casu* Article 85 of the *EEC Treaty*)(ibid at p 3826, paragraphs 9-10 of the Court's judgment).

In reality, however, there is no necessary link between specific manifestations in the Treaty of the Community's legislative competence and the duties arising under or derived from Article 5 (second paragraph) of the *EC Treaty*. This is apparent from the wording of the provision itself. Whereas Article 5 (first paragraph) imposes certain positive duties on Member States to, *inter alia*, "ensure fulfilment of the *obligations arising out of this Treaty* or resulting from *action taken by the institutions*", Article 5 (second paragraph) requires abstinence on the part of Member States from measures "which could jeopardise the attainment of the *objectives* of this Treaty".

Indeed in *France v United Kingdom*[1] the Court of Justice said that a Council resolution laying down certain consultation procedures concerning the enactment of national fisheries conservation measures "makes specific the duties of co-operation which the Member States assumed under Article 5 of the EEC Treaty when they acceded to the Community".[2] The Court was expressly adopting the submissions of the Commission which had argued that "agreements which would not in themselves be legally binding may be sufficient to make concrete and specific the legal duty, imposed by Article 5, to co-operate and not to hinder the realization of the objectives of the Treaty".[3] The national legislation successfully impugned in *Re Belgian Family Allowances* was enacted in an area within the Member State's legislative competence as was the administrative measure successfully challenged in *Re Italian Wine Imports*.

There is thus no necessity for a specific grant to the Community of legislative power in respect of nationality before Article 5 (second paragraph) becomes relevant. Provided it can be shown that a State measure regarding nationality "could jeopardise the attainment of the objectives" of the *EC Treaty*, Article 5 (second paragraph) will render that national measure incompatible with the Treaty. What is meant by "objectives of this Treaty" in Article 5 (second paragraph)? According to P.J.G. Kapteyn (now a Judge of the Court of Justice) and P. Verloren van Themaat:

> ... Article 5 ... requires the Member States to abstain from any measures which could jeopardise the attainment of the objectives of the Treaty. The term 'objectives' in this context embraces not only the

[1]Case 141/78 [1979] ECR 2923.

[2]ibid at p 2942, paragraph 8 of the Court's judgment.

[3]ibid at p 2933. See also Case 124/80 *Officier van Justitie v J van Dam & Zonen* [1981] ECR 1447 at pp 1464-1465, the opinion of Advocate General Reischl. The duty of solidarity also affects national economic policy as it relates to each Member State's balance of payments and confidence in its currency. Until the *Union Treaty* these aspects of policy remained within the exclusive legislative competence of the Member States. Nevertheless in Case 95/81 *Commission v Italy* ("*Re Advance Payments for Imports*") [1982] ECR 2187 the Court of Justice said that Article 104 of the *EEC Treaty* "sets out the general objectives of the economic policy which the Member States must pursue, regard being had to their membership of the Community" (ibid at p 2201, paragraph 16 of the Court's judgment). That Member States *must* have had an economic policy which pursued the prescribed objectives strongly implies that failure to comply would have placed a delinquent Member State in breach of its duty of solidarity. The fact that a Member State pursued a policy which tried, but simply failed, to achieve the mandated objectives would not have placed it in breach of its duty. But pursuit of a policy which at least avowedly disregarded the mandated objectives in favour of others (eg the State ownership of the means of production, distribution and exchange) would have exposed the delinquent State to a charge that it was in breach of its duty of solidarity.

> objectives mentioned in Article 2, but also the means mentioned in Article 3 for the attainment of these objectives and the non-discrimination provision of Article 7 [of the *EEC Treaty* - now Article 6 of the *EC Treaty*]. An example of measures which are clearly prohibited by the second limb of Article 5 is measures which, without patently conflicting with the free movement of goods or the non-discrimination principle laid down in Article 7 will lead, experience shows, in a number of situations or after a certain period of time, to restrictions on inter-state commerce or to prohibited discrimination. In more general terms, this obligation makes it at least desirable that the Member States consider whether economic or financial policy measures which they propose to adopt may jeopardise the attainment of the objectives of the Treaty.[1]

Thus if a national measure could jeopardise any of the basic objectives contained in either Articles 2 or 3 of the *EC Treaty* (or, since the *Union Treaty*, Article 3a of the *EC Treaty*) the relevant Member State will be in breach of its obligations under Article 5 (second paragraph). This approach is consistent with the decision in *Schlüter v Hauptzollamt Lörrach*[2] in which the Court of Justice said that, until the procedures envisaged by Article 3(g) of the *EEC Treaty* were enacted, Articles 5 and 107 (Member States to treat their exchange rates policies as a matter of "common concern") could not confer on individuals rights which the national courts were bound to protect when Member States made adjustments to their exchange rates. This absence of direct effect, however, did not diminish the Member States' and institutions' duty to co-operate:

> One of the cardinal aims of the Treaty is to create a single economic region, free from internal restrictions, in which economic and customs union may be progressively achieved.
>
> This requires the parities between the currencies of the various Member States to remain fixed; as soon as this requirements [*sic*] ceases to be met, the process of integration envisaged by the Treaty will be retarded and prejudiced.
>
> It is therefore the duty of the Community Institutions and of Member States to cooperate in and to ensure the creation and maintenance of these conditions.[3]

If, as Judge Kapteyn and Professor Verloren van Themaat maintain, Article 5 prohibits Member States from adopting measures which, while not "patently conflicting" with the free movement of goods, could lead to restrictions on interstate commerce, why

[1] P.J.G. Kapteyn and P. Verloren van Themaat, "*Introduction to the Law of the European Communities*" (1990), 2nd ed, at p 90. Footnote omitted.

[2] Case 9/73 [1973] ECR 1135.

[3] ibid at p 1161, paragraph 39 of the Court's judgment. See also Case 10/73 *Rewe-Zentral AG v Hauptzollamt Kehl* [1973] ECR 1175 at p 1194, paragraph 26 of the Court's judgment.

should Article 5 not operate in a similar way with respect to the free movement of persons? In other words, why should Article 5 not prohibit Member States from adopting or maintaining in force national measures which, while not patently conflicting with the free movement of persons, could nevertheless lead to a disruption of such basic Treaty objectives as the harmonious and balanced development of economic activities, a high level of employment and of social protection, the raising of the standard of living and quality of life, and solidarity among Member States?

There is, of course, no reason in principle for answering this question in the negative. We have already seen how it is conceivable that a measure adopted by a Member State with regard to the conferral of its nationality might jeopardise the basic objectives of the Treaty. Accordingly, it cannot be said that Article 5 does not create obligations binding on the Member States because nationality does not fall within a field of Community legislative competence specifically granted by the Treaty. It is not necessary that matters of nationality should fall within a specific legislative Community competence. Provided a conferral (either *en masse* or to an individual) by a Member State of its nationality "could jeopardise the attainment of the objectives" of the *EC Treaty* by damaging either the "harmonious and balanced development of economic activities, ... a high level of employment and of social protection, the raising of the standard of living and quality of life" or the "solidarity among Member States", Article 5 will be infringed and the Member State will be in breach of its obligations under the Treaty.

Genuine link in Community law

Whereas international law permits States to refuse recognition of nationality conferred by other States on individuals in certain circumstances, Community law requires Member States always to recognise and give full effect to the nationality conferred on a person by another Member State merely upon production of a valid identity card or passport. Member States nevertheless owe each other, and the Community institutions, a duty of solidarity when making dispositions of their nationality.

We have seen that the duty of solidarity imposed on the Member States includes an obligation not to confer their nationalities on persons who do not enjoy a genuine link to the conferring State. The purpose of this constraint is, *inter alia*, to avoid allowing Member States the opportunity of constructing 'ephemeral, abusive, and simulated creations' in the realm of Community law.[1] Whether the conferral by a

[1]This was impliedly the basis for dismissing the argument of the Irish government in Case 249/81 *Commission v Ireland* (*"Re 'Buy Irish' Campaign"*) [1982] ECR 4005 that the activities of the Irish Goods Council, which activities had an equivalent effect to quantitative restrictions on imports, could not be imputed to the Irish government. The Irish Goods Council was in form a non-government body registered in accordance with Irish company law, and which encouraged Irish consumers to buy Irish made products. Notwithstanding its formal independence from government, the Council's management committee was appointed by government, it received generous government subsidies and the broad outline of its public campaign was defined by government. In this connection the Court of Justice said (ibid at p 4020, paragraph 15 of the Court's judgment); "In the circumstances the Irish Government cannot rely on the fact that the campaign was conducted by a private company in order to escape any liability it may have under the provisions of the Treaty".

Member State of its nationality involves the necessary genuine link will depend on whether the conferral is ephemeral, abusive or simulated.

In *Re Nottebohm* the links between Liechtenstein and Mr Nottebohm were extremely marginal, and the abusive purpose underlying the conferral was apparent. Indeed, the marginality of the links made it easier to discern the abusive purpose. None of the criteria which States ordinarily apply in conferring their nationality were present in the case of Mr Nottebohm. Although *Re Nottebohm* is sometimes criticised as laying down an overly restrictive definition of nationality for the purposes of international law,[1] or for prescibing a test which is vague and subjective,[2] it has been rightly argued that "to dismiss *Nottebohm* as an old chestnut is to overlook the usefulness of an effective link-type test as an equitable and logical means to regulate who benefits from free movement and Community citizenship".[3]

The latitude which international law allows States in making dispositions of their nationality such as to produce effects on the plane of international relations is very wide. Indeed, international law does not prescribe how nationality is to be acquired. Nor does it even demand that States ensure that everyone has a nationality.[4] It is nevertheless here submitted that if a Member State confers its nationality by applying criteria commonly employed by States it will be very difficult, and perhaps virtually impossible, to infer a deceptive or abusive purpose sufficient to regard the conferral as a breach of the Member State's duty of solidarity.

Oppenheim writes that the five most common forms of acquiring nationality are birth, naturalisation, redintegration, annexation and cession.[5]

Annexation and Cession. Acquisition of nationality by annexation follows upon subjugation, ie the appropriation of territory by conquest. In the contemporary Western European context subjugation is, fortunately, no longer of any practical concern and need not detain us here.[6] Acquisition of nationality by cession results from the transfer of sovereignty over territory from one State to another. Such a transfer may or may not be pursuant to a peace treaty putting an end to armed hostilities. Again, this mode of acquiring nationality is of little or no practical concern in the contemporary Western European context.[7]

[1]eg J.H.W. Verzijl, "*International Law in Historical Perspective*", Vol V (1972) at p 6.

[2]eg the dissenting decision of Judge Read in *Re Nottebohm* at p 46.

[3]Siofra O'Leary, "*Nationality Law and Community Citizenship: A Tale of Two Uneasy Bedfellows*", (1992) 12 Yearbook of European Law 353 at p 368.

[4]*Oppenheim's International Law*, 9th ed (1992), Vol 1 at p 869.

[5]ibid.

[6]For a discussion of this mode of acquisition see ibid at pp 700-701 and the materials there cited.

[7]For a discussion of this mode of acquisition see ibid at pp 683-686 and the materials there cited. There is no reason why a treaty of cession could not stipulate that the inhabitants of the ceded territory could not retain their original nationality as well as, or instead of, acquiring the nationality of the acquiring State. It cannot be entirely ruled out that the United Kingdom might one day cede Gibraltar to Spain or the province of Northern Ireland to the Republic of Ireland. In either case most of the inhabitants of the ceded territory would, if they acquired the nationality of the acquiring State at all, already have been nationals of a Member State. Subject to any provisions laid down in the Treaty of cession, the acquiring

Redintegration. Redintegration involves a person resuming a nationality which he had earlier lost for some reason. Section 13(1) of the *British Nationality Act 1981*, for example, allows a person of full capacity who lost his British citizenship by renunciation to apply for registration as a British citizen if the renunciation was necessary to enable him to retain or acquire some other citizenship or nationality. A further example is provided by Article 116(2) of Germany's *Grundgesetz* (Basic Law) which allows former German citizens who had been deprived of their citizenship on political, racial or religious grounds during the period of the Nazi regime to be regranted their German nationality upon application.[1]

Birth. At the moment of a person's birth he is obviously in no position to make a choice as to his nationality. This fact attracts added significance when one considers that the vast majority of people acquire their nationality (or nationalities), without their consent, at birth and retain only that nationality (or those nationalities) throughout their lives.

The reason that a person might occasionally acquire more than one nationality at birth derives partly from the fact that State laws are not uniform. Almost all States apply one or both of two principles in conferring nationality upon new-borns.[2] The first principle is that the child acquires the nationality of the State in whose territory he is born (*iure soli*), so that every child born in such a State's territory automatically acquires its nationality irrespective of his parents' nationality.[3] The second principle is that the child acquires the nationality of his parents irrespective of the child's place of birth (*iure sanguinis*).[4]

A large and increasing number of States apply both principles[5] in various combinations and degrees, so that a child born either on their territories (sometimes subject to conditions as to the parents' length of residence) or to parents possessing their nationalities (sometimes subject to the parents not themselves being nationals purely *iure sanguinis*) will become their nationals.

State would be free to confer its nationality on any inhabitant of the ceded territory, including persons who were not nationals of the United Kingdom.

[1]For a discussion of this provision of the *Grundgesetz* and its interpretation by the German courts see *Oppenheim's International Law*, 9th ed (1992), Vol 1 at p 879 n 15.

[2]An exception is that of the Vatican City State which applies neither the *ius sanguinis* nor the *ius soli* principle. Instead, tenure of nationality is determined by the holding of a Vatican office and residence on the territory: P. Weis, "*Nationality and Statelessness in International Law*", 2nd ed (1979), p 96. Thus, a person cannot be born a national of the Vatican City State.

[3]Special rules may be made for children born of diplomats from other States, and for children born on the high seas aboard vessels flying the State's flag. Detailed consideration of these rules is beyond the scope of this thesis.

[4]That children are born with multiple nationalities is only *partly* due to a lack of uniformity among nationality laws arises from the fact that a uniform application of one of the available principles - *ius sanguinis* based on the nationality of either parent - could still result in instances of dual nationality at birth, ie the nationality of each parent.

[5]See P. Weis, "*Nationality and Statelessness in International Law*", 2nd ed (1979), at p 95.

Thus it is entirely possible for a child to acquire multiple nationalities at birth. For example a child born in the United Kingdom of an Italian father and a mother possessing both British and Australian nationality would possess British (*iure soli* and *iure sanguinis*, father or mother),[1] Italian (*iure sanguinis*, father only before 1983)[2] and Australian (*iure sanguinis*, father or mother)[3] nationalities. If either of the child's parents in our example possessed other nationalities, then the child might also acquire those additional nationalities if the relevant States applied some version of the *ius sanguinis* principle.[4]

Although there is no rule of international law providing that nationality at birth must be imposed in accordance only with either or both the *ius soli* or *ius sanguinis* principles,[5] they accord with State practice.[6]

Involuntary Naturalisation. The vast majority of people who acquire a nationality after birth do so as the result of an act of naturalisation. Naturalisation can be either involuntary or by application.

An individual acquires a new nationality by involuntary naturalisation most commonly by marriage to a national of the State conferring the nationality[7] (eg

[1]*British Nationality Act 1981* section 1 (*ius soli* - either parent must be a British citizen or "settled" in the United Kingdom). The United Kingdom also applies the *ius sanguinis* principle if either parent is a British citizen born in the United Kingdom or if either parent is a British citizen performing certain kinds of Crown, Community or prescribed employment: *British Nationality Act 1981*, section 2.

[2]*Legge 13 giugno 1912, n. 555.*, Article 1. In 1983, this provision was extended by the *Corte Costituzionale* to include Italian mothers: Corte cost., sent. 9 febbraio 1983 n. 30).

[3]A person acquires Australian citizenship at birth if either his father or his mother is an Australian citizen otherwise than by descent (ie either parent must have been born in Australia), or an Australian citizen by descent if certain residence requirements have been met: *Australian Citizenship Act 1948*, section 10B. Australia also applies the *ius soli* principle if the child is of an Australian parent or if the parent has been "ordinarily resident" in Australia for ten years immediately preceding the child's birth: *Australian Citizenship Act 1948*, section 10.

[4]It is equally possible, because of the absence of a uniform practice among States, for a child to 'fall between the stools' and be born without having any nationality automatically conferred on him at birth. Thus a child born in Australia of British parents, neither of whom were born in the United Kingdom or had been ordinarily resident in Australia for the previous ten years, would himself be stateless until the Australian Minister for Immigration decided to register him as an Australian citizen, as in certain circumstances the Minister must: *Australian Citizenship Act 1948*, section 23D read together with section 10(2)(b). Such an action would be in accordance not only with that State's domestic law, but also with Article 1 of the *Convention on the Reduction of Statelessness* (989 UNTS 175, UKTS 158 (1975), done at New York on 30 August 1961, entered into force 13 December 1975) to which several Member States are also parties (Denmark, Germany, Ireland, the Netherlands and the United Kingdom), and which provides that a child born in the territory of a State must be granted the nationality of that State if he would otherwise be stateless. Article 14 of the *Convention on Nationality* provides that a "child whose parents are both unknown shall have the nationality of the country of birth". The *Protocol Relating to a Certain Case of Statelessness* (179 LNTS 115, UKTS 31 (1937), done at the Hague on 12 April 1930, entered into force on 1 July 1937) also provides at Article 1 that "(i)n a State whose nationality is not conferred by the mere fact of birth in its territory, a person born in its territory of a mother possessing the nationality of that State and of a father without nationality or of unknown nationality shall have the nationality of the said State". The Member State parties are the Netherlands and the United Kingdom.

[5]P. Weis, "*Nationality and Statelessness in International Law*", 2nd ed (1979), at p 96; *Oppenheim's International Law*, 9th ed (1992), Vol 1 at p 869.

[6]J.G. Starke, "*Introduction to International Law*", 10th ed (1989), at p 344.

[7]See more particularly *Oppenheim's International Law*, 9th ed (1992), Vol 1 at pp 872-874.

Airola, *Van den Broeck* and *Devred*) and, where the person being involuntarily naturalised is a child, by adoption by a national of the State conferring the nationality or upon naturalisation of a parent. Oppenheim also writes that involuntary naturalisation is also often provided for where the recipient has been appointed as a government official or upon "acquisition of domicile in the naturalising state".[1]

Naturalisation upon Application. It is clearly in the area of naturalisation upon application, however, that the risk of 'ephemeral, abusive or simulated creations' is most likely to occur, as it did in *Re Nottebohm*. The circumstances in *Re Nottebohm* were peculiar, involving as they did a conferral of nationality on a person with no substantial links to the conferring State for the obvious sole purpose of permitting him to avoid adverse legal consequences in another State with which he enjoyed very substantial links. There are two principles to be drawn from *Re Nottebohm*.

The first principle is very narrow in scope and is closely connected with the peculiar facts of the case: In an international claim where a State brings an action on behalf of a person who is its national by application, the defendant State need not recognise the plaintiff State's standing where the person has no substantial links to the plaintiff State but does have substantial links to the defendant State. This narrowly framed principle has very little significance for Community law, within whose scope the traditional diplomatic machinery for legal redress of wrongs has no place.[2]

The second principle is broader and does have implications for the way in which the Member States' duty of solidarity affects the exercise of their reserved domain power of conferring nationality upon those who apply for naturalisation.

The International Court of Justice in *Re Nottebohm*, it will be recalled, regarded nationality as "a legal bond having as its basis a social fact of attachment, a genuine connection of existence, interests and sentiments, together with the existence of reciprocal rights and duties" and that it "may be said to constitute the juridical expression of the fact that the individual upon whom it is conferred, either directly by the law or as a result of an act of the authorities, is in fact more closely connected with the population of the State conferring nationality than with that of any other State".[3] In the context of the facts in *Re Nottebohm*, this passage should be seen as prescribing the circumstances in which a State may confer its nationality upon application such as to produce obligatory effects on the level of international relations.

How does the attachment or connection between the applicant for naturalisation and the conferring State manifest itself? In *Re Nottebohm* the International Court of Justice referred expressly to the fact that at the time of his naturalisation Mr

[1]ibid at pp 872-873.

[2]By virtue of Article 219 of the *EC Treaty* the Member States have undertaken "not to submit a dispute concerning the interpretation or application of this Treaty to any method of settlement other than those provided for therein".

[3]*Liechtenstein v Guatemala (Second Phase)* (*Re Nottebohm*) [1955] International Court of Justice Reports 4 at p 23.

Nottebohm had never resided in Liechtenstein, he had not been born there and none of his business interests were located there. In short, Mr Nottebohm's "naturalization was not based on any real prior connection with Liechtenstein".[1]

Oppenheim comments that "[m]ost states naturalise only such persons as have been residing there for some length of time, or have in some other way (eg by service for the state) given evidence of their attachment to the state".[2] Ruth Donner writes of the practice of States showing that a period of residence in the country of naturalization is normally required before nationality is conferred[3] and that:

> Of the various definitions of the link that have been handed down [in numerous decisions of international tribunals] two ingredients are essential. There must be the fact of permanent residence in a State and also it must be evident that in that State lies the centre of the individual's interests.[4]

The fact that the naturalising State has become the centre of the new citizen's interests or the focus of his national loyalty is symbolised, but not proved, by the usual practice of the naturalised person swearing an oath or making a declaration of allegiance to his new State or its sovereign.

Member State nationals and the right of abode

Even when a Member State confers its nationality on an individual in circumstances which, in international law, do not raise a doubt about the conferral's authenticity, it may still fail to conform with the Member State's duties under Article 5 of the *EC Treaty*.

We have already considered the hypothetical case of a Member State conferring its nationality *en masse* on the inhabitants of former imperial possessions. How much worse would be the breach of duty under Article 5 if, for example, the same Member State were to deny those new nationals the right of abode in any of its territory to which the Community's freedom of personal movement applied? The result of such an act would be that the new Member State nationals would be entitled to enjoy movement and residence rights under Community law in every Member State except the one whose nationality they possessed.[5] Such an act would amount to a kind of 'social dumping'; ie by forcing the other Member States to receive newly-created Member State nationals while escaping the same consequence itself.

[1]ibid at p 26.

[2]*Oppenheim's International Law*, 9th ed (1992) at p 876.

[3]Ruth Donner, "*The Regulation of Nationality in International Law*" (1983), at p 45.

[4]ibid at p 95.

[5]Since the decision of the Court of Justice in Case C-370/90 *R v Immigration Appeal Tribunal and Surinder Singh ex parte Secretary of State for the Home Department* [1992] 3 CMLR 358, it is almost certain that a Member State national would be entitled to the rights of movement and residence in his own Member State after having taken advantage of them in another Member State.

The principle would be the same even where the conferral was not *en masse* and a genuine link between the individual and the conferring State could be established. A breach of the duty of solidarity would occur whenever an individual was conferred with Member State nationality when the individual concerned lacked the right of abode in any part of the conferring Member State territory to which the Community's freedom of movement applies.[1]

This implies an additional Community law criterion for the conferral by a Member State of its nationality. A 'citizen', or 'subject' or 'national', however described in national law, should not be clothed with the garments of a 'national of a Member State' if he has no right of abode in any part of his Member State's territory which is subject to the Community's free movement provisions. This Community criterion finds reflection in the two United Kingdom declarations on nationality[2] which restrict United Kingdom nationality for Community purposes to those citizens or subjects who have a right of abode in at least part of the United Kingdom's territories to which the Community's free movement provisions apply, ie the United Kingdom itself or Gibraltar.[3]

That a right of abode in any part of the conferring Member State's territory which is subject to the free movement provisions is sufficient for Community purposes is implicit in *R v Saunders*.[4] The Court of Justice said that a national measure,[5] preventing a British national who was resident in Northern Ireland from entering England and Wales for a period of three years, did not infringe Community law if the restriction arose from a "wholly domestic situation" falling "outside the scope of the rules contained in the Treaty on freedom of movement for workers".[6] It would be strange if the United Kingdom authorities were, as a result of such a restriction on one of its nationals' right of abode, to be under a Community law obligation to deprive him of his Member State nationality for Community purposes.

Thus a British 'citizen' or 'subject', however described in national law, whose right of abode is restricted to, say, Gibraltar (which is within the territorial scope of the Community's free movement provisions)[7] is properly endowed with the accoutrements of a 'national of a Member State'. By contrast a British 'citizen' or 'subject', however

[1] Guido Van den Berghe says that one of the reasons the United Kingdom, upon acceding to the Community, made its 1972 declaration on the meaning of nationality (see Appendix, § 1) was that "to apply the meaning most commonly ascribed to the expression in the conduct of international relations would have entailed extending freedom of movement to persons who do not enjoy the right of abode in the United Kingdom": "*Political Rights for European Citizens*" (1982) at p 13.

[2] See Appendix, §§ 1 and 2. The second declaration replaced the first.

[3] In Case 257/78 *Devred v Commission* [1979] ECR 3767 at p 3790, Advocate General Warner noted that the first United Kingdom declaration on nationality (Appendix, § 1) linked British nationality for Community purposes with the possession of a nationality status giving the right of abode in either the United Kingdom or Gibraltar.

[4] Case 175/78 [1979] ECR 1129.

[5] *in casu* an enforceable undertaking given to an English court.

[6] Case 175/78 *R v Saunders* [1979] ECR 1129 at p 1135, paragraph 12 of the Court's judgment.

[7] See Article 227(4) of the *EC Treaty*: Gibraltar is a European territory for whose external relations the United Kingdom is responsible.

described in national law, whose right of abode is restricted to, say, Hong Kong could not be properly so endowed.

Summary and conclusion

The conferral by a State of its nationality, according to international law, is a matter which falls within the reserved domain of States. In this, Community law follows international law.

Although a State's conferral of its nationality ought, in international law, to be recognised by other States, a conferral in certain circumstances relieves other States of an obligation to recognise it. In particular, if a State confers its nationality without conformity to the usual practice of States and thereby exposes a want of genuine connection between the conferring State and its new citizen, a question may arise as to whether the nationality was conferred for an abusive purpose. If, in such circumstances, an abusive purpose does lie behind the conferral, another State may not be obliged to recognise it.

Here, the position in Community law differs from that of international law. The Court of Justice requires a host Member State to extend to any person possessing the status of 'national of a Member State' all the rights due to such a person simply upon production of a valid identity card or passport from another Member State. The status of 'national of a Member State' is held by any person who holds the nationality of one of the Member States according to the law of that Member State.

The Member States nevertheless owe each other a duty of solidarity and co-operation which derives from Article 5 of the *EC Treaty*. In particular they must abstain from "any measure" which "could jeopardise" the attainment of the Treaty's objectives. The Treaty's objectives include, according to Article 2, promoting "throughout the Community a harmonious and balanced development of economic activities, ... a high level of employment and of social protection, the raising of the standard of living and quality of life, and ... solidarity among Member States". Any measure which could jeopardise these objectives is one from which the Member States are enjoined to refrain.

A breach of the duty occurs where a Member States adopts a measure which could jeopardise the Community's fundamental economic objectives. Given that many measures which are not within the Community's legislative competence, such as those relating to nationality or most elements of national macro-economic policy, could have a theoretically adverse impact to greater or lesser degrees on the Community's basic economic objectives, the concept of 'jeopardy' in Article 5 would need to imply a 'real and serious threat' if Article 5 were not to operate as a vehicle for the complete destruction of national sovereignty.[1] An obvious example of such a real and serious threat might be a decision by a Member State to extend its nationality, and

[1]Such an approach would accord with Article 3b (first paragraph) of the *EC Treaty* which provides that the Community "shall act within the limits of the powers conferred upon it by this Treaty and of the objectives assigned to it therein".

hence the Community status of 'national of a Member State', to all the inhabitants of its former colonial possessions. Less extreme measures could also suffice.

A breach of the duty also occurs when a Member State adopts a measure, affecting a matter falling within the scope of the treaties, which deceives or misleads other Member States or the Community institutions in order to effect an abusive purpose. A Member State which confers its nationality on a person who possesses no genuine links with it, thereby clothing that person with the status of 'national of a Member State' for the purpose of entitling him to take advantage of the Community's freedoms of movement, may be engaging in behaviour which deceives or misleads the other Member States and the Community institutions in order to effect an abusive purpose.

There can be no question of deception or abusive purposes, however, if the conferral of nationality is founded upon a genuine link between the person and the conferring State, and provided that the person receiving the nationality has a right of abode in any part of the conferring Member State's territory which is subject to the Community's free movement provisions. If nationality is conferred in accordance with criteria commonly employed among States, it will be practicably impossible to demonstrate deception or abuse.

Thus, nationality conferred at birth in accordance with either or both of the *ius soli* or *ius sanguinis* principles will not create a difficulty with Article 5. It is to be noted that in *Micheletti* entitlement to Italian nationality had been conferred at birth *iure sanguinis*. Similarly no problem arises if nationality is conferred as the result of an act of redintegration. Involuntary naturalisation should not present a problem if nationality is imposed upon adults as the result of marriage to a national or appointment to an official post, or upon children when they are adopted by a national or when their parents are naturalised, or upon either adults or children when they establish their domicile in the naturalising State's territory. An involuntary naturalisation will not, however, be applied in Community law if it results in an infringement of the general principles of law upheld by the Court of Justice, notably the principle against sex discrimination.

Voluntary naturalisation is the most potentially problematic area, latent as it is with the opportunity for abuse (as in *Re Nottebohm*). The practice of States is that naturalisation upon application is usually approved only after a period of residence in the naturalising State's territory (most commonly), or as the result of service rendered to the naturalising State. Other connections, such as birth in the naturalising State's territory or the location there of business interests are also sometimes criteria for the grant of nationality upon application.

As the gravamen of any breach of solidarity arising from a conferral of nationality without a genuine link would be the deceptive or misleading conduct involved, the breach could be avoided by informing or consulting the Commission about the proposed conferral.

The mere act of informing or consulting the Commission would not, however, avoid the breach of solidarity if it is occasioned by an act which could jeopardise the harmonious and balanced development of economic activities, a high level of employment and of social protection and the raising of the standard of living and quality of life throughout the Community. Nor would it avoid the breach of solidarity if the recipient of the nationality has no right of abode in any part of the conferring Member State's territory which is subject to the Community's free movement provisions, for here the abuse arises primarily from social dumping or a refusal to accept symmetrical obligations rather than from deception.

It is finally worth noting that the Member States are obliged to treat an individual as a national of a Member State only if the identity card or visa which he presents is "valid". Thus a forged document obviously does not oblige the host Member State to treat its bearer as a national of a Member State. Similarly a document which has expired could not be regarded as "valid" for the purposes of *admitting* a Union citizen,[1] but secondary legislation forbids the *expulsion* of a person covered by Articles 48-66 of the Treaty merely because the identity card or passport with which he entered the host country has expired.[2]

Less clear is the case of a document which has been issued as the result of fraud against the issuing Member State. Although the matter cannot be regarded as free from doubt, the better view is probably that an identity card or passport obtain by fraud is not "valid". Certainly, in the context of international claims, international law regards a nationality obtained in violation of the conferring State's laws as grounds depriving that State of its standing.[3]

Such an approach also accords with the *Declaration on Nationality of a Member State*[4] by which the Member States agreed that the question whether an individual possesses the nationality of a Member State shall be settled solely by reference to the national law of the Member State concerned. The declaration accurately reflects the position in Community law as regards the *conferring* of nationality. If a person has procured an identity card or passport from a Member State when the laws of that Member State do not entitle him to be a national, the identity card or passport will not be 'valid' and the holder cannot be regarded as a national of the Member State regardless of what documents he produces.

[1]Support for this view can be found in Article 2(3) of *Directive 68/360* which provides in part that where a passport is the only document on which the holder may lawfully leave the country, its period of validity shall be not less than five years.

[2]Article 3(3) of *Directive 64/221*. In Case C-376/89 *Giagounidis v Stadt Reutlingen* [1991] ECR I-1069 the Court of Justice tacitly accepted that an expired passport could not be used to obtain a Community residence permit under Article 4(3)(a) of *Directive 68/360*.

[3]eg *Flegenheimer Claim* (1958-I) 25 ILR 91 (Italian-United States Conciliation Commission), and *Flutie Cases* (1903) RIAA vol ix p 148 (American-Venezuelan Commission).

[4]See this Chapter, post.

CONDITIONS FOR LOSS OF NATIONALITY

The latitude which Community law permits Member States in bestowing their nationality such as to endow the recipients with the status of 'national of a Member State', and thus of citizen of the Union, is wide indeed. It will be only in the most extraordinary or extreme of cases that a conferral will be assailable on the grounds that it threatens the Community's basic economic objectives, although the impending decolonisations of Hong Kong and Macau may yet be of significance in this regard. Nor will a conferral of nationality on an individual in the absence of a genuine link create a potential problem for the conferring Member State provided it first discharges its duty to inform or consult with the Commission, even assuming that the Commission or another Member State could be moved for some reason to challenge an individual conferral. In any event, the individual who has been endowed with the nationality would be entitled to be treated as a citizen of the Union by the mere production of a valid identity card or passport until his nationality is revoked by the conferring State. The practical consequences of these constraints are thus likely to be very minimal.

The position is different, however, when we consider the constraints which limit the Member States' power to withdraw nationality such as to deprive an individual of his status of citizen of the Union.

Denationalisation and Fundamental Rights

The withdrawal by any State of its nationality from an individual may give rise to a question as to whether one of the denationalised individual's fundamental rights have been infringed. Some authoritarian and totalitarian States engage in, or have engaged in, the practice of depriving individuals of their nationality on grounds of political opinion or activity, religious belief, race or ethnicity. People are sometimes rendered stateless by such denationalisations. Even now in some European countries, including present and applicant Member States of the European Union, there are elected politicians calling for the expatriation and denationalisation of certain classes of citizens on grounds which raise serious human rights concerns.

When a person acquires the nationality of a Member State he also acquires citizenship of the Union. What would be the effect on this status were a person to be deprived of his Member State nationality on grounds which violated his fundamental rights? In particular, could such a deprivation of nationality operate so as to deprive him of his citizenship of the Union?

At first blush, it might appear that the denationalised individual must lose his Union citizenship whatever the grounds for his denationalisation. After all, Article 8(1) of the *EC Treaty* provides that every person holding the nationality of a Member State shall be a citizen of the Union. There is no suggestion in the text that former Member State nationals will continue to be citizens of the Union, and there is no provision laying down separate Community rules for the loss of union Citizenship. The Treaty, it might be said, therefore leaves both the acquisition and loss of Union citizenship entirely to the operation of national laws. Such a view might, moreover, be said to accord with the *Declaration on Nationality of a Member State* which states that the question whether an individual possesses the nationality of a Member State shall be settled solely by reference to the national law of the Member State concerned.

Yet there are good reasons for believing that a denationalised individual need not always be deprived of his citizenship of the Union. This belief arises from a consideration of the way in which fundamental freedoms are protected in Community law. In this connection it will be argued that individuals may not be deprived of their Union citizenship, or even of their Member State nationality, by an act of denationalisation which violates the fundamental freedoms protected by the Court of Justice.

Community Protection of Fundamental Freedoms

That fundamental human rights are among the general principles of law which the Court of Justice will uphold is now perfectly well established. The foundation case is *Stauder v City of Ulm, Sozialamt*[1] in which the Court of Justice first indicated that it would protect "the fundamental human rights enshrined in the general principles of Community law".[2] In *Internationale Handelsgesellschaft mbH v Einfuhr- und Vorratsstelle für Getreide und Futtermittel*[3] the Court of Justice said that in protecting fundamental rights it was "inspired by the constitutional traditions common to the Member States",[4] and in *J Nold, Kohlen- und Baustoffgroßhandlung v Commission*[5] it added that "international treaties for the protection of human rights on which the Member States have collaborated or of which they are signatories, can supply guidelines which should be followed within the framework of Community law".[6]

Convention on the Reduction of Statelessness

Article 8(1) of the United Nations *Convention on the Reduction of Statelessness*[7] provides that a Contracting State "shall not deprive a person of its nationality if such deprivation would render him stateless".

There are several exceptions to this rule. It does not apply if the nationality was obtained by misrepresentation or fraud.[8] It does not apply if a naturalised citizen has lived abroad for more than seven consecutive years and he has not notified the Contracting State of his intention to retain his nationality.[9] It does not apply in respect of persons who were born as nationals outside the Contracting State's territory

[1]Case 29/69 [1969] ECR 419.
[2]ibid at p 425, paragraph 7 of the Court's judgment.
[3]Case 11/70 [1970] ECR 1125.
[4]ibid at p 1134, paragraph 4 of the Court's judgment.
[5]Case 4/73 [1974] ECR 491.
[6]ibid at p 507, paragraph 13 of the Court's judgment.
[7]Done at New York on 30 August 1961, 989 UNTS 175.
[8]Article 8(2)(b).
[9]Articles 8(2)(a) and 7(4).

and who have not taken up residence in the Contracting State's territory within one year of attaining their majority.[1] It does not apply in respect of persons who have taken an oath, or made a formal declaration, of allegiance to another State, or given definite evidence of their determination to repudiate their allegiance to the Contracting State.[2] It does not apply in respect of persons who, inconsistently with their duty of loyalty to the Contracting State, have rendered or continued to render services to, or received or continued to receive emoluments from, another State in disregard of an express prohibition from the Contracting State.[3] Nor does it apply in respect of persons who, inconsistently with their duty of loyalty to the Contracting State, have conducted themselves in a manner prejudicial to the vital interests of the State.[4]

Article 9 of the same Convention provides that a Contracting State "may not deprive any person or group of persons of their nationality on racial, ethnic, religious or political grounds". This provision is not subject to any exceptions, and it is applicable whether or not the person is rendered stateless.

Although the European *Convention for the Protection of Human Rights and Fundamental Freedoms* ("*ECHR*")[5] and its protocols are usually the international agreements which provide guidelines in defining and applying general principles of Community law in the field of human rights protection, there is no reason in principle why agreements concluded under other auspices, such as those of the United Nations, could not equally serve.[6]

The *Convention on the Reduction of Statelessness* was concluded in 1961, entered into force in 1975 and includes among its parties Denmark, Germany, Ireland, the Netherlands and the United Kingdom. France is a signatory, but not yet a party. Of the European Union's Member States which have not signed the Convention, all except Greece participated in one or both of the sessions of the United Nations conference[7] whose Final Act included the Convention. Thus, all the Member States except Greece have collaborated on or signed the Convention.

[1] Articles 8(2)(a) and 7(5).

[2] Article 8(3)(b).

[3] Article 8(3)(a)(i).

[4] Article 8(3)(a)(ii).

[5] Done at Rome on 4 November 1950, 213 UNTS 221.

[6] eg Case 149/77 *Defrenne v Société Anonyme Belge de Navigation Aérienne Sabena* [1978] ECR 1365 at p 1378; ILO *Convention (No 111) Concerning Discrimination in Respect of Employment and Occupation* (done at Geneva on 25 June 1958, 362 UNTS 31) referred to in support of the elimination of discrimination on grounds of sex as a fundamental right of Community law. Also Case 374/87 *Orkem v Commission* [1989] ECR 3283 at p 3351, paragraph 31 of the Court's judgment and Joined Cases C-297/88 and C-197/89 *Dzodzi v Belgian State* [1990] ECR I-3763 at p I-3800, paragraph 68 of the Court's judgment; Article 14 of the *International Covenant on Civil and Political Rights* considered, but regarded as inapplicable on the facts.

[7] The United Nations Conference on the Elimination or Reduction of Future Statelessness. See Paul Weis, "*The United Nations Convention on the Reduction of Statelessness*", (1962) 11 ICLQ 1073 at pp 1078-1080.

At the time of Greece's accession to the Community in 1981, the Nine had all collaborated on or signed the *Convention on the Reduction of Statelessness.* Article 9 of the Convention thus provided guidelines for the general principles of law which the Court protected within the framework of Community law. As a guideline for the general principles of Community law Articles 8 and 9 formed part of the *acquis communautaire* which Greece agreed to observe upon accession.[1] In any event, it can hardly be said that Community principles of human rights cease to be protected when a State, which has not signed or collaborated on a relevant international treaty providing guidelines, subsequently joins the Union. An acceding Member State must take the Community's extant general principles of law as it finds them.

Consequently, Articles 8 and 9 of the *Convention on the Reduction of Statelessness* can supply guidelines for human rights protection which should be followed within the framework of Community law.

International Covenant on Civil and Political Rights

All the European Union's Member States are parties to the United Nations *International Covenant on Civil and Political Rights* ("*ICCPR*"),[2] Article 26 of which provides as follows:

> All persons are equal before the law and are entitled without any discrimination to the equal protection of the law. In this respect, the law shall prohibit any discrimination and guarantee to all persons equal and effective protection against discrimination on any ground such as race, colour, sex, language, religion, political or other opinion, national or social origin, property, birth or other status.

In *Arantzamendi-Osa v Procureur de la République*,[3] a fisheries case involving the validity of national licensing requirements for non-Community nationals operating in a Member State's waters, Advocate General Capotorti referred to Article 26 of the *ICCPR* as a provision which guarantees "the formal equality of persons with regard to each legal order considered as a whole but only in order to preclude the legislature from introducing arbitrary discrimination or differences in treatment without any objective justification whatever".[4] The Advocate General thought that the impugned national measures in the case before him were justified by conservation considerations so that Article 26 was not helpful and the Court of Justice did not find it necessary to refer to the provision in its judgment. Nevertheless, Article 26 is clearly a provision which, in the right circumstances, could supply guidelines which should be followed within the framework of Community law.

If within the framework of Community law a legislature passes a measure arbitrarily discriminating against a person on any of the grounds specified in Article 26, and if

[1] Article 2 of the *Act of Accession 1979*.

[2] Done at New York on 16 December 1966, 999 UNTS 171.

[3] Joined Cases 13-28/82 [1982] ECR 3927.

[4] ibid at p 3943, paragraph 5 of the opinion.

there is no objective justification for that measure, the guidelines supplied by Article 26 would suggest an infringement of a fundamental principle of Community law. There is nothing in the *ICCPR* which expressly renders Article 26 inapplicable to denationalisation laws. Indeed the preamble to the *ICCPR* refers to the *Universal Declaration of Human Rights*,[1] Article 15(2) of which provides in part that "[n]o one shall be arbitrarily deprived of his nationality".

Convention on Racial Discrimination

The United Nations *International Convention on the Elimination of all Forms of Racial Discrimination*[2] provides, if it is needed, additional authority for the proposition that a deprivation of nationality can, at least in certain cases, be a violation of human rights. Article 2(1)(a) provides that each State Party undertakes to engage in no act or practice of racial discrimination against persons, groups of persons or institutions. Article 5(d)(ii) commits States parties to eliminate racial discrimination in all its forms and to guarantee the right of everyone to equality before the law without distinction as to race, colour, or national or ethnic origin in the enjoyment of the right to nationality. Article 1(1) defines 'racial discrimination' to mean any distinction, exclusion, restriction or preference based on race, colour, descent, or national or ethnic origin which has the purpose or effect of nullifying or impairing the recognition, enjoyment or exercise, on an equal footing, of human rights in the political, economic, social, cultural or any other field of public life.

That the definition of 'racial discrimination' is wide enough to include certain acts of denationalisation is implicit in Article 1(3) which provides that nothing in the Convention may be interpreted as affecting in any way the legal provisions of State Parties concerning nationality, citizenship or naturalization, *provided that such provisions do not discriminate against any particular nationality.* Thus a denationalisation measure which singled out persons who also hold, and possibly who have held, the nationality of another particular State or of other particular States would be an infringement of the convention. All the European Union's Member States have signed the convention, which can therefore supply guidelines for human rights protection which should be followed within the framework of Community law.

European Convention on Human Rights

All the European Union's Member States are parties to the *ECHR*, which is a well established and preferred source of inspiration for the protection of fundamental freedoms within the framework of Community law.[3] The preamble to the *Single European Act* records the determination of the Member States to promote democracy on the basis of the fundamental rights recognised in, *inter alia*, the *ECHR*. Article F(2) of the *Union Treaty* also provides that the Union shall respect fundamental rights

[1]UN Doc A/811.

[2]Done at New York on 7 March 1966, 60 UNTS 195.

[3]See especially Case 222/84 *Johnston v Chief Constable of the Royal Ulster Constabulary* [1986] ECR 1651 at p 1682, paragraph 18 of the Court's judgment, and Case C-260/89 *Elliniki Radiophonia Tileorassi AE v Dimotiki Etairia Pliroforissis* ("*ERT*") [1991] ECR I-2925 at pp I-2963 - I-2964, paragraph 41 of the Court's judgment. See also A.G. Toth, "*Human Rights*" in the "*Encyclopaedia of European Community Law*" (1990), pp 284 *et seq*.

as guaranteed in, *inter alia*, the *ECHR* as general principles of Community law.[1] Article 14 of the *ECHR* provides as follows:

> The enjoyment of the rights and freedoms set forth in this Convention shall be secured without discrimination on any ground such as sex, race, colour, language, religion, political or other opinion, national or social origin, association with a national minority, property, birth or other status.

As the language of the provision suggests, it is intended to supplement rights already set out elsewhere in the convention. Indeed, the European Court of Human Rights has said that "Article 14 has no independent existence, it is complementary to the other normative provisions of the Convention and Protocols".[2] Hence, in proceedings brought before the institutions established by the *ECHR* it is of no avail to allege an infringement of Article 14 without being able to point to another right guaranteed by the convention or its protocols to which Article 14 can be attached.

This, combined with the fact that neither the *ECHR* nor any of its protocols specify standards for either the acquisition or loss of nationality, might seem strongly to suggest that Article 14 is of no assistance in deciding whether there are circumstances in which a withdrawal of nationality by a Member State will always have the effect of depriving the individual concerned of his citizenship of the Union.

Yet there is reason to believe that Article 14 of the *ECHR*, whatever its *rôle* in the convention, may provide guidelines for human rights protection which should be followed within the framework of Community law generally. If this is the case, it may have something to tell us about the impact on Community law of a Member State's withdrawal of nationality in violation of human rights principles.

Article 6 of the *EC Treaty* prohibits any discrimination on grounds of (Community) nationality within the scope and application of the Treaty, subject to any special provisions on nationality discrimination such as those contained in Articles 8a, 48, 52 and 59. The vast majority of complaints about discrimination brought before or referred to the Court of Justice are about nationality discrimination. The legal bases for dealing with such complaints are usually clear and involve applying provisions of the treaties or of secondary legislation. There is also explicit authority in the *EC Treaty* against discrimination on the grounds of sex in the field of pay for work of equal value (Article 119), and secondary legislation has been adopted extending the

[1]That Article F(2) specifically provides that the *ECHR*'s fundamental rights shall be respected as "general principles of Community law" probably means that the Court can refer to Article F(2) notwithstanding Article M of the *Union Treaty* which provides that some provisions of that Treaty (including Article F) shall not affect the Treaties establishing the Communities or the subsequent Treaties and Acts modifying them.

[2]*National Union of Belgian Police Case*, (1975) Series A, No 19 at p 19, paragraph 44 of the Court's judgment. Similar pronouncements exist in numerous other cases before the European Court of Human Rights and the European Commission of Human Rights. See also the opinion of Advocate General Van Gerven in Case C-262/88 *Barber v Guardian Royal Exchange Assurance Group* [1990] ECR I-1889 at p I-1941, paragraph 53 of the opinion.

prohibition against sex discrimination into other contexts.[1] Discrimination between producers and consumers in the context of the common agricultural policy is also forbidden by the *EC Treaty* (Article 40(3)).

All these provisions are obviously helpful if a person has been discriminated against on grounds of his Community nationality, sex or *rôle* in the market and to the extent that the discrimination occurs in a context prohibited by Community legislation. But what relief in Community law is available if a person is denied a right under Community law, not because he is a foreign (Community) national or because of sex, but because of his religion, race, or political views? The Community treaties and secondary legislation are silent.

One instinctively expects that the Court of Justice would reply in the negative if it were to be confronted, for example, with a reference asking whether it is compatible with Community law to deny a foreign Community student access to vocational training because of his colour.[2] The same instinct underpins a belief, even if there were no suggestion of covert nationality discrimination, that the Court would not be sympathetic to a plea that all students, not just foreign ones, were subject to the same discrimination. Would there be legal warrant for the Court of Justice to deal with this hypothetical case in a way consistent with our instinctive expectations?

In *Royal Scholten-Honig (Holdings) Limited v Intervention Board for Agricultural Produce* ("*Re Isoglucose*")[3] the Court of Justice said that Article 40(3) of the Treaty "is merely a specific enunciation of the general principle of equality which is one of the fundamental principles of Community law", which principle "requires that similar situations shall not be treated differently unless the differentiation is objectively justified".[4] Thus a system of levies and subsidies established by secondary legislation, under which the manufacturers of glucose subsidised their competitors in the sugar industry, was held invalid for violation of the general principle of equality. The discrimination struck down in *Re Isoglucose* was of a type not expressly forbidden by Article 40(3). The rule of equality of treatment is a fundamental principle of Community law,[5] which applies to forbid not only overt discrimination but also all covert forms of discrimination involving the application of other criteria leading in fact to the same discriminatory result.[6]

[1]eg *Directive 76/207* (access to employment, vocational training, promotion and working conditions) and *Directive 79/7* (social security).

[2]The student would need to be a foreign Community national - if he was a local national he would probably find that the situation would be regarded as entirely internal to the Member State and unconnected with Community law: Case 180/83 *Moser v Land Baden-Württemberg* [1984] ECR 2539.

[3]Joined Cases 103 and 145/77 [1978] ECR 2037.

[4]ibid at p 2072, paragraphs 26-27 of the Court's judgment. See also Case 300/86 *Van Landschoot v Mera NV* [1988] ECR 3443 at p 3460, paragraph 9 of the Court's judgment.

[5]Case 1/72 *Frilli v Belgian State* [1972] ECR 457 at p 466, paragraph 19 of the Court's judgment.

[6]Case 152/73 *Sotgiu v Deutsche Bundespost* [1974] ECR 153 at p 164, paragraph 11 of the Court's judgment.

A differentiation will not be objectively justified if it is based on an arbitrary distinction.[1] In this context it is well to note that Article 14 of the *ECHR* catalogues the most common arbitrary distinctions. It is, moreover, a non-exhaustive catalogue as the provision's language suggests.

Secondary legislation indirectly discriminating against women in their conditions of employment with the Community was, without express authority in the Treaty or secondary legislation, disallowed by the Court of Justice in *Sabbatini v European Parliament*.[2]

In the field of sex discrimination it is at least possible to point to Article 119 of the *EC Treaty* as being a source of inspiration for a broader general principle.[3] In *Prais v Council*,[4] however, the Court of Justice went further and said that the Community must take reasonable steps to ensure that adherents of different religious faiths have equal opportunity to participate in the process for recruitment to the Community service by endeavouring not to set dates for tests which coincide with holy days.[5] Although Article 9 of the *ECHR* (freedom of religion) was referred to in argument, it was not part of the *ratio decidendi*, and Article 9 in its terms was not apt to be of assistance on the facts of the case.[6] The Court's judgment should therefore be seen as an expression of the fundamental principle of equality, rather than of a discrete Community freedom of religion; applicants for Community employment must not be treated differently on account of an arbitrary distinction such as religious belief.

Thus the Court of Justice is quite prepared to strike down measures which discriminate arbitrarily on the grounds of Community nationality, for which explicit textual authority exists in Community legislation. It is also prepared to strike down measures which arbitrarily discriminate on grounds of sex, even in contexts where the Community legislative authority is at most only analogous. It will even strike down measures which arbitrarily discriminate, even indirectly, on grounds of religion in the absence of any express Community legislative authority whatever. In the context of the Community's tasks it is difficult to conceive of circumstances in which a difference in treatment based on a ground like religion could ever be objectively justified. Consequently such differentiation is, in the Community context, arbitrary *per se*.

But why stop at religion? There is no reason in principle why discrimination based on race, colour, language, political or other opinion, national or social origin (as distinct

[1] Case 11/74 *L'Union des Minotiers de la Champagne v French Government* [1974] ECR 877 at p 886, paragraph 22 of the Court's judgment.

[2] Case 20/71 [1972] ECR 345.

[3] The Court of Justice did not, however, do so in *Sabbatini*.

[4] Case 130/75 [1976] ECR 1589.

[5] ibid at p 1599, paragraph 16 of the Court's judgment. The Community's duty is a very qualified one. If a candidate does not advise "in good time" that a particular date is unsuitable for religious reasons, the Community need not set another date. Even if the advice is received in good time, the Community need only "take this into account in fixing the date for written tests, and endeavour to avoid such dates".

[6] This, at least, was the view of Advocate General Warner at pp 1607-1608.

from nationality), association with a national minority, property, birth or other status should not likewise be forbidden by the general principle of equality. All of these grounds are, of course, among those mentioned in Article 14 of the *ECHR*. Differentiation on some of these grounds might, in some Community contexts, conceivably be objectively justifiable; eg refusing to employ a worker because he does not speak a language essential for the performance of his job. Differentiation on some of the other grounds would, like religion, almost certainly be arbitrary *per se* in any conceivable Community law context; eg race.

In *Administrateur des Affaires Maritimes, Bayonne v Dorca Marina*[1] the Court of Justice expressly left open the question as to whether Article 14 of the *ECHR* is applicable to economic activities[2] after the Advocate General had argued that it was of no assistance because, on the facts, it could not be linked to any of the other rights protected in that convention.[3] This question can safely be left open, for it is the wrong question to ask. It is not necessary, in order to link Article 14 of the *ECHR* to the protection of the Community's human rights, to ask whether Article 14 can apply to economic activities. Nor is it necessary, as the Advocate General argued, to allege a breach in the context of Community law of another provision of the *ECHR* before Article 14 can act as a guideline to be followed in Community law.

The first question is misplaced because Article 14, like all provisions of international human rights treaties, does not apply of its own force within the Community legal order. It merely furnishes guidelines which should be followed by Community law. To the extent that it is followed, it is by force of Community law itself. The second argument is misplaced because the real significance of Article 14 lies not in linking it to an alleged infringement of another *ECHR* provision within a Community context; although such a linkage, where it could be made, would certainly make Article 14 relevant. Rather its real significance lies in it providing guidelines for applying the Community's general principle of equality. Article 14 is, indeed, the *ECHR*'s functional equivalent to the Community's general principle of equality.

Thus Article 14 of the *ECHR* supplies guidelines for human rights protection which should be followed within the framework of applying Community law's general principle of equality. This is what the Court of Justice effectively did in *Sabbatini* and *Prais*. It is what the Court would do again if confronted with our hypothetical student denied access to his vocational training course because of his colour. Similarly a national measure which arbitrarily denationalises a person on the sorts of grounds referred to in Article 14, thereby affecting his status as a citizen of the Union, raises a question about the person's Community right to equal treatment.

[1]Joined Cases 50-58/82 [1982] ECR 3949.

[2]ibid at p 3959, paragraph 11 of the Court's judgment.

[3]ibid at pp 3942-3943, paragraph 5 of Advocate General Capotorti's opinion.

The 'Framework of Community law'

In *Nold*, it will be recalled, the Court of Justice said that "international treaties for the protection of human rights on which the Member States have collaborated or of which they are signatories, can supply guidelines which should be followed within the framework of Community law".[1] Even given that Articles 8 and 9 of the *Convention on the Reduction of Statelessness*, Article 26 of the *ICCPR*, Articles 2(1)(a) and 5(d)(iii) of the *International Convention on the Elimination of all Forms of Racial Discrimination*, and Article 14 of the *ECHR* as it informs the general principle of equality can supply Community law with guidelines for the protection of human rights, the measure affected must fall within the "framework of Community law". Could a Member State's act of denationalisation be said to fall within this framework such as to attract the application of Community law's general principles of law upholding fundamental freedoms?

That the validity of Community secondary legislation is subject to conformity with the Community's human rights principles was clear from the beginning; *Stauder*, in 1969, involved the validity of a provision in a Commission decision addressed to the Member States and *Internationale Handelsgesellschaft*, decided in 1970, involved the validity of provisions in Council and Commission regulations.

But what about national measures which are inconsistent with the human rights standards protected by Community law? In 1984 the Court of Justice held in *R v Kirk*[2] that the fundamental freedoms protected by Community law prevented a Community measure from retrospectively authorising the adoption of a national measure imposing criminal liability in a field of unexercised Community legislative competence. Thus national measures can indirectly be struck down when an authorising Community measure fails to meet the Community's human rights standards.

The following year the Court of Justice, in *Cinéthèque SA v Fédération nationale des cinémas français*,[3] signalled that this might be as far as it was prepared to go. The Court refused to declare as inconsistent with the Treaty French measures forbidding the commercial release on video of cinematographic works within one year of issue of their cinema performance certificates. The complaint was, *inter alia*, that the restriction was inconsistent with freedom of expression as guaranteed by Article 10 of the *ECHR*.

In this connection the Court said that although it had a duty to ensure the observance of the Community's fundamental rights "in the field of Community law", it had no power to do so in "an area which falls within the jurisdiction of the national legislator".[4] The impugned French measures did 'enter the field of Community law';

[1]Case 4/73 *J Nold, Kohlen- und Baustoffgroßhandlung v Commission* [1974] ECR 491 at p 507, paragraph 13 of the Court's judgment.

[2]Case 63/83 [1984] ECR 2689.

[3]Joined Cases 60 and 61/84 [1985] ECR 2605.

[4]ibid at p 2627, paragraph 26 of the Court's judgment.

the Court expressly acknowledged that measures of the sort under challenge "may create barriers to intra-Community trade in video-cassettes".[1] But they were still measures which the Member State was entitled to adopt. The *Cinéthèque* Court was therefore saying, consistently with *Kirk*, that any attack on grounds of human rights violations must be directed at measures adopted by the Community institutions, and that national measures are unimpeachable on these grounds even if they 'enter the field of Community law'.

There has been a recent subtle, but highly significant, reorientation in the Court's approach to the application of the Community's fundamental rights principles to national measures.[2]

A hint of a change in the Court's direction appeared in *Demirel v Stadt Schwäbisch Gmünd*[3] in 1987, two years after *Cinéthèque*. The Court of Justice was asked whether Article 8 of the *ECHR* (right to respect for private and family life) affected a decision by German authorities to order a Turkish national, the wife of a Turkish worker resident in Germany, to leave the country. The Court held that no relevant provision of the *EEC-Turkey Association Agreement* was directly effective and there was no legislation adopted under that agreement which could confer on the Turkish woman a right to remain in the Community on family reunion or other grounds. After repeating the formula in *Cinéthèque* the Court said:

> In this case ... there is at present no provision of Community law defining the conditions in which Member States must permit the family reunification of Turkish workers lawfully settled in the Community. It follows that the national rules at issue in the main proceedings did not have to implement a provision of Community law. In those circumstances, the Court does not have jurisdiction to determine whether national rules such as those at issue are compatible with the principles enshrined in Article 8 of the European Convention on Human Rights.[4]

Although apparently following *Cinéthèque*, the Court was actually signalling an imminent departure. Now it was suggested, for the first time, that certain national measures could be tested against the Community's human rights standards. National measures implementing Community rules might have to pass the test.

The Court's reorientation manifested itself openly in 1989 in *Wachauf v Federal Republic of Germany*.[5] The Court of Justice was invited to invalidate a Council regulation which allegedly authorised the adoption of a German order depriving

[1] ibid at p 2626, paragraph 22 of the Court's judgment.

[2] see Jason Coppel and Aidan O'Neill, "*The European Court of Justice: Taking rights seriously?*", (1992) 12 Legal Studies 227.

[3] Case 12/86 [1987] ECR 3719.

[4] ibid at p 3754, paragraph 28 of the Court's judgment.

[5] Case 5/88 [1989] ECR 2609.

compensation to tenant farmers who, without their landlords' consent, surrendered their milk production quotas. The regulation was asserted to be invalid for violation of a fundamental right against unconstitutional expropriation without compensation:

> [I]t must be observed that Community rules which, upon the expiry of the lease, had the effect of depriving the lessee, without compensation, of the fruits of his labour and of his investments in the tenanted holding would be incompatible with the requirements of the protection of fundamental rights in the Community legal order. Since those requirements are also binding on the Member States when they implement Community rules, the Member States must, as far as possible, apply those rules in accordance with those requirements.[1]

The Court ruled that the regulation, properly construed, did not have the effect imputed to it and that it did not permit landlords to deprive tenants of the fruits of their labours. The Council regulation was therefore valid. However the German order was, by necessary implication, incompatible with Community law for violation of fundamental rights.

At one level the Court's decision in *Wachauf* appears to be nothing more than '*Stauder* revisited'. In both cases a Community measure was attacked for alleged violation of fundamental rights and in both cases the Community measure was interpreted in a way which avoided the alleged violation. There is, however, a critical differencc between the two cases.

In *Stauder* the Court said that the German authorities, in implementing the Commission decision, were by Community law neither required to adopt nor prohibited from adopting a rule that the socially disadvantaged recipients of reduced-price butter identify themselves by name at the point of purchase.[2] The same identification requirement, had it been contained in the challenged Commission decision which authorised the German measure, would probably have been invalid for violation of a right to human dignity. In *Wachauf*, by contrast, the Court effectively held a national measure adopted in implementation of a Community rule inconsistent with Community law for infringing a fundamental right protected by Community law.

The next encroachment made by the Court of Justice into State jurisdiction came two years after *Wachauf* on a reference from the Thessaloniki Regional Court in *Elliniki Radiophonia Tileorassi AE* ("*ERT*") *v Dimotiki Etairia Pliroforissis*.[3] The Court of Justice was asked whether a Greek law conferring a broadcasting monopoly on a State broadcasting company (ERT) contravened Article 10 of the *ECHR* and, if so, what were the implications in Community law.

[1] ibid at pp 2639-2640, paragraph 19 of the Court's judgment.

[2] Case 29/69 *Stauder v City of Ulm, Sozialamt* [1969] ECR 419 at p 425, paragraph 6 of the Court's judgment.

[3] Case C-260/89 [1991] ECR I-2925.

The *ERT* Court started by putting a gloss on its decision in *Wachauf*, which case was interpreted as meaning that "the Community cannot accept measures which are incompatible with observance of the human rights ... recognized and guaranteed" in the constitutional traditions common to the Member States, international treaties which they have signed or on which they have collaborated, and especially the *ECHR*.[1] The passage in *Wachauf* to which the *ERT* Court refers in making this comment indicates that its use of the word "measures" is a reference to both national and Community measures.

The Court then said that while it has no power to examine the compatibility with the *ECHR* of national rules which do not fall within the scope of Community law;

> ... where such rules do fall within the scope of Community law, and reference is made to the Court for a preliminary ruling, it must provide all the criteria of interpretation needed by the national court to determine whether those rules are compatible with the fundamental rights the observance of which the Court ensures and which derive in particular from the European Convention on Human Rights.[2]

In particular, the Court said, when a Member State relies on the public policy provisos to derogate from a fundamental Community freedom, any derogations must not infringe the general principles of law and particularly fundamental rights.[3] Whether an infringement was actually involved in the present case was a matter left to the Greek court.

Thus any national measure which 'falls within the scope of Community law', in the sense of derogating from a Community right on grounds permitted by Community law, must be consistent with the Community's general principles on fundamental rights.[4]

A national measure will "fall within the scope of Community law" if it implements a Community rule (*Demirel*, *Wachauf*) or if it derogates from a Community rule on grounds permitted by Community law (*ERT*). Thus the potential for national measures to fall foul of the fundamental rights protected by Community law is now wider than it appeared in the early days of *Stauder*, *Internationale Handelsgesellschaft* and *Nold*. We can therefore perceive a recent expansion in the types of national measures which will be subject to Community control on fundamental rights grounds. Jason Coppel and Aidan O'Neill have recently commented that:

[1] ibid at pp I-2963 - I-2964, paragraph 41 of the Court's judgment.

[2] ibid at p I-2964, paragraph 42 of the Court's judgment.

[3] ibid, paragraph 43 of the Court's judgment.

[4] See also the opinion of Advocate General Van Gerven in Case C-159/90 *Society for the Protection of Unborn Children Ireland Ltd v Grogan* [1991] ECR I-4685 at p I-4723, paragraph 31 of the opinion.

> The only Member State actions which the Court might decline to vet on human rights grounds are ... those which occur in an area of exclusive Member State jurisdiction. This concept of Member State jurisdiction may itself be open to future redefinition by the Court.[1]

That Community law has developed in this direction should not have been, however, wholly unexpected. As early as 1974 the *Nold* Court, it will be recalled, said that "international treaties for the protection of human rights on which the Member States have collaborated or of which they are signatories, can supply guidelines which should be followed within the framework of Community law".[2] The phrase "within the framework of Community law" indicates something more than simply legislation adopted by Community institutions. Developments post-*Cinéthèque* may be seen as a realisation of what the *Nold* Court meant.

Citizenship and the Framework of Community law

Does any of this help us in resolving the main issue; whether the fundamental rights which the Court of Justice protects circumscribe the ability of Member States to deprive persons of their Union citizenship by depriving them of their Member State nationality?

Measures adopted by Member States will be subject to Community supervision for conformity with fundamental rights if the national measures fall within the scope of Community law. National measures will fall within the scope of Community law if they implement a Community rule or derogate from a Community rule on grounds permitted by Community law. The only national measures exempt from Community supervision on fundamental rights grounds are those which fall within the Member States' exclusive jurisdiction. The concept of exclusive Member State jurisdiction cannot be regarded as being permanently fixed at its present boundaries.

Citizenship of the Union is a status created by and held under Community law. It is Article 8(1) of the *EC Treaty* which both creates the status and determines the possessors of it. It chooses to make this determination by referring to national law, which in turn determines the conditions for acquisition and loss of nationality. Any national of a Member State is, by force only of Article 8(1), a citizen of the Union. National law does not of its own force create, confer or withdraw citizenship of the Union.

A national measure which withdraws a person's nationality is one which produces effects in an area covered by Community law. But at the current stage of development of Community law this is not enough to place it 'within the scope of Community law'.

[1] Jason Coppel and Aidan O'Neill, "*The European Court of Justice: Taking rights seriously?*", (1992) 12 Legal Studies 227 at p 236.

[2] Case 4/73 *J Nold, Kohlen- und Baustoffgroßhandlung v Commission* [1974] ECR 491 at p 507, paragraph 13 of the Court's judgment.

A Member State's denationalisation measure does more, however, than simply produce effects in an area covered by Community law. It affects the very operation of Community law itself, and is comparable in its effects to a national measure derogating from Community rights. A Member State's denationalisation measure may, accordingly, be said to fall 'within the scope of Community law'. Falling within the scope of Community law, it would be subject to Community law supervision for consistency with the fundamental rights which Community law protects.

It should also be remembered that in *Micheletti* the Court of Justice said that Member States, in exercising their competence to make dispositions of nationality must have due regard to Community law ("*qui doit être exercée dans le respect du droit communautaire*").[1]

Summary and Conclusion

It now remains to determine the implications of these findings for both Community law and national law. What would be the legal consequences of a Member State's denationalisation measure which was inconsistent with Articles 8 or 9 of the *Convention on the Reduction of Statelessness*, Article 26 of the *ICCPR*, Articles 2(1)(a) or 5(d)(iii) of the *International Convention on the Elimination of all Forms of Racial Discrimination*, or Article 14 of the *ECHR* as it informs the Community's general principle of equality?

If, as is here suggested, a denationalisation measure is within the scope of Community law, it can be scrutinised for consistency with the fundamental rights which the Court of Justice upholds as part of the Community's general principles of law. If such a national measure fails the standard set by the Community's general principles of law, it is inconsistent with Community law and cannot be applied by any national court, including the courts of the Member State responsible for the delinquent measure.

In the case of a reference under Article 177 of the Treaty, the Court of Justice would give all the criteria of interpretation needed by the national court to determine whether the national rules are compatible with the fundamental rights the observance of which the Court ensures.[2] Moreover, in the event of proceedings successfully brought by the Commission under Articles 169 of the Treaty or by another Member State under Article 170, the offending Member State would be obliged by Article 171 to take immediate steps to remedy the violation of fundamental rights.

A national measure which is within the exclusive jurisdiction of the Member States cannot, however, be regarded as falling 'within the scope of Community law' and therefore cannot be subject to the Community's general principles of law. The argument that denationalisation measures are inconsistent with Community law when

[1] CJ CE 7 July 1992, *Micheletti / Delegación del Gobierno en Cantabria* (C-369/90, Rec. p I-4239) at paragraph 10 of the Court's judgment.

[2] Case C-260/89 *Elliniki Radiophonia Tileorassi AE ("ERT") v Dimotiki Etairia Pliroforissis* [1991] ECR I-2925 at p I-2964, paragraph 42 of the Court's judgment.

they violate the general principles of law protected by the Court of Justice must fail if such measures are properly classified as falling within the Member States' exclusive jurisdiction.

In this connection it is well to recall the view expressed by the Permanent Court of International Justice that the "question whether a certain matter is or is not solely within the jurisdiction of a State is an essentially relative question; it depends upon the development of international relations" but that "in the present state of international law, questions of nationality are ... in principle within this reserved domain".[1] The Permanent Court's pronouncement, made in 1923, was effectively endorsed as still valid in the Community context as recently as 1992 when the Court of Justice said "*[l]a définition des conditions d'acquisition et de perte de la nationalité relève, conformément au droit international, de la competence de chaque Etat membre*".[2]

So, as late as 1992, nothing connected with the Community constituted a sufficiently important development in international relations as to displace "questions of nationality" from the reserved domain of States.

The coming into force of the *Union Treaty* on 1 November 1993, however, alters the picture. A Community of States, each with its own personality in international law, has conferred a common citizenship on their nationals. There has certainly been no similar phenomenon since the Permanent Court's pronouncement in 1923. Laden with symbolic power, linked to the enjoyment of the Community's fundamental freedoms and made conditional on possession of a Member State's nationality, the advent of a *de jure* transnational citizenship within the European Union must, if ever anything can, constitute a sufficiently important development in international relations as to displace questions of nationality from the reserved domain of States.

The fact that nationality is, in the context of the Community, no longer within the Member States' reserved domain does not mean that they lack competence to make dispositions of their nationality. But in the context of the Community, it does mean that their dispositions are subject to Community supervision.

The possibility cannot be ignored, however, that denationalisation measures are not properly to be regarded as falling within the scope of Community law. This could be because the analogy between denationalisation measures and national measures derogating from Community rights is on balance not regarded as sufficiently compelling. It might also be because the advent of *de jure* Union citizenship does not

[1] *Nationality Decrees Issued in Tunis and Morocco*, [1923] Permanent Court of International Justice, Series B, No 4 at p 24.

[2] 'The definition of the conditions of acquisition and loss of nationality is, in conformity with international law, within the competence of each Member State' (author's translation). CJ CE 7 July 1992, *Micheletti / Delegación del Gobierno en Cantabria* (C-369/90, Rec. p I-4239) at paragraph 10 of the Court's judgment.

on balance compel the view that questions of nationality have ceased to be in the reserved domain of the Member States.

If denationalisation measures are not within the scope of Community law they will not depend for their validity on consistency with the requirements of Community law, including its protection of human rights. But this is not to say that their inconsistency with the Community's human rights principles is without importance in Community law.

Such a national measure could not be allowed to produce effects at the level of Community law. In *Airola* the Court of Justice refused to give effect, at the level of Community law, to an unrequested and unrenounceable Italian naturalisation when to do so would have resulted in an infringement of the general Community principle against sex discrimination. The Advocate General, in the same case, argued that the Court should decline to give Community effect to any conferral of naturalisation which was itself done in violation of a fundamental human right. There was in that case no suggestion that the violative naturalisation could not continue to be valid at the level of domestic law.

If the Court of Justice can refuse to give Community effect to a naturalisation done in violation of human rights or which would violate human rights if given effect to, there can be no reason in principle why it cannot do the same with a denationalisation in like circumstances. Indeed, with a violative denationalisation the case for refraining from giving it Community effect is, if anything, stronger. It will, from a human rights perspective, ordinarily be a much more serious matter to be deprived of a nationality than to gain one.

Such an approach would mean that no person could be deprived of his Union citizenship as the result of a Member State's denationalisation measure which violated the Community's fundamental rights. National authorities, including national courts, would consequently be obliged to treat a person as a citizen of the Union notwithstanding that he was the subject of such a measure.

Consequently a person who is the subject of a Member State's denationalisation measure which violates the Community's fundamental rights would, in another Member State, be entitled to exactly the same rights under Community law that he possessed before the denationalisation measure became effective. Article 8(2) of the *EC Treaty* extends all the rights "conferred by this Treaty" on citizens of the Union. This includes not only those rights contained in Part Two of the Treaty, but also those contained in provisions such as Articles 6, 48, 52 and 59. He would continue to enjoy those rights as a citizen of the Union.

Even if the validity of the denationalisation measure remained unaffected at the level of domestic law, a citizen of the Union would retain that status in his (former) own Member State. In these circumstances the Member State could not treat any claim of Community right made by the denationalised person as outside the scope of

Community law on the grounds that it involved a situation entirely internal to itself; the denationalised person would be a Union citizen in a Member State of which he was not a national. The denationalised Union citizen would thus be entitled to enjoy in his (former) own Member State exactly the same rights that applied to Union citizens who were nationals of other Member States.

On this view, however, the denationalised Union citizen will effectively be assimilated to the same position as a Union citizen possessing the nationality of another Member State and will be liable to expulsion or exclusion in certain circumstances (eg public policy, public security, public health, or failure to meet requirements as to financial self sufficiency or health insurance). This will, under the present state of Community law, be an inevitable consequence of lacking the nationality of the host Member State. In the words of Advocate General Trabucchi:

> So long as there is no Community nationality, nationals of other Member States will always have a different status from that of a national of the State concerned even where he enjoys the right of free movement and residence on conditions of parity with such a national.[1]

If the Member State to which he was expelled or to whose territory he was refused entry could similarly exclude or expel him the absurd spectacle of an endless shuffle between Member States could ensue, for no State is under an absolute obligation to accept any person into its territory unless he possesses the nationality of that State.[2]

This tends to confirm the view that a denationalisation measure inconsistent with the human rights protected by the Court of Justice ought be regarded as falling within the scope of Community law so as to be unenforceable by the national authorities.

Furthermore if the Court of Justice can give no judicial remedy as regards the domestic effect of a denationalisation measure which violates the Community's human rights principles, but which is valid within the framework of the domestic legal order, then the denationalised Union citizen will probably lack any judicial remedy. The *ECHR* does not prescribe standards for the withdrawal of nationality so that the European Court of Human Rights will probably be of no assistance. Even in the unlikely event that the European Court of Human Rights were to interpret Article 2(1) of Protocol 4 to the *ECHR*[3] very creatively (the European Commission of Human Rights has adopted a very narrow and literal interpretation of the provision) so as to imply human

[1]Case 118/75 *Watson and Belmann* [1976] ECR 1185 at p 1210.

[2]See eg Case C-192/89 *Sevince v Staatssecretaris van Justitie* [1990] ECR I-3461 at p I-3494, paragraph 66 of Advocate General Darmon's opinion; Article 2(1) of the United Nations *Declaration on the Human Rights of Individuals Who are not Nationals of the Country in which They Live*, (1985) General Assembly Resolution 144 (XL), GAOR, 40th session, Supp 53, p 253; Application 9285/81 *X, Y and Z v United Kingdom* (1982) 29 DR 205 and Application 12068/86 *Paramanathan v Germany* (1986) 51 DR 237 (European Commission of Human Rights).

[3]"Everyone lawfully within the territory of a State shall, within that territory, have the right to liberty of movement and freedom to choose his residence".

rights standards for denationalisation, three of the Union's Member States (Greece, Spain and the United Kingdom) are not parties to it.[1]

Accordingly, the better view is that a Member State's denationalisation measure falls within the scope of Community law so that a violation of the human rights protected by the Court of Justice will cause it to be unenforceable by the national authorities.

Fundamental Principle of Democracy. Among the general principles which the Court of Justice upholds is the "fundamental democratic principle that the peoples should take part in the exercise of power through the intermediary of a representative assembly".[2] The Court of Justice has, in the name of this principle, been prepared to annul Community legislation adopted in disregard of the proper *rôle* to be performed in the legislative process by the European Parliament.[3]

As the principle of democratic participation in the exercise of Community power through the European Parliament is regarded by the Court of Justice as "fundamental", the Court could be expected to annul any Community measure which, without objective justification, violated the principle by depriving Union citizens of their right to vote or to stand for office in European Parliamentary elections.[4] A national measure which did the same thing would fall within the scope of Community law on the test we have formulated and could not be applied by Member State authorities.

A denationalisation measure done in violation of the human rights protected in the Community legal order would also constitute an infringement of the Community's principle of democracy to the extent that it operated to deprive the denationalised person of his franchise in European Parliamentary elections.

Since the *Union Treaty*, a citizen of the Union resident in a Member State of which he is not a national has the right to vote and to stand in European Parliamentary elections in his host Member State under the same conditions as nationals of that State.[5] This reinforces the view that the principle of democratic participation includes a right for Union citizens to vote in and stand for European Parliamentary elections.

[1]Furthermore, four of the Union's Member States (Belgium, Germany, Greece, and the United Kingdom) are not parties to the optional protocol to the *ICCPR* by which individuals have a right of petition to the United Nations Human Rights Committee for breaches of the *ICCPR*, including its Article 26.

[2]Case 138/79 *SA Roquette Frères v Council* [1980] ECR 3333 at p 3360, paragraph 33 of the Court's judgment; Case 139/79 *Maizena GmbH v Council* [1980] ECR 3393 at p 3424, paragraph 34 of the Court's judgment; Case C-300/89 *Commission v Council* ("*Re Titanium Dioxide*") [1991] ECR I-2867 at p I-2900, paragraph 20 of the Court's judgment.

[3]See previous footnote.

[4]See also Article 3 of Protocol 1 to the *ECHR* (obligation to hold free elections to the legislature).

[5]Article 8b(2) of the *EC Treaty*.

DECLARATIONS ON NATIONALITY

In considering the ways in which Community law circumscribes Member States in making dispositions of nationality, it is impossible to disregard the several joint and unilateral declarations made by the Member States which touch upon the subject.[1]

The Declarations

The earliest of these is the unilateral declaration made by Germany upon signing the *EEC Treaty* and the *Euratom Treaty* in 1957, by which it was declared that "[a]ll Germans as defined in the Basic Law for the Federal Republic of Germany shall be considered nationals of the Federal Republic of Germany". Declarations to identical effect were made by Germany upon signing the *Treaty of Accession 1979* and the *Treaty of Accession 1985*.[2]

The United Kingdom made a unilateral declaration on nationality upon signing the *Treaty of Accession 1972*.[3] It replaced that declaration in 1983 with another unilateral declaration[4] upon the entry into force of the *British Nationality Act 1981*.

Upon the signing of the *Union Treaty* the Member States, meeting in the Intergovernmental Conferences on Political Union and on Economic and Monetary Union, jointly adopted a *Declaration on Nationality of a Member State* which provides as follows:

> The Conference declares that, wherever in the Treaty establishing the European Community reference is made to nationals of the Member States, the question whether an individual possesses the nationality of a Member State shall be settled solely by reference to the national law of the Member State concerned. Member States may declare, for information, who are to be considered their nationals for Community purposes by way of a declaration lodged with the Presidency and may amend any such declaration when necessary.[5]

Some eleven months after the signing of the *Union Treaty*, and between the first and second Danish referendums on ratification, the European Council meeting at Edinburgh adopted a Declaration on Citizenship ("*Edinburgh Declaration*") as part of a decision on problems raised by Denmark concerning the *Union Treaty*. The *Edinburgh Declaration* says:

[1] As to the effect of declarations on the treaties see Richard Plender, "*An Incipient Form of European Citizenship*", in F. Jacobs (ed), "*European Law and the Individual*" (1976), p 39 at p 44; A.G. Toth, "*The legal status of the declarations annexed to the Single European Act*", (1986) 23 CML Rev 803; H.G. Schermers, "The effect of the date 31 December 1992", (1991) 28 CML Rev 275 at pp 275-277.

[2] See the Final Act of each intergovernmental conference.

[3] For the full text see Appendix, § 1 or the Final Act of the intergovernmental conference.

[4] For the full text see Appendix, § 2 or OJ C23 of 28 January 1983.

[5] See the Final Act of the conferences.

> The provisions of Part Two of the Treaty establishing the European Community relating to citizenship of the Union give nationals of the Member States additional rights and protection as specified in that Part. They do not in any way take the place of national citizenship. The question whether an individual possesses the nationality of a Member State will be settled solely by reference to the national law of the Member State concerned.[1]

Do the unilateral declarations on nationality made by Germany and the United Kingdom or the *Declaration on Nationality of a Member State* or the *Edinburgh Declaration* alter any of the conclusions reached earlier in this Chapter?

Constitutional Charter

We must start with the proposition that at the pinnacle of the Community legal system are the constitutive Community treaties. These treaties are analogous to a national constitution and authorise the enactment of subsidiary measures which are not inconsistent with the constitutional instrument. According to the Court of Justice:

> [T]he European Economic Community is a Community based on the rule of law, inasmuch as neither its Member States nor its institutions can avoid a review of the question whether the measures adopted by them are in conformity with the basic constitutional charter, the Treaty.[2]

The *EC Treaty* is a constitutional charter notwithstanding that it is concluded in the form of an international agreement.[3] No measures which are inconsistent with the constitutive treaties can have any legal validity within the Community legal order. Our conclusions about the constraints Community law places on the ability of Member States in making dispositions of their nationality is based on an analysis of the treaties. If the various declarations on nationality are to modify the rules derived from the treaties, they must do so by means permitted by the treaties.

Four types of Declaration

For the purpose of deciding whether the declarations might hypothetically modify the effect of the treaties, it is possible to divide them into four types.

[1]OJ C 348/2 of 31.12.92. At the same European Council meeting, Denmark also unilaterally adopted a *Declaration on Citizenship of the Union* (for the full text see Appendix, § 3 or OJ C 348/4 of 31.12.94), none of whose provisions are relevant for present purposes.

[2]Case 294/83 *Parti écologiste 'Les Verts' v European Parliament* [1986] ECR 1339 at p 1365, paragraph 23 of the Court's judgment. See also Case C-2/88 Imm *Zwartveld* [1990] ECR I-3365 at p I-3372, paragraph 16 of the Court's judgment, and Opinion 1/91 *Re Draft EEA Treaty* [1991] ECR I-6079 at p I-6102, paragraph 21 of the Court's judgment.

[3]Opinion 1/91 *Re Draft EEA Treaty* [1991] ECR I-6079 at p I-6102, paragraph 21 of the Court's judgment.

Firstly the *Edinburgh Declaration*, being a multilateral act of all the Member States done after the signing of the *Union Treaty*, might be construed as an amendment to the treaties.

Secondly the *Declaration on Nationality of a Member State*, being a multilateral act of all the Member States done simultaneously with signing the *Union Treaty*, might be construed as forming part of the treaties.

Thirdly the three German declarations and the first United Kingdom declaration, being unilateral acts done simultaneously with signing various treaties, could be construed as reservations to those treaties.

Fourthly and finally, there is the second United Kingdom declaration. Being a unilateral act done after the signing of the treaties to which it refers it cannot even hypothetically qualify as an amendment to, an integral part of, or a reservation from, the treaties. If it has any authority to modify the effect of the treaties with respect to nationality, it can only be as an interpretative aid. The declarations in the first three groups might likewise serve as interpretative aids if they fail to qualify as amendments to, terms of, or reservations from, the treaties.

Amendment to the Treaties?

Nothing in the *Edinburgh Declaration* is inconsistent with our conclusions about the way in which Community law circumscribes the power of Member States to make conferrals of their nationality. Whether a person has been conferred with the nationality of a Member State such as to produce immediate effects for him in Community law is a matter to be determined solely by reference to the national law of the Member State concerned. Whether, in making a particular conferral either individually or *en masse*, the Member State has breached a duty under the treaties is another matter.

The *Edinburgh Declaration* does, however, potentially have an impact on our conclusions about the Member States' power to withdraw nationality. In saying that the question whether an individual possesses the nationality of a Member State will be settled *solely* by reference to the national law of the Member State concerned, the *Edinburgh Declaration* could be regarded as denying the power of Community law to override a withdrawal of nationality when the national measure conflicts with Community human rights principles. On this interpretation, if the *Edinburgh Declaration* amends the treaties then Community law loses the power to override such denationalisation measures.

Article N(1) of the *Union Treaty* lays down the procedure for amending the "Treaties on which the Union is founded".[1] This provision replaces Article 96 of the *ECSC Treaty*, Article 236 of the *EEC Treaty and* Article 204 of the *Euratom Treaty*, so that

[1]Article A of the *Union Treaty* provides that the Union is founded on the European Communities supplemented by the policies and forms of cooperation established by the *Union Treaty*.

there is now a uniform amendment procedure for the treaties establishing the Union and the three Communities.

The *Edinburgh Declaration* did not of course comply with the amendment procedure. In particular it was not ratified in accordance with the Member States' respective constitutional requirements. Indeed the only Union institution involved in adopting the *Edinburgh Declaration* was the European Council, which is not given any formal *rôle* at all in the Treaty amendment procedure of Article N(1).

In *Defrenne v Société Anonyme Belge de Navigation Aérienne Sabena*[1] it was contended that a resolution of the Member States was effective to extend the deadline, prescribed by Article 119 of the *EEC Treaty*, for application of the principle that men and women should receive equal pay for equal work. The Court of Justice had no difficulty in rejecting the contention:

> Without prejudice to its possible effects as regards encouraging and accelerating the full implementation of Article 119, the Resolution of the Member States ... was ineffective to make any valid modification of the time-limit fixed by the Treaty.
>
> In fact, apart from any specific provisions, the Treaty can only be modified by means of the amendment procedure carried out in accordance with Article 236.[2]

The same principle applies with equal force to resolutions or declarations of Member States, whether or not acting within the European Council, seeking to modify the rules on nationality derived from the treaties. Accordingly, the *Edinburgh Declaration* cannot be effective to amend the treaties.

Integral Part of the Treaties?

Whether the *Declaration on Nationality of a Member State* forms part of the *Union Treaty* is relevant to our enquiry for exactly the same reasons as those applying to the *Edinburgh Declaration*. It has no potential impact on our conclusions about the conferral of nationality, but it potentially destroys our conclusions about the withdrawal of nationality.

If it is to form part of the *Union Treaty* it must be among those provisions amending the *EEC Treaty*. As an amendment to the *EEC Treaty*, it fails for exactly the same reasons as apply to the *Edinburgh Declaration*.

It is also likely that the *Declaration on Nationality of a Member State* does not form part of the *EC Treaty* because, while Article 239 of the *EC Treaty* says that the Protocols attached to the Treaty "shall form an integral part thereof", the Treaty is

[1]Case 43/75 [1976] ECR 455.

[2]ibid at p 478, paragraphs 57-58 of the Court's judgment.

conspicuously silent about declarations. It is reasonable to infer, on the basis of this omission alone, that the *Declaration on Nationality of a Member State* is not part of the *EC Treaty*.

There is, however, the additional consideration that a reference in the *ECSC Treaty* to 'this Treaty' is a reference to the "Treaty and its Annexes, of the Protocols annexed thereto and of the Convention on the Transitional Provisions" (Article 84). In *Groupement des Industries Sidérurgiques Luxembourgeoises v High Authority*[1] the Court of Justice, referring to the documents mentioned in Article 84 of the *ECSC Treaty*, said that they were all "equally binding" because they had been expressly incorporated into the Treaty.[2] There is no express incorporation of declarations into the *EC Treaty*. By analogy with the *ECSC Treaty*, the *Declaration on Nationality of a Member State* is not "equally binding" with the provisions of the *EC Treaty*. If it is not "equally binding" it is, at most, 'less binding' or subordinate. If it is subordinate, it will not be effective to modify the constitutional rules we identified as restricting Member States' powers to adopt acts of denationalisation.

The same considerations prevent the *Declaration on Nationality of a Member State* from being part of the *Union Treaty*. Whereas the Final Act expressly annexes all the Protocols adopted at the intergovernmental conference to either the *EC Treaty* (Protocols 1-16) or both the *EC Treaty* and the *Union Treaty* (Protocol 17), the declarations are pointedly annexed only to the Final Act. Neither the Final Act nor the declarations annexed thereto were subject to the Treaty amendment procedure, including ratification in accordance with the Member States' respective constitutional requirements.

If the Member States had intended the *Declaration on Nationality of a Member State* to be part of the *EC Treaty* or the *Union Treaty* they could quite easily have incorporated it into the relevant treaty's text, or called it a 'Protocol' and subjected it to ratification.

Finally, there is the not insignificant matter that the *Declaration on Nationality of a Member State* makes no express claim to be part of either the *EC Treaty* or the *Union Treaty*.

Accordingly the *Declaration on Nationality of a Member State* cannot be regarded as being part of either the *EC Treaty* or the *Union Treaty*.

Reservation to the Treaties?

Nor can the *Declaration on Nationality of a Member State* be regarded as a reservation to the treaties. Article 2(1)(d) of the *Vienna Convention on the Law of Treaties*[3]

[1] Joined Cases 7 and 9/54 [1956] ECR 175.

[2] ibid at p 194.

[3] Done at Vienna on 23 May 1969, 1155 UNTS 331. The Convention entered into force in 1980. Its parties include Germany, Greece, Italy, the Netherlands, Spain and the United Kingdom. Its signatories include Luxembourg.

defines "reservation" as meaning "a unilateral statement, however phrased or named, made by a State, when signing, ratifying, accepting, approving or acceding to a treaty, whereby it purports to exclude or to modify the effect of certain provisions of the treaty in their application to that State". The *Declaration on Nationality of a Member State* is not a unilateral statement. Furthermore, it is impossible simply as a matter of logic to regard the *Declaration on Nationality of a Member State* as a reservation - how can *all* the parties to a treaty agree to exclude or modify the effect of a treaty which they are simultaneously signing? Why do they not simply agree on a different text? The same objections apply to treating the *Edinburgh Declaration* as a reservation, with the additional reason that it was not made when signing, ratifying etc the Treaty.

These objections do not, however, apply to the three German declarations and the first United Kingdom declaration. All of them are unilateral statements made when signing a treaty. But do they purport to exclude or modify the effect of any treaty provisions with respect to the State making them?

The three German declarations refer the reader to the Basic Law, Article 116(1) of which provides as follows:

> *Deutscher im Sinne dieses Grundgesetzes ist vorbehaltlich anderweitiger gesetzlicher Regelung, wer die deutsche Staatsangehörigkeit besitzt oder Vertriebener deutscher Volkszugehörigkeit oder als dessen Ehegatte oder Abkömmlimg in dem Gebiete des Deutschen Reiches nach dem Stande vom 31. Dezember 1937 Aufnahme gefunden hat.*[1]

The German declarations and the first United Kingdom declaration all make the possession of nationality for Community purposes dependent on domestic legal provisions.

To the extent, however, that the declarations might be construed as permitting a change in domestic law *always* to effect a withdrawal of nationality and of citizenship of the Union, they do conflict with the Community principles we have identified as they apply to Germany and the United Kingdom. They might thus constitute reservations to the treaties to which they refer. Assuming such an interpretation can properly be placed on these unilateral declarations, are they effective as reservations to the Community treaties to which they refer?

[1]'Unless otherwise provided by law, a German within the meaning of this Basic Law is a person who possesses German citizenship or who has been admitted to the territory of the German Reich within the frontiers of 31 December 1937 as a refugeee or expelee of German stock or as the spouse or descendant of such a person'.

Richard Plender has taken the view that none of the declarations made in respect of the founding treaties or the *Treaty of Accession 1972* can be effective as reservations.[1] Writing of the unilateral declarations accompanying the *Single European Act*, A.G. Toth rejected them as constituting reservations. Such an acceptance, he argued, would entail the invalidity of the *Single European Act* itself:

> This is because those provisions of the Act which constitute amendments to the Treaties establishing the European Communities ... can, by virtue of an express requirement laid down in those Treaties, only be determined by "common accord" of all the Member States (Articles 96 ECSC, 236 EEC and 204 Euratom). By its very nature, a reservation proper would signify the lack of such "common accord". ... Thus, while the Act itself is silent as to the possibility of reservations, this consideration alone would seem to exclude any such possibility.[2]

These observations are equally applicable to the second and third German declarations and the first United Kingdom declaration (made in respect of the *Treaty of Accession 1979*, the *Treaty of Accession 1985* and the *Treaty of Accession 1972* respectively), but not in respect of the first German declaration. This is because only the first German declaration was made upon the signing of treaties which were not themselves subject to the treaty amendment procedures, ie the original *EEC Treaty* and *Euratom Treaty*.

So although the second and third German declarations and the first United Kingdom declaration are eliminated as candidates for the status of reservation, the first German declaration is still a possibility.

It will be recalled, however, that while the foundation treaties are in the form of international agreements they are in reality part of the Community's constitutional charter. Any act which is inconsistent with that charter cannot possess validity within the Community's legal order. It therefore becomes important to inquire whether the first German declaration forms part of the constitutional charter, and specifically the three founding treaties. If it is not part of those treaties it cannot produce any effects which are inconsistent with them within the Community legal order.

The first German declaration has never been annexed or attached to any Treaty. It was, instead, annexed only to the Final Act of the Intergovernmental Conference on the Common Market and Euratom. Whereas both the *EEC Treaty* and the *Euratom Treaty* were signed by the Member States and required ratification in accordance with their respective constitutional requirements (Articles 247 and 224 respectively), the Final Act was neither signed nor subject to ratification. Furthermore the Final Act itself

[1]Richard Plender, "*An Incipient Form of European Citizenship*", in F. Jacobs (ed), "*European Law and the Individual*" (1976), p 39 at p 44.

[2]A.G. Toth, "*The legal status of declarations annexed to the Single European Act*", (1986) 23 CML Rev 803 at p 806.

says that the intergovernmental conference merely 'took note' of Germany's declaration.

In this connection it is worth recalling that Article 239 of the *EEC Treaty* and Article 207 of the *Euratom Treaty* say that the protocols "annexed ... by common accord of the Member States" form an integral part of those treaties. This strongly implies that only those provisions adopted by common accord of the Member States can form part of the treaties. The first German declaration, being merely 'noted' by the other Member States, not being signed by them, and not subject to their ratification requirements, can hardly be said to represent their "common accord". The effect of not annexing the first German declaration to the treaties is exactly the same for it as for the *Declaration on Nationality of a Member State*.[1] Furthermore it is generally accepted that a reservation "is a declaration which is external to the text of a treaty".[2]

The first German declaration cannot, therefore, be regarded as forming part of the Community's constitutional charter. To the extent that it might purport to modify the charter's rules about denationalisation as they apply to Germany, the declaration is ineffective.

Interpretative Aid?

The only way in which the second United Kingdom declaration could affect the operation of the treaties is as an interpretative aid. This is also a residual possibility for the other declarations.

Professor Plender has remarked that where a declaration made in respect of the founding treaties or the *Treaty of Accession 1972* amounts to a description of a point of Community law it possesses some persuasive value, though less than where the declaration makes a statement about the declarant's own national law.[3]

None of the unilateral declarations are, when properly construed, really making any sort of statement about Community law at all. This is in fact the most compelling reason of all for not regarding them as reservations. Rather they are making a statement about their declarants' domestic legal arrangements; ie that German nationals are those regarded as such by the Basic Law which in turn partly refers to enacted German law, and that United Kingdom nationals are certain classes of citizens or subjects (basically those with a right of abode in the United Kingdom or Gibraltar) as provided for under United Kingdom law.

The unilateral declarations are really doing nothing more than supplying the reader with certain information about the relevant national legal orders. This is all that such

[1] See the discussion of Joined Cases 7 and 9/54 *Groupement des Industries Sidérurgiques Luxembourgeoises v High Authority* [1956] ECR 175 (infra p XXX).

[2] Sir Ian Sinclair, "*The Vienna Convention on the Law of Treatiies*", 2nd ed (1984), at p 51 and material there noted.

[3] Richard Plender, "*An Incipient Form of European Citizenship*", in F. Jacobs (ed), "*European Law and the Individual*" (1976), p 39 at p 44.

a declaration can actually do, as is confirmed by the European Council in the *Declaration on Nationality of a Member State*:

> ... Member States may declare, for information, who are to be considered their nationals for Community purposes by way of a declaration lodged with the Presidency and may amend any such declaration when necessary.

That a declaration may be amended "when necessary" anticipates that the information it contains may become outdated upon a change in national law. The question of the 'validity' of the unilateral declaration does not really therefore arise. It cannot produce legal effects; it can merely supply information. The declaration can be accurate or inaccurate, but it cannot be 'effective' or 'ineffective'. The information it contains is, nevertheless, not lightly to be discounted. According to Professor Plender, when a declaration "amounts to a Member State's objective statement of its own law on a point from which there is a remission from the Communities' legal order it will be conclusive in the absence of very persuasive evidence to the contrary".[1] To the extent, however, that such a declaration excludes persons who have been denationalised as the result of measures incompatible with the Community's basic principles, it will simply be inaccurate and can be disregarded.

The unilateral declarations should therefore not be regarded as providing interpretative aids in respect of the treaties to which they refer.

The *Declaration on Nationality of a Member State* and the *Edinburgh Declaration* are a different matter. These statements make a claim about the operation of Community law. In each declaration it is proclaimed that the "question whether an individual possesses the nationality of a Member State shall be settled solely by reference to the national law of the Member State concerned". We have already seen that nothing in this statement is inconsistent with the Community's rules concerning conferral of nationality.

Even in the case of denationalisations, a Member State's act must be regarded as *prima facie* valid, and for this purpose reference must be made to the national law of the Member State concerned. When the declarations are applied to denationalisation measures, however, their use of the word "solely" might be construed as representing a direct challenge to the supervisory principles derived from the treaties. According to such an interpretation of the declarations, denationalisation measures, regardless of how violently they collide with the human rights principles protected by the Court of Justice, are beyond Community supervision.

It is clear that in international law statements of the sort contained in the *Declaration on Nationality of a Member State* and the *Edinburgh Declaration* can, and should, be

[1] ibid.

taken into account in interpreting the treaties to which they refer. Article 31 of the *Vienna Convention on the Law of Treaties* provides in part as follows:

> 1. A treaty shall be interpreted in good faith in accordance with the ordinary meaning to be given to the terms of the treaty in their context and in the light of its object and purpose.
>
> 2. The context for the purpose of the interpretation of a treaty shall comprise in addition to the text, including its preamble and annexes:
>
> (a) any agreement relating to the treaty which was made between all the parties in connection with the conclusion of the treaty; ...
>
> 3. There shall be taken into account, together with the context;
>
> (a) any subsequent agreement between the parties regarding the interpretation of the treaty or the application of its provisions; ...
>
> 4. A special meaning shall be given to a term if it is established that the parties so intended.

Thus, international law requires treaties to be interpreted in their context (Article 31(1)). The context includes statements like the *Declaration on Nationality of a Member State* (Article 31(2)(a)). Additionally, account must be taken of statements like the *Edinburgh Declaration* (Article 31(3)(a)). Assuming these declarations have given a special meaning to the term 'nationals of Member States' and its cognates, effect must be given to that meaning (Article 31(4)).

There are thus two questions to be answered. Firstly, is the intention of the declarations to confer a special meaning on the term 'nationals of Member States' such as to exclude denationalisation measures from Community scrutiny for conformity with the human rights principles protected by the Court of Justice? Secondly, and assuming an affirmative answer to the first question, can the declarations produce such an effect in Community law?

The first question should be answered in the negative. It is most unlikely that the Member States intended that the two declarations should operate so as to protect the validity of denationalisations done in violation of the Community's human rights. We have already seen that the Member States have already committed themselves at the level of international law not to effect denationalisations which violate human rights. Furthermore upon signing the *Union Treaty* they committed themselves to the objective of strengthening "the protection of the rights and interests of the nationals of its Member States through the introduction of a citizenship of the Union"[1] and

[1] Article B, third indent.

recommitted themselves to respect the fundamental rights as guaranteed in the *ECHR* and the constitutional traditions common to the Member States.[1]

It is more likely that the declarations were intended to clarify the position with respect merely to the conferral of nationality, and to allay potential or actual concern in some sectors of public opinion that Union citizenship would replace State citizenship and that the Community would assume competence to confer citizenship. That this was the Member States' real concern is evident from the terms of the *Edinburgh Declaration* which partly restates the *Declaration on Nationality of a Member State* and partly amplifies the latter's reassuring signals. The *Edinburgh Declaration* was adopted after the first unsuccessful Danish referendum on ratification of the *Union Treaty*, during the campaign for which those opposed to ratification raised persistent concerns about Denmark's sovereignty in the field of conferring national citizenship.

The view that the *Declaration on Nationality of a Member State* and the *Edinburgh Declaration* are really concerned only with the conferral of nationality is reinforced by reference to the *Declaration on Citizenship of the Union*[2] adopted unilaterally by Denmark at the same European Council meeting which adopted the *Edinburgh Declaration*. The Danish declaration is completely silent about Denmark's continuing power to withdraw its citizenship, but is at pains to emphasise that "[c]itizenship of the Union in no way in itself gives a national of another Member State the right to obtain Danish citizenship or any of the rights, duties, privileges or advantages that are inherent in Danish citizenship by virtue of Denmark's constitutional, legal and administrative rules".

The *Declaration on Nationality of a Member State* and the *Edinburgh Declaration* should not, therefore, be construed as intended to modify the effect of the treaties or to give the term 'nationals of Member States' any special meaning which it did not already possess under the treaties.

Even if, however, the *Declaration on Nationality of a Member State* and the *Edinburgh Declaration* are interpreted as intending to shield denationalisations from Community scrutiny for conformity with its human rights principles, they cannot have that effect. If legislation adopted by the Community institutions and the Member States cannot produce results which are inconsistent with the fundamental freedoms protected by the Court of Justice, then neither can a mere interpretative aid.

Conclusion

Every citizen of the Union possesses the rights set out in Article 8a of the *EC Treaty*. In determining the personal scope of Article 8a it is necessary to know who is endowed with the status of citizen of the Union. Article 8(1) makes it plain that every

[1] Article F(2).
[2] OJ C 348/4 of 31.12.94 or Appendix § 3.

person holding the nationality of a Member State is a citizen of the Union. Therefore, every person holding the nationality of a Member State is within the personal scope of Article 8a.

In Chapter 2 we saw that there are good reasons for thinking that, in principle, Community law circumscribes the power of Member States to make dispositions of their nationality. This principle has been actualised in the context of compulsory naturalisations which the recipient is unable to renounce. Where such a naturalisation occurs, Community law will not give it effect if it was done in violation of the fundamental rights protected by the Court of Justice or where, in its Community application, it violates such rights.

In *Micheletti* the Court of Justice held that any person presenting in a host Member State a valid identity card or passport from another Member State is to be accorded all the rights due to a national of a Member State under Community law. National laws to the contrary are inconsistent with the Treaty and are not to be applied by the national authorities. The Court emphasised that the definition of the conditions of acquisition and loss of nationality is, in conformity with international law, within the competence of each Member State. This recognition was, however, accompanied by the important caveat that the Member States' competence must be exercised with due regard to Community law. This caveat strongly implies the existence of Community constraints on the Member States' power to make dispositions of their nationalities.

These constraints differ according to whether the Member State is conferring or withdrawing its nationality. In accordance with *Micheletti* any conferral must be recognised and given full effect merely upon production of a valid identity card or passport. The Community constraints on both the conferral and withdrawal of nationality to which the Court of Justice alludes must, however, have some meaning in connection with the conferral of nationality.

In this connection Article 5 of the *EC Treaty* and the international law requirement for a genuine link between the State conferring nationality and the recipient of that nationality become important. The duty of solidarity inherent in Article 5 prevents Member States from making conferrals of nationality which are deceptive or misleading *vis-á-vis* other Member States or the Community. A conferral which is made according to criteria commonly applied by States will not be deceptive or misleading and will not infringe the duty of solidarity. Since the gravamen of a conferral made in the absence of a genuine link would be the deceptive or misleading nature of it, the breach of duty could be avoided by informing or consulting the Commission.

Even where the conferring Member States informs before conferring its nationality in the absence of a genuine link, or where a genuine link exists and no consultation is required, a breach of solidarity will occur when a conferral is made which threatens the basic economic objectives of the Community. This problem might present itself in the case of certain conferrals of nationality *en masse*.

In any event, a breach of duty will occur if a conferral of nationality is made, with Community effect, on a person who lacks a right of abode in any part of the conferring Member State's territory which is subject to the Community's freedom of movement provisions.

Whether the breach of solidarity arising from a conferral of nationality is occasioned by a want of genuine link or damage to the Community's basic economic objectives or problems associated with right of abode, the recipients must be treated as nationals of Member States upon production of a valid identity card or passport. The remedy for the breach of duty lies in proceedings under Articles 169 or 170 of the Treaty.

Of potentially more practical significance are the Community constraints on the power of Member States to withdraw their nationalities. Because possession of a Community status, ie citizenship of the Union, is at stake a Member State may not withdraw its nationality where to do so would involve infringing the human rights protected as being among the Community's general principles of law.

Thus a Member State cannot deprive a person of his Union citizenship by a denationalisation measure which, subject to certain exceptions, renders the denationalised person stateless. Nor may a denationalisation, without objective justification, deprive any person or group of persons of their nationality on racial, ethnic, religious or political grounds or on grounds of their colour, sex, language, association with a national minority, national or social origin, property, birth or other status. In the case of a denationalisation based on some of these grounds, it is not possible to conceive of circumstances when objective justification might exist. Such a denationalisation would also involve a violation of the Community principle of democracy to the extent that the denationalised person was disenfranchised in respect of European Parliamentary elections.

Although it is possible that a denationalisation done in violation of human rights remains valid within the domestic legal order (so that a person is effectively denationalised but retains his citizenship of the Union), the better view is that the offending denationalisation measure is inconsistent with the Treaty and must not be given effect to by national authorities.

The various unilateral and multilateral declarations on nationality do not alter this picture. The unilateral declarations are sources of information and are not intended to, and are not capable of, producing legal effects. To the extent that the information they contain is inaccurate, they can be disregarded.

The multilateral declarations are interpretative aids to the treaties. Nothing in them is inconsistent with the Community rules identified with respect to conferring nationality. Nor are they intended to alter the rules with respect to denationalisations. Even if they are intended to alter the denationalisation rules they are incapable of doing so.

CHAPTER 4

MATERIAL SCOPE OF CITIZENSHIP MIGRATION RIGHTS

Union Citizen's Right to Move and Reside

The rights actually granted by Article 8a of the *EC Treaty* are "to move and reside freely within the territory of the Member States". They are therefore somewhat different in their material scope to those available to the economic migrants covered by Articles 48-66.

The economic migrants covered by Community law are entitled to a raft of rights extending beyond the mere right to move and reside.

Workers are entitled to certain rights in the field of "employment, remuneration, and other conditions of work and employment".[1] They are also entitled, subject to public policy exceptions, to accept offers of employment actually made[2] and to remain in the territory of the host Member State after having been employed there.[3]

Establishers who are nationals of a Member State are entitled to found primary and secondary establishments in Member States of which they are not nationals,[4] and service providers who are nationals of a Member State are free to provide services in another Member State.[5] Both sets of freedoms are subject to public policy exceptions.[6]

Neither establishers nor service providers are expressly granted a right to move and reside within the territory of the Member States by the *EC Treaty* itself, although it is clearly arguable that these rights are necessarily implicit in the Treaty.[7] An express grant of establishers' and service providers' (and service recipients') freedom to move and reside is made in *Directive 73/148*.[8] This grant was made pursuant to Articles 54(2) and 63(2) of the *EEC Treaty*[9] which provide for the issuing of directives "in

[1] Article 48(2).

[2] Article 48(3)(a).

[3] Article 48(3)(d). This right is expressed to be "subject to conditions which shall be embodied in implementing regulations to be drawn up by the Commission". The conditions are contained in *Regulation 1251/70.*

[4] Article 52.

[5] Article 59.

[6] Articles 56 and 66.

[7] In Case C-357/89 *Raulin v Minister van Onderwijs en Wetenschappen* [1992] ECR I-1027 the Court of Justice said that a right of access to vocational training necessarily implied a right to enter into and reside within the territory in which the vocational training is to be undertaken.

[8] Articles 2-5.

[9] First recital of *Directive 73/148*.

order to implement" the Community right of establishment and freedom of services respectively.

The *EC Treaty* does, however, expressly give workers the right to move and reside freely within the territory of Member States.[1] Article 49 empowers the Council, by issuing regulations and directives, to adopt the measures "required to bring about ... freedom of movement for workers". The detailed application of workers' rights to move and reside is dealt with by directive.[2]

If a person benefiting from Article 8a were to become employed in the host Member State there is no reason to suppose that he would not attract the additional rights conferred on workers. Similarly if a beneficiary of Article 8a were to become an establisher there is no reason to suppose that he would not attract the additional rights conferred on such persons. If, however, a person benefiting from Article 8a were to become a service provider in the same host Member State in which he resides he would not be subject to the provisions on the free movement of services, but would be covered by the provisions on workers or establishers depending on the case.[3]

The public policy exceptions applicable to the free movement of workers are described by Article 48(3) of the *EC Treaty* as "limitations", and it is to such exceptions that the reference in Article 8a to limitations laid down in the Treaty should be taken to refer. Although the word "limitations" is not used to describe the equivalent exceptions applicable in the field of establishment and services,[4] they should also be regarded as limitations to which Article 8a(1) refers.[5]

The "conditions" to which Article 8a(1) refers are also to be found in the Treaty provisions dealing with workers, establishment and services. Thus Article 48(3)(d) requires the Commission to draw up regulations containing the conditions on which workers can remain in the territory of a Member State after having been employed there.[6] In the field of establishment and services, the *EC Treaty* requires the Commission to draw up general programmes "which shall set out the general conditions under which" the right of establishment and liberalisation of services are to be achieved.[7] The Council is then directed to implement these general programmes, including their 'conditions', by issuing directives.[8]

[1]Article 48(3)(b), (c).

[2]*Directive 68/360.*

[3]Case 196/87 *Steymann v Staatssecretaris van Justitie* [1988] ECR 6159 at pp 6173-6174, paragraphs 16-17 of the Court's judgment.

[4]See Articles 56(1) and 66 of the *EC Treaty.*

[5]In Case 48/75 *Royer* [1976] ECR 497 at p 509, paragraph 12 of the judgment, the Court of Justice said that the Treaty provisions dealing with the free movement of workers and services and the right of establishment "are based on the same principles both in so far as they concern the entry into and residence within the territory of Member States of persons covered by Community law and the prohibition of all discrimination between them on grounds of nationality".

[6]These conditions are contained in *Regulation 1250/71.*

[7]Article 54(1) (establishment) and Article 63(1) (services).

[8]Article 54(2) (establishment) and Article 63(2) (services).

It therefore appears that the "limitations and conditions" to which Article 8a(1) refers can be found in the context of the Treaty provisions on the free movement of workers and services and the right of establishment.

Limitations on Union Citizens' Rights

Assuming for present purposes that Article 8a of the *EC Treaty* is directly effective,[1] an important question arises. To what limitations and conditions, if any, are citizens of the Union subject in exercising their Article 8a rights of movement and residence within the territory of the Member States? In particular are they subject to, or can they be made subject to, the limitations on the grounds of public policy, public security and public health to which persons exercising migration rights under Articles 48-66 of the *EC Treaty* are subject? Furthermore, can they be made subject to conditions concerning financial self-sufficiency and health insurance if not engaged in economic activity within the scope of Articles 48-66?

We shall see that the answer to this question is related to the resolution of a different problem; namely the appropriate legal basis for the adoption of the "measures" referred to in Article 8a(1).

ARTICLE 8A NOT AN ABSOLUTE RIGHT

A useful starting point might be the proposition that, there being no limitations or conditions expressly applicable to Union citizens exercising their rights under Article 8a, the citizen's right to move and reside freely within the territory of the Member States cannot be encumbered by limitations or conditions. In other words, it is an absolute right which permits of no restrictions by the Community institutions or Member States.

This initial proposition could be supported by arguing that the use of the word "facilitating" in Article 8a(2) implies that the Council may act only to assist, and not restrict, the effective exercise of the citizen's rights of movement and residence. Such an approach has the advantage of according with the ordinary meaning of "facilitating", and of the equivalent expressions in the other language versions of the *EC Treaty*.[2] On this analysis, any legislation adopted under Article 8a(2) can serve - as in the case of secondary legislation implementing the directly effective freedom of movement provisions in Articles 48, 52 and 59 - only to determine "the scope and detailed rules for the exercise of rights conferred directly by the Treaty".[3]

[1] In Chapter 5 it will be shown that Article 8a is directly effective.

[2] Dutch, *vergemakkelijken*. French, *faciliter*. German, *erleichtert*. Italian, *facilitare*.

[3] Case 48/75 *Royer* [1976] ECR 497 at p 512, paragraph 28 of the Court's judgment. By contrast, Article 48(3)(d) of the *EEC Treaty* confers on workers a right to remain in the territory of a Member State after having been employed there "subject to conditions which shall be embodied in implementing regulations". This implies that the right in question may be restricted, rather than merely 'facilitated', by the foreshadowed regulations. Restrictions on the right contained in Article 48(3)(d) were imposed by Article

However this first proposition is, as presently formulated, unsatisfactory. It would be most incongruous if the *EC Treaty* could subject the narrower category of Articles 48-66 economic migrants to a raft of limitations and conditions when the broader category of Article 8a Union citizens was free from the possibility of being subject to any similar limitations. This could result in serious distortions in the operation of Community law.

For example, a would-be economic migrant can be refused entry into the territory of a Member State if he suffers from one of the diseases mentioned in Annex A to *Directive 64/221* (eg., syphilis or tuberculosis).[1] Can it really be maintained that a person seeking, under Article 8a, merely to move and reside in a Member State cannot be made subject to a similar limitation? Would such a person, residing in a host Member State, pose any less danger to public health than a resident economic migrant?

If the Article 8a rights could not be made subject to public health exceptions, then a person suffering from syphilis or tuberculosis could enter and reside in the host Member State under Article 8a, obtain a residence permit under secondary legislation to be adopted under Article 8a(2), and then undertake an economic activity within terms of Articles 46-66. He would then be entitled to the additional advantages afforded by Community law to economic migrants, for *Directive 64/221* permits the refusal only of a first residence permit on public health grounds.[2] The result would be to circumvent the public health exceptions to the free movement of economic migrants.

And what of public security? Surely it cannot be the case that a known terrorist could be refused entry if seeking to undertake an economic activity within terms of Articles 48-66, but would have to be admitted if he intended merely to move and reside within the host Member State under Article 8a.

A similar problem would also arise in the context of retired workers and retired establishers who wish to remain permanently in the territory of a host Member State after having been economically active there. Is it possible that a such person, who was ineligible to remain under Community secondary legislation regulating that right,[3] could be refused permission to remain while another person who had never been employed in the host Member State could be entitled to remain by invoking his unqualified residence right in Article 8a(1) of the *EC Treaty*?

2(1) of *Regulation 1251/70* (OJ Sp Ed 1970, L 142/24, p 402) which has the effect of excluding from enjoyment of the right several categories of persons who would otherwise fall within the scope of the Treaty provision.

[1] Article 4(1) of *Directive 64/221* and Annex A points 2 and 3.

[2] Article 4(1).

[3] Because, for example, he has not attained the legal retiring age in the host Member State: Article 2(1)(a) of *Regulation 1251/70* (OJ Sp Ed 1970, L 142/24, p 402), and Article 2(1)(a) of *Directive 75/34* (OJ 1975, L 14/10).

Further examples of the distortive effect on Community law, should it be maintained that there are no limitations actually or potentially applicable to the Union citizen's Article 8a(1) rights, could be all too easily multiplied.

Moreover, an analysis of Article 8a(1) which postulated that the provision conferred an unqualified right would implicitly be asserting that the provision's qualifying words are meaningless.

THE THREE MOVEMENT AND RESIDENCE DIRECTIVES

The *Union Treaty* was signed against the background of the enactment of EEC *Directives 90/364*[1] (residence rights for persons of independent means), *90/365*[2] (residence rights for pensioners), and *90/366*[3] (residence rights for students) which were all required to be implemented by not later than 30 June 1992,[4] after which date *Directives 90/364* and *90/365* probably became directly effective. The Court of Justice has held that Article 7 of the *EEC Treaty*[5] was directly effective so as to confer on nationals of Member States who have been admitted to a course of vocational training in a host Member State a right of residence in the host Member State,[6] and that *Directive 90/366* merely "aims to give effect to and organise the right of residence"[7] conferred by the Treaty itself.

The movement and residence rights contained in these three Directives are subject to certain restrictions.

In the case of Member State nationals who have "pursued an activity as an employed or self-employed person", covered by *Directive 90/365*, they must be in receipt of "an invalidity or early retirement pension, or old age benefits, or of a pension in respect of an industrial accident or disease".[8] There is no requirement that they need have pursued their employment in the territory of the host Member State.[9] This directive would therefore appear to be outside the scope of Article 48 of the *EEC Treaty*, which confers on persons who have been employed in a host Member State a qualified right to remain in that State. Although the Commission's proposal for *Directive 90/365*

[1] OJ 1990, L 180/26.

[2] OJ 1990, L 180/28.

[3] OJ 1990, L 180/30.

[4] Article 5 of each directive.

[5] Article 7 of the *EEC Treaty* became Article 6 of the *EC Treaty* after the coming into force of the *Union Treaty*.

[6] Case C-357/89 *Raulin v Minister van Onderwijs en Wetenschappen* [1992] ECR I-1027.

[7] Case C-295/90 *European Parliament v Council* ("*Re Students' Rights*") [1992] 3 CMLR 281 at p 300, paragraph 14 of the Court's judgment.

[8] Article 1(1) of *Directive 90/365*.

[9] In the case of workers, the right to remain in a host Member State after having been employed in the same Member State is covered by Article 48(3)(d) of the *EEC Treaty* and *Regulation 1251/70* (OJ Sp Ed 1970, L 142/24, p 402). The corresponding right for self-employed persons is covered by *Directive 75/34* (OJ 1975, L 14/10).

was based on Articles 49 and 54 of the *EEC Treaty*, the Council refused to adopt it on this basis.

In the case of students, covered by *Directive 90/366*, they must be "enrolled in a recognized educational establishment for the purpose of following a vocational training course" in the host Member State.[1]

The right of residence[2] is also granted "to nationals of Member States who do not enjoy this right under other provisions of Community law".[3]

The rights enjoyed by all three categories of persons are additionally enjoyed by certain members of their families.[4]

In the case of *Directive 90/364*, the beneficiaries of these movement and residence rights must show that "they themselves and the members of their families are covered by sickness insurance in respect of all risks in the host Member State and have sufficient resources to avoid becoming a burden on the social assistance system of the host Member State during their period of residence".[5] Similar conditions are imposed in respect of pensioners and students.[6]

Finally the three EEC non-economic residence directives permit Member States to derogate from their provisions on grounds of public policy, public security and public health. In that event, the three Directives apply the provisions of *Directive 64/221*.[7]

[1]*Directive 90/366*, Article 1(1). As to the meaning of "vocational training" see eg Nicholas Green, Trevor C. Hartley and John A. Usher, *The Legal Foundations of the Single European Market*, (Oxford University Press, 1992), pp 179-181.

[2]The right of residence is granted by Article 1 of each directive. The right of movement is granted by the first paragraph of Article 2(2) of *Directives 90/364* and 90/365, which apply Articles 2, 3, 6(1)(a), 6(2) and 9 of *Directive 68/360* mutatis mutandis to the beneficiaries of those Directives. Article 2(2) of *Directive 90/366* does not extend Articles 6(1)(a) and 6(2) of *Directive 68/360* to the students covered by the former directive, thereby implying that such beneficiaries do not enjoy a freedom to move ***within*** the territory of the host Member State.

[3]*Directive 90/364*, Article 1(1).

[4]Article 1 of each directive. The family provision is rather less liberal in the case of *Directive 90/366* than in the case of *Directives 90/364* and *90/365*. Whereas only a student's spouse and dependent children may accompany him, the beneficiaries under the other two Directives may be accompanied by their spouses and dependent 'descendants' as well as dependant relatives in the ascending line of the beneficiary (but not, it seems, of the beneficiary's spouse).

[5]The first paragraph of Article 1(1).

[6]The first paragraph of Article 1(1) of *Directive 90/365* and Article 1 of *Directive 90/366*. Curiously, these Directives do not expressly require the beneficiaries' accompanying families to be covered by sickness insurance. Furthermore in the case of pensioners, the pensions which they are required to be receiving must themselves be of a sufficient amount to prevent the pensioner from becoming a burden on the host Member State's social security system. Consequently a pensioner who is not in receipt of a sufficiently lucrative pension, but who has sufficient income from his pension combined with income from other sources as would prevent him from becoming a burden on the host Member State's social security system, would need to rely on *Directive 90/364* should he desire to reside in a Member State of which he is not a national.

[7]The third paragraph of Article 2(2) of each directive. In the case of students, only Articles 2 to 9 of *Directive 64/221* apply.

THE SCOPE OF SECONDARY LEGISLATION ADOPTED UNDER ARTICLE 8A

It will be recalled that the Union citizen's right under Article 8a(1) to move and reside freely within the territory of the Member States is made subject to "limitations and conditions laid down in this Treaty and by the measures adopted to give it effect". Article 8a(1) does not expressly provide a procedure by which 'measures' 'giving effect' to the right to move and reside may be adopted. Article 8a(2), however, provides for a procedure by which 'provisions' 'facilitating' the exercise of the Article 8a(1) rights may be adopted.

It would therefore seem that the Union citizen's right to move and reside under Article 8a(1) can be made subject to only: (i) Article 8a(2) provisions adopted "with a view to facilitating" the exercise of those rights, and (ii) limitations and conditions laid down elsewhere in the *EC Treaty*. If "facilitating" is understood to mean that Article 8a(2) cannot be employed as a legal basis to enact measures limiting or conditioning the rights referred to in Article 8a(1), this approach would exclude a contrary argument that Article 8a(1), either through Article 8a(2) or on some other legal basis, authorises the adoption of secondary measures limiting or conditioning the Union citizen's right of movement and residence. A significant consequence hinges on the choice to be made between these two opposed readings of Article 8a.

If the former reading were to prevail, secondary legislation which had the effect of limiting or conditioning the Union citizen's movement and residence rights could not validly be adopted under Article 8a. Such measures could subject those rights only to provisions 'facilitating' their exercise.

If the latter reading were to prevail, then secondary legislation could effectively place potentially significant limitations and conditions on the exercise of the Union citizen's movement and residence rights which go beyond provisions necessary for merely 'facilitating' them. For reasons which will follow, it is here argued that the latter reading of Article 8a(1) is preferable, and that the provision authorises the adoption of secondary legislation restricting the exercise of the Union citizen's right to move and reside.

It is convenient firstly to consider whether the former reading, restricting the operation of any secondary legislation to a facilitating *rôle*, in the narrow sense that the secondary legislation may not impose limitations and conditions on the rights referred to in Article 8a(1), is the preferable one. There are a number of things which can be said in favour of this proposition.

As has already been indicated, the only legislative procedure apparently available for the adoption of "measures'" under Article 8a(1) is that specified for the adoption of "provisions" under Article 8a(2), and that procedure permits the legislator merely to 'facilitate' the Union citizen's movement and residence rights. It could also be said to be incongruous if the *EC Treaty* were to confer an apparently new right of movement and residence on Member State nationals while simultaneously providing the means by which that new right could be effectively annulled. Furthermore in both the French and Italian versions of the *EC Treaty*, the nouns corresponding to "measures" in Article 8a(1) and "provisions" in Article 8a(2) are rendered as the same word,[1] thereby suggesting that the special legislative procedure prescribed by Article 8a(2) is applicable to the adoption of the "measures" referred to in Article 8a(1).

THE MOVEMENT AND RESIDENCE DIRECTIVES APPLY TO UNION CITIZENS

Each of the three EEC movement and residence directives was enacted under Article 235 of the *EEC Treaty*.

Directive 90/366 was annulled by the Court of Justice on 7 July 1992 because it was adopted under the wrong provision of the *EEC Treaty*, although it was continued in force until the entry into force of a replacement directive adopted on the appropriate legal basis, ie Article 7 of the *EEC Treaty*.[2] No legal challenge has thus far been mounted in respect of the legal bases for *Directives 90/364* and *90/365*.[3]

A question immediately arises as to whether the three movement and residence directives can limit the rights conferred by Article 8a of the *EC Treaty* especially if that Article provides a procedure for enacting legislation different from that provided for under Articles 7 and 235 of the *EEC Treaty*.

In particular, Article 8a(2) of the *EC Treaty* requires the assent of the European Parliament before the adoption of legislation thereby affording the European Parliament a veto even in the face of a unanimous Council, whereas legislation adopted under Article 7 of the *EEC Treaty* merely required observance of the co-operation procedure.[4] The co-operation procedure enables, in certain circumstances, the European Parliament to block proposed legislation unless it meets with unanimity on the Council. Similarly, Article 235 of the *EEC Treaty* merely required that in

[1]French: *dispositions*. Italian: *disposizioni*. The German text, like the English, uses different nouns, with "*Durchführungsvorschriften*" corresponding to "measures" and "*Vorschriften*" corresponding to "provisions". It would be difficult on this basis alone, however, to mount a convincing argument to the effect that the use of these similar nouns signified an intention on the part of the Treaty draftsman to make the adoption of Article 8a(1) measures/ *Durchführungsvorschriften* the subject of a different and unspecified procedure to that of Article 8a(2) provisions/ *Vorschriften*.

[2]Case C-295/90 *European Parliament v Council* ("*Re Students' Rights*") [1992] 3 CMLR 281. The Commission has since made a proposal for a new Council directive (COM (93) 209 final, 14 May 1993) expressed to rest upon the legal base approved by the Court.

[3]The Commission originally proposed Article 100 of the *EEC Treaty* as the correct legal basis for *Directive 90/364* and Articles 49 and 54 of the *EEC Treaty* as the correct legal bases for *Directive 90/365*: The opinion of Advocate General Jacobs in Case C-295/90 *European Parliament v Council* [1992] 3 CMLR 281 at p 290.

[4]The co-operation procedure was set out in Article 149(2) of the *EEC Treaty*. After the coming into force of the *Union Treaty* Article 7 of the *EEC Treaty* became Article 6 of the *EC Treaty* and Article 149(2) of the *EEC Treaty* is repealed. Article 6 of the *EC Treaty* requires that legislation adopted thereunder be enacted in accordance with the procedure referred to in Article 189c of the *EC Treaty* which is identical to that contained in Article 149(2) of the *EEC Treaty*.

adopting any legislation under it the European Parliament be consulted.[1] The European Parliament's *rôle* is therefore greater in the case of legislation adopted under Article 8a of the *EC Treaty* than in the case of legislation adopted under either Article 7 or Article 235 of the *EEC Treaty*.

In *Commission v Council ("Re Generalised Tariff Preferences")*,[2] the Court of Justice invalidated a Council Regulation which had been adopted under Article 235 of the *EEC Treaty* when power to enact the Regulation existed under Article 113. A proposal requires Council unanimity to be adopted under Article 235, but only a qualified majority of the Council to be adopted under Article 113. The Court of Justice referred to this difference in the voting procedures and also said;

> It follows from the very wording of Article 235 that its use as the legal basis for a measure is justified only where no other provision of the Treaty gives the Community institutions the necessary power to adopt the measure in question.[3]

If a power to enact legislation in respect of the rights in Article 8a(1) is contained in Article 8a(2), resort to Article 235 would seem unjustified and therefore liable to lead to the legislation being annulled.[4]

Furthermore, the enactment of any measure under either Article 7, when Article 8a(2) provided the appropriate legal basis, could likewise lead to the annulment of the measure. This is because resort to Article 7 would, in these circumstances, involve an infringement of the European Parliament's prerogative of giving or withholding assent to the measure in contravention of the principle that the European Parliament's powers and prerogatives must be respected in the interests of preserving the Community's institutional balance.[5]

Nevertheless, even if Article 8a(2) is the appropriate legal basis for enactment of the "measures" referred to in Article 8a(1), it is probable that the three movement and residence directives are effective to impose limitations - including limitations on the grounds of public policy, public security and public health - on the enjoyment of the

[1] Article 235 of the *EEC Treaty* became Article 235 of the *EC Treaty* without amendment.

[2] Case 45/86 [1987] ECR 1493.

[3] ibid at p 1520, paragraph 13 of the Court's judgment.

[4] One might argue that the procedural differences between Articles 8a(2) and 235 do not in the present instance pose a difficulty because the Article 8a(2) procedure applies only where it is sought to facilitate the exercise of the Article 8a(1) rights. If one seeks to limit or restrict those rights, such an argument might run, Article 8a(2) does not provide the power and it is necessary to resort to Article 235. The problem with this argument is that to limit or restrict the Article 8a rights amounts to an amendment to the treaty if one accepts that Article 8a confers an absolute right on Union citizens. This being so, only the treaty amendment procedure contained in Article 236 can be employed: see eg Case 43/75 *Defrenne v Société Anonyme Belge de Navigation Aérienne Sabena* [1976] ECR 455 at p 478, paragraph 58 of the Court's judgment.

[5] See Case C-70/88 *European Parliament v Council ("Chernobyl")* [1990] ECR I-2041 and Case C-295/90 *European Parliament v Council ("Re Students' Rights")* [1992] 3 CMLR 281.

Union citizen's right to move and reside freely within the territory of the Member States.

This is so firstly, and most importantly, because the three directives were adopted before the coming into force of the *Union Treaty* and Article 8a of the *EC Treaty*. Secondly the European Union, of which the European Community forms one of the foundations,[1] is bound by the *acquis communautaire*.[2] Indeed, the *Union Treaty* did not repeal the *EEC Treaty*. While the name of the treaty is changed to *Treaty Establishing the European Community*, there is no break in the existence of the Community. It is therefore probable that all existing EEC law applies to the EC even without express reference to the *acquis communautaire*.

The limitations and conditions imposed on Member State nationals' migration and residence rights under the three migration and residence directives therefore continue to apply after the coming into force of the *Union Treaty*. These limitations and restrictions will be picked up and applied to the Union citizen's migration and residence rights by Article 8a(1) of the *EC Treaty*, for such limitations and restrictions will be among the measures adopted to give effect to the Treaty.[3] This is especially true of *Directive 90/364* which confers the right of residence on nationals of Member States who do not enjoy the right under other provisions of Community law.[4] The question of a conflict between the three movement and residence directives and Article 8a of the *EC Treaty* does not, therefore, arise. The limitations and restrictions contained in the three movement and residence directives are thus incorporated into the Union citizen's right to move and reside freely within the territory of the Member States by the terms of Article 8a itself.[5]

[1] Third paragraph of Article A of the *Union Treaty*.

[2] Article B (fifth point) and Article C (first paragraph) of the *Union Treaty*.

[3] In Chapter 5 it is demonstrated that the pronoun "it" in Article 8a(1) refers to the noun "Treaty", and not to the noun "right".

[4] Article 1(1) (first paragraph).

[5] In contradiction to this proposition, it might rationally be suggested that the three EEC residence directives do not 'give effect' to the Union citizen's movement and residence rights under Article 8a of the *EC Treaty*. Such an objection could be founded upon an argument that the three directives, in so far as they are expressed to apply to only limited categories of Member State nationals, are not co-extensive *ratione personae* with the Article 8a right. Thus the requirement in Article 1(1) of *Directive 90/364* that the directive's beneficiaries "have sufficient resources to avoid becoming a burden on the social assistance system of the host Member State", it could be suggested, is not a limitation or condition on the exercise of the rights conferred by the directive; rather, it defines the personal scope of the directive. A proponent of this view might rely on the opinion of Advocate General Jacobs in his opinion to the Court in Case C-295/90 *European Parliament v Council* ("*Re Students' Rights*") [1992] 3 CMLR 281. The Advocate General argued (at p 295 of the report) that, in restricting access to the students' right of residence to the duration of the course and to those who could assure the relevant national authority that they had sufficient resources to avoid becoming a burden on the social assistance system of the host Member State during their period of residence and that they and their families were covered by sickness insurance in respect of all risks in the host Member State, the directive did no more than limit the right of residence to those who were entitled to receive it directly under the effect of Article 7 of the *EEC Treaty*. In these respects, then, no limitations of the Treaty's residence rights for students were actually imposed by the directive. In connection, however, with the directive's authorisation to limit students' residence rights on grounds of public policy, public security and public health, the directive was doing more than merely recognising the boundaries of the Treaty right. Rather the directive was, according to the Advocate General, expressly authorising derogations from that right. On this analysis, it could be argued, the directive fails to give effect to the rights contained in Article 8a of the *EC Treaty* because it does not

It therefore seems that there are at present two sets of limitations and conditions applicable to the exercise of Article 8a movement and residence rights. The first set refers to the Treaty's limitations and conditions laid down in respect of economic migration covered by Articles 48, 52 and 59, which limitations and conditions continue to apply to economic migrants. The second set of limitations refers both to secondary legislation applicable to the economic migrants covered by Articles 48, 52 and 59 and to the migrants covered by EEC *Directives 90/364*, *90/365* and *90/366*. These three directives[1] restrict the Union citizen's right to move and reside freely within the territory of the Member States under Article 8a by, *inter alia*, permitting Member States to derogate from that right on grounds of public policy, public security and public health subject to the provisions of *Directive 64/221* and by imposing certain conditions concerning the citizen's financial self-sufficiency and health insurance status.

This reformulation of our hypothetical argument brings us closer to an understanding of the limitations which may apply to the exercise of movement and residence rights under Article 8a of the *EC Treaty*. Yet the picture is still not complete. If Community law must rely exclusively upon the terms of *Directives 90/364*, *90/365*, and *90/366* for the application of exceptions to Article 8a migration rights, then what would happen to such exceptions if the three directives were to be annulled by the Court of Justice (without their effects being maintained until replaced by valid measures) or if they were to be repealed by the Community's legislative process?

---

truly extend to "(e)very citizen of the Union" as stipulated by Article 8a(1). Although this argument is attractive in so far as it is limited to interpreting *Directive 90/366*, it cannot convincingly be analogised to *Directive 90/364*. In the first place, the rights conferred by the latter directive were not conferred directly by the *EEC Treaty* (the directive being correctly based on Article 235). Instead it created new rights which extended to all nationals of Member States, subject to them satisfying certain conditions. This difference in approach between, on the one hand, *Directive 90/366* and, on the other hand, *Directive 90/364*, is furthermore reflected in the language employed in them. In the case of *Directive 90/366*, a right of residence is conferred on "*any student* who is a national of a Member State and who does not enjoy this right under other provisions of Community law" (Article 1) and who meets certain additional qualifications corresponding to the scope of the rights conferred directly by Articles 7 and 128. In the case of *Directive 90/364*, by contrast, a right of residence is conferred on "*nationals of Member States* who do not enjoy this right under other provisions of Community law" and who meet certain additional conditions (Article 1(1) (first paragraph)). Accordingly even if the restrictions imposed on the exercise of residence rights imposed by Article 1 of *Directive 90/366* are merely definitive of the directive's personal scope, and not limitations and conditions upon the exercise of the rights, a similar analysis is not valid for *Directive 90/364*. On the contrary, both the language and purpose of *Directive 90/364* indicate that the rights contained therein are to be enjoyed by all Member State nationals subject to limitations and conditions attaching to, *inter alia*, their financial self-sufficiency and health insurance status. In any event, the objection that the three EEC residence directives do not affect the Union citizen's movement and residence right conferred by Article 8a(1) assumes that the "measures" therein referred to are adopted to give effect to that right. Such an assumption is misplaced. In Chapter 5 it is demonstrated that the pronoun "it" in Article 8a(1) is a reference to the noun "Treaty" rather than to the noun "right". Thus the Union citizen's right to move and reside is subject to the limitations and conditions laid down in the *measures adopted to give effect to the Treaty* (not the measures adopted to give effect to the Union citizen's right of movement and residence). Clearly, the three EEC residence directives are adopted to give effect to the *Treaty*. Thus it is not to the point to argue that they do do not give effect to the *right*.

[1] It is possible that only *Directive 90/364* has this effect (see previous footnote). Because, however, *Directive 90/364* is expressed to apply its right of movement and residence to "nationals of Member States who do not enjoy this right under other provisions of Community law", it would alone serve the same purpose.

The answer to this question must be that if the three EEC directives really are the sole source of such exceptions, and if Article 8a permits only the adoption of legislation "facilitating" (in the narrow sense) the exercise of movement and residence rights, then the Union citizen's rights under Article 8a would be unencumbered unless they were being exercised in the context of economic migration under Articles 48-66, in which case Articles 48(3), 56(1) and 66 of the *EC Treaty* and *Directive 64/221* would continue to apply. Such a result would return us to the dilemma identified at the outset of this discussion on the limits applicable to the rights conferred under Article 8a(1); namely the severely distortive effects on Community law of subjecting the narrower class of economic migrants to restrictions on their rights to move and reside while the broader category of Union citizens are subject to no similar restrictions.

Even if the three EEC directives were not annulled or repealed, it would not be possible to enact limitations and conditions that go further than those already embodied in the three directives.

AN EXCURSION INTO THE HINTERLAND

This dilemma can be overcome only if the three movement and residence directives are not regarded as the sole source of possible limitations and restrictions on the migration rights conferred by Article 8a(1). But if not those three directives, then what else? Article 8a(2) appears, at least for the moment, to remain a poor candidate because of its restriction as a legal basis to the adoption of provisions "facilitating" (in the narrow sense) the rights referred to in Article 8a(1). Can we nevertheless save our hypothetical argument, in favour of a narrowly-construed Article 8a(2) being the appropriate legal basis for the "measures" referred to in Article 8a(1), by looking for limitations and conditions applicable to the Union citizen's right to move and reside elsewhere in the *EC Treaty* itself? If we can find any such limitations and conditions, we may be able to rescue our hypothetical argument by avoiding the dilemma to which it appears to give rise.

Let us, then, embark on an excursion into the constitutional hinterland of Article 8a in search of implied limitations applicable to the citizenship right of movement and residence.

A LACUNA IN THE TREATY?

The right conferred by Article 8a(1) is expressed to be subject not only to the measures adopted to give effect to the Treaty, but also to the "limitations and conditions laid down in this Treaty". We have already seen that Articles 48(3), 56(1) and 66 of the *EC Treaty* and *Directive 64/221* will continue to apply to Union citizens who are exercising economic migration rights under Articles 48, 52 and 59. But does the reference in Article 8a(1) to "limitations and conditions laid down in this Treaty" have any implications for the exercise by Union citizens of migration and residence rights, independently of any economic activity?

One might first be tempted to answer this question by suggesting that the reference to "limitations and conditions laid down in this Treaty" in Article 8a(1) operates so as to pick up the limitations and conditions applicable under Articles 48(3), 56(1) and 66 and to apply them to the citizen's rights under Article 8a. In particular, the public policy provisos in Articles 48(3), 56(1) and 66 could be said to apply *mutatis mutandis* to the citizen's rights to move and reside freely. This suggestion might be supported by pointing out that the Court of Justice does, on occasion, address *lacunae* in Community legislation by applying analogous Community legislative provisions.[1]

The Court of Justice suggested, in *Germany and Bundesanstalt für Arbeit v Commission*[2] that if there were to be a *lacuna* in the *EEC Treaty* which deprived persons of the "effective protection of their rights" it might be appropriate for the Court to fill that *lacuna*.[3] Where the treaties are silent in the protection of individual rights, the Court has tended, however, to fill the apparent gap by reference to some overriding general principle of Community law rather than by resort to the mechanical application of analogous Community legislation. Moreover we are here concerned not with an apparent gap which diminishes citizens' rights but, on the contrary, we are concerned to establish whether there is a gap which effectively enhances those rights by failing expressly to provide for the imposition of certain possible limitations.

Although there is no reason in principle why the Court of Justice could not have recourse by analogy to Articles 48(3), 56(1) and 66 for the purpose of enhancing the right of Union citizens to move and reside freely within the territory of the Member States, it is most unlikely to do so for the opposite purpose of permitting Member States to limit the right. The Court would need to be satisfied, moreover, that the absence of an unambiguous power in Article 8a permitting Member States to limit the Union citizen's movement and residence rights on public policy grounds is a genuine *lacuna* in the *EC Treaty*, and this is a matter which remains to be established.

[1]This method has been particularly evident where the lacuna involves the remedies made available by the treaties to parties before the Court of Justice. Thus in Case 4/79 *Société Coopérative "Providence Agricole de la Champagne" v Office National Interprofessionel des Céréales (ONIC)* [1980] ECR 2823 the Court of Justice applied by analogy Article 174 (second paragraph) of the *EEC Treaty*, which enables the Court of Justice to declare definitive certain effects of regulations which have been declared void as a result of annulment proceedings brought under Article 173, to the performance of its functions under Article 177 where the validity of a regulation is in question (at p 2855, paragraph 45 of the Court's judgment). See also Case 112/83 *Société des Produits de Maïs SA v Administration des douanes et droits indirects* [1985] ECR 719 at p 748, paragraph 18 of the Court's judgment; Case 41/84 *Pinna v Caisse d'allocations familiales de la Savoie* [1986] ECR 1 at p 26, paragraphs 26-28 of the Court's judgment; Joined Cases C-38 and C-151/90 *R v Lomas* [1992] ECR I-1781 at p I-1816, paragraph 23 of the Court's judgment. In Case 34/86 *Council v European Parliament* [1986] ECR 2155 Article 174 (second paragraph) was also expressly invoked as an appropriate analogous provision empowering the Court of Justice to partly annul, under Article 173, an act of the President of the European Parliament declaring the Community's 1986 budget finally adopted (at p 2212, paragraph 48 of the Court's judgment). In Case C-295/90 *European Parliament v Council ("Re Students' Rights")* [1992] 3 CMLR 281, Article 174 (second paragraph) was applied by analogy in such a way as to permit the partial annulment of a directive in proceedings brought under Article 169 (at p 302, paragraph 26 of the Court's judgment).

[2]Case 44/81 [1982] ECR 1855.

[3]ibid at p 1875, paragraph 7 of the Court's judgment.

The Court of Justice is, moreover, generally reluctant to concede the existence of *lacunae* in the constitutive treaties.[1]

Accordingly, we must look elsewhere if we are to retain a narrow interpretation of Article 8a(2) of the *EC Treaty* such that, because of the word "facilitating", it cannot be used as a legal basis for the adoption of provisions limiting or conditioning the rights contained in Article 8a(1).

We shall therefore turn our attention elsewhere and venture somewhat further into the constitutional hinterland of Article 8a. We will do this firstly by establishing that, when it is confronted by a textual deficiency in the treaties, the Court of Justice will try to fill it by reference to fundamental constitutional principles which can be derived from the scheme of the treaties as a whole.

We will then enquire whether there is a fundamental constitutional principle which permits the Member States to protect themselves from threats to their public policy, public security and public health such as to warrant derogations from the enjoyment of Article 8a non-economic migration rights. This will involve asking whether any such power is reserved to the Member States, or whether they retain a merely residual power which they may exercise until the Community acts (eg under Article 235).

All of this is of course predicated on an assumption that there really is a *lacuna* or textual deficiency in the Treaty such that no special provision is made for the adoption of limitations and conditions on the rights contained in Article 8a. After our return from the constitutional hinterland, we will consider whether this assumption is valid and identify how the limitations and conditions we are interested in can be adopted.

PROTECTION OF FUNDAMENTAL CONSTITUTIONAL PRINCIPLES

When the Court of Justice recognises the existence of a textual deficiency in the treaties it tends if possible to avoid the technique of filling the gap by direct borrowings from analogous legislation, preferring if possible to derive from the scheme of the treaties some constitutional principle which it will strive to protect.[2] The Court's technique in four illustrative cases is of interest in this connection.

In *Commission v Council* ("*Re ERTA*")[3] the Court of Justice interpreted the text of the *EEC Treaty* in order to give effect to a fundamental objective of the Treaty as derived from a legislative scheme therein. In casu, Articles 164 and 173 read conjointly evidencing a Treaty objective of observance of 'the law' in connection with

[1]See eg the reasoning of the Court of Justice in Case 21/64 *Macchiolarti Dalmas e Figli v High Authority* [1965] ECR 175 at pp 190-191.

[2]This technique is to be distinguished from the technique of using secondary legislation as an aid in interpreting treaty provisions. Even in Case 4/79 *Société Coopérative "Providence Agricole de la Champagne" v Office National Interprofessionel des Céréales (ONIC)* [1980] ECR 2823 and other cases involving the application by analogy of Article 174 (second paragraph), the Court justified its use of this technique by reference to wider considerations of maintaining the general principle of legal certainty.

[3]Case 22/70 [1971] ECR 263.

annulment proceedings, thereby allowing proceedings for annulment of Community acts which are not specifically named in Article 189 but which are intended to have legal effect.[1]

Similarly, in *Parti écologiste 'Les Verts' v European Parliament*[2] the Court of Justice said that it would ensure that the powers of, *inter alia*, the Member States will be protected from the unlawful actions of a Community institution even where the treaties provide no explicit textual authority so to do. Accordingly Article 173 of the *EEC Treaty* was interpreted so as to permit annulment proceedings to be brought against acts of the European Parliament which were intended to have legal effects *vis-à-vis* third parties[3] notwithstanding that such acts were not among those which the provision expressly stipulated could be challenged.[4] This will be done in order to protect what is essentially a fundamental constitutional principle derived from the scheme of the treaty.

In *European Parliament v Council* ("*Chernobyl*"),[5] another case involving the interpretation of the Treaty's annulment proceedings provision (*in casu* Article 146 of the *Euratom Treaty*, then in identical terms to Article 173 of the *EEC Treaty*), the Court of Justice allowed the European Parliament standing to challenge acts of the other institutions where its prerogatives were at stake notwithstanding that it was not named among those entities possessing standing.[6] The Court filled the gap in the Treaty provision in order to preserve "the institutional balance created by the Treaties".[7] If the Court will act to preserve the balance of power among the Community institutions without express textual authority so to do, it is probable that the Court would also act to protect the balance established by the scheme of the treaty between the Community institutions on the one hand and the Member States on the other.[8]

[1] ibid at pp 276-277, paragraphs 40-42 of the Court's judgment.

[2] Case 294/83 [1986] ECR 1339.

[3] ibid at p 1366, paragraph 25 of the Court's judgment.

[4] Article 173 of the *EC Treaty* now expressly includes acts of the European Parliament intended to produce legal effects vis-à-vis third parties.

[5] Case C-70/88 [1990] ECR I-2041.

[6] Article 173 of the *EC Treaty* and Article 146 of the *Euratom Treaty* now expressly grant the European Parliament standing for the purpose of protecting its prerogatives.

[7] Case C-70/88 *European Parliament v Council* ("*Chernobyl*") [1990] ECR I-2041 at p I-2072, paragraph 21 of the Court's judgment. See also Case 230/81 *Luxembourg v European Parliament* [1983] ECR 255, Case 108/83 *Luxembourg v European Parliament* [1984] ECR 1945 and Joined Cases C-213/88 and C-39/89 *Luxembourg v European Parliament* [1991] ECR I-5643 in which the Court of Justice said that the Community institutions must respect the institutional balance created among them by the treaties. Article 4(1) of the *EC Treaty* now expressly provides that "(e)ach institution shall act within the limits of the powers conferred upon it by this Treaty".

[8] That the Community is not entitled to legislate in fields not conferred on it by the treaties, and which therefore remain within the sole competence of the Member States, is made clear in Joined Cases 281, 283, 285 and 287/85 *Germany, France, Netherlands, Denmark and United Kingdom v Commission* ("*Re Immigration Policy*") [1987] ECR 3203. Article 3b (first paragraph) of the *EC Treaty* now also expressly provides that the Community "shall act within the limits of the powers conferred upon it by this Treaty and of the objectives assigned to it therein". The Court of Justice has, furthermore, interpreted Article 5 of the *EEC Treaty* as meaning that the Community institutions owe a duty of sincere co-operation to the Member States: Case 230/81 *Luxembourg v European Parliament* [1983] ECR 255 at p 287, paragraph 38 of the

More recently, in *Francovich v Italian Republic*[1] the Court of Justice held that, in certain circumstances, a Member State which had failed in its obligation under Community law to implement a directive would be liable in damages to individuals upon whom the directive intended to confer rights. This was so notwithstanding the absence of any express provision in the treaties entitling an individual to recover damages from Member States as a consequence of their failure to fulfil their obligations under Community law. The Court reasoned that the right of individuals to damages from a Member State in default of its Community legal obligations arose from the scheme of the *EEC Treaty*, and the need to ensure full and uniform effectiveness of rights conferred on individuals by the Community legal order.[2]

PUBLIC POLICY A FUNDAMENTAL CONSTITUTIONAL PRINCIPLE?

But is there, specifically in connection with the Member States' defence of their public policy, public security and public health, a fundamental Treaty objective or a fundamental constitutional principle derived from the scheme of the treaty in conformity with which the Member States will be justified in excluding persons seeking to exercise migration and residence rights under Article 8a? It is at least possible to make out a coherent affirmative case.

Article 2 of the *EC Treaty* sets out the tasks of the European Community which include the promotion throughout the Community of "a harmonious and balanced development of economic activities" and "economic and social cohesion and solidarity among the Member States". Article 3(c) of the same Treaty goes on to include among the Community's activities an internal market characterised by the abolition of obstacles to the interstate free movement of persons "[f]or the purposes set out in Article 2" and "as provided in this Treaty".[3] Being located in Part I of the *EC Treaty* ("Principles"), Articles 2 and 3 are among the fundamental provisions of the Community legal order.[4]

Court's judgment; Case C-2/88 Imm *Zwartveld* [1990] ECR I-3365 at p I-3372, paragraph 17 of the Court's judgment.

[1]Joined Cases C-6 and C-9/90 [1991] ECR I-5357.

[2]In Joined Cases 80 and 81/77 *Société Les Commissionnaires Réunis Sàrl and Sàrl Les Fils de Henri Ramel v Receveur des Douanes* [1978] ECR 927, the Court of Justice declared invalid a provision of a Council Regulation. The Regulation purported to authorise the maintenance of certain measures having effects equivalent to customs duties on agricultural products. The Court invalidated the provision on the ground that it violated a "fundamental principle of the Common Market applicable to all products and goods", derived from the scheme of the *EEC Treaty*, requiring the abolition of all such measures: [1978] ECR 927 at p 945, paragraph 24 of the Court's judgment.

[3]In Case 249/81 *Commission v Ireland* ("*Re 'Buy Irish' Campaign*") [1982] ECR 4005 at p 4023, the Court of Justice said that Article 3 of the Treaty 'enlarges upon' the aims of the Community as set out in Article 2.

[4]Case 43/75 *Defrenne v Société Anonyme Belge de Navigation Aérienne Sabena* [1976] ECR 455 at p 474, paragraph 28 of the Court's judgment. In Case 167/73 *Commission v France* ("*Re French Sailors*") [1974] ECR 359 at p 373, paragraph 43 of the judgment, the Court of Justice said that Article 3(c) of the *EEC Treaty* indicates that the Treaty provisions on the free movement of workers are among the foundations of the Community. Similarly, in Case 118/75 *Watson and Belmann* [1976] ECR 1185 at p 1198, paragraph 16 of the judgment, the Court of Justice said that the activities contained in Article 3(c) of the *EEC Treaty* are a fundamental principle of Community law. Semble the opinion of Advocate

Articles 48(3), 56(1) and 66 of the *EC Treaty* permit the Member States to continue subjecting Community economic migration rights to exceptions on the grounds of public policy, public security and public health. In *Rutili v Minister for the Interior*[1] the Court of Justice said that Article 48(3) of the Treaty justifies Member States in imposing restrictions on a Community worker's right to enter, remain in and move within their territories where "his presence or conduct constitutes a genuine and sufficiently serious threat to public policy".[2] A similar chord was struck in *R v Bouchereau*[3] when the Court of Justice said that a Member State is justified in restricting the Community free movement of persons where "in addition to the perturbation of the social order which any infringement of the law involves" there exists "a genuine and sufficiently serious threat to the requirements of public policy affecting one of the fundamental interests of society".[4]

Both *Rutili* and *Bouchereau* indicate that the public policy exceptions applicable under the *EEC Treaty* to economic migration rights serve a fundamental interest of the Member States in protecting themselves and their populations from serious social disruption occasioned by the influx of certain Community nationals.

Furthermore, public policy restrictions on Community rights are not confined to the free movement of persons. Article 36 of the *EC Treaty*, which is to be found under the Treaty Chapter dealing with the elimination of quantitative restrictions on the free movement of goods, also provides that prohibitions or restrictions on imports, exports or goods in transit will be allowed when they can be justified on grounds of, *inter alia*, "public morality, public policy or public security".

Similar limitations are also placed on many of the human rights and fundamental freedoms protected by the European *Convention for the Protection of Human Rights and Fundamental Freedoms* ("*ECHR*").[5] Thus exceptions on the grounds of public safety, public order (or the prevention of disorder), health and morals are permitted in respect of the freedoms guaranteed by *ECHR* Protocol 4 Articles 2(1) (freedom of movement and residence) and 2(2) (freedom to leave any country) and *ECHR* Articles 8 (respect for private and family life, home and correspondence), 9 (freedom of thought, conscience and religion), 10 (freedom of expression), and 11 (freedom of assembly and association).[6]

General Tesauro in Case C-68/89 *Commission v Netherlands* ("*Re Dutch Border Controls*") [1991] ECR I-2637 at p I-2646, paragraph 6 of the opinion. Article 3(c) was described as setting out fundamental objectives of the Community in Case 36/74 *Walrave and Koch v Association Union Cycliste Internationale* [1974] ECR 1405 at p 1419, paragraph 18 of the Court's judgment.

[1] Case 36/75 [1975] ECR 1219.

[2] ibid at p 1231, paragraph 28 of the Court's judgment.

[3] Case 30/77 [1977] ECR 1999.

[4] ibid at p 2014, paragraph 35 of the Court's judgment.

[5] Done at Rome on 4 November 1950, 213 UNTS 221.

[6] In Case C-260/89 *Elliniki Radiophonia Tileorassi AE v Pliroforissis* [1991] ECR I-2925 at p I-2948, paragraph 49 of the opinion, Advocate General Lenz said that the rules of the *ECHR* "are to be regarded as part of the Community legal order". He goes on, however, to make it plain that those rules do not apply by force of the *ECHR*, but by force of the Community's own legal order. Moreover, while he seeks

Comparable reservations are also to be found in Articles 223 and 224 of the *EC Treaty*. Article 223 expressly preserves the Member States' prerogatives (i) not to disclose any information which they consider contrary to the essential interests of their security and (ii) to take such measures as they consider necessary for the protection of the essential interests of their security which are connected with the production of or trade in arms, munitions and war material. Article 224, which requires the Member States to consult with each other and act together in order to preserve the functioning of the common market, presupposes that the Member States retain a power to take measures prejudicial to the functioning of the common market in the event of serious internal disturbance affecting the maintenance of the law and order, war, serious international tension constituting a threat of war, or in order to carry out obligations they have accepted for the purpose of maintaining peace and international security.

The existence of Articles 36, 48(3), 56(1), 66, 223 and 224, of the *EC Treaty*, it could be rationally argued, tends to indicate that the Member States' right to protect their fundamental social interests from genuine and serious threats to public policy, public security and public health arising from the Community freedoms of movement across Member State frontiers is to be respected as a fundamental principle of Community law arising from the scheme of the Treaty. This conclusion would also tend to accord with the Article 2 objectives of harmony, cohesion and solidarity among the Member States and with the exceptions permissible in respect of the freedom of movement and other important freedoms under the *ECHR* system.

That the movement and residence rights conferred by Article 8a are expressed to be subject to "the limitations and conditions laid down in this Treaty" may therefore indicate that those rights are intended to be subject to more than just the Treaty limitations and conditions expressly limiting the Union citizen's rights of economic migration. They may also be intended to be subject to such limitations and conditions applicable to migration as emerge from the scheme of the Treaty as a whole, including the Member States' right to protect themselves and their populations from a genuine and sufficiently serious threat to the requirements of public policy affecting one of the fundamental, but non-economic,[1] interests of society.

Assuming this view to be correct, and if *Directives 90/364*, *90/365*, and *90/366* were not to provide the necessary means, then it would be open to the Court of Justice to act so as to uphold an exercise of the Member States' power, derived from the scheme of the Treaty as a whole and the language of Article 8a(1), to restrict the Union

---

guidance from the case law of the European Court of Human Rights and the European Commission of Human Rights as to the meaning of Article 10 of the *ECHR*, he clearly does not regard the Court of Justice as being in any way bound thereby. The Court of Justice (at p I-2964, paragraph 44 of the judgment) seems to have accepted the Advocate General's approach on this point. For a discussion of the significance of the *ECHR* public policy exceptions in Community law see; Stephen Hall, *The European Convention on Human Rights and Public Policy Exceptions to the Free Movement of Workers under the EEC Treaty*, (1991) 16 European Law Review 466. See also the preamble to the *Single European Act* and Article F(2) of the *Union Treaty*.

[1] That the disruption to be avoided cannot be economic is made clear by Article 2(2) of *Directive 64/221*.

citizen's right of migration and residence on grounds of national security, public policy, public security and public health.

Support for this view is additionally available from the decision of the Court of Justice in *Germany, France, Netherlands, Denmark and United Kingdom v Commission* ("*Re Immigration Policy*").[1] The Commission adopted a decision,[2] in purported pursuance of Article 118 of the *EEC Treaty*, imposing on Member States a mandatory communication and consultation procedure prior to the adoption of draft measures and draft agreements with regard to workers from non-member countries and members of their families relating to their entry, residence, employment, living and working conditions, wages and economic rights, voluntary return to countries of origin and integration into the workplace, society and cultural life. The Members States sought annulment of the decision on the grounds, *inter alia*, that the Commission had exceeded its competence in adopting the decision and that it had trespassed upon territory which was within the sole power of the Member States.

France argued that the whole area of policy on foreign nationals falls outside the field of social policy inasmuch as it involves questions of public security for which the Member States are alone responsible. The Court partly annulled the decision, but rejected this part of France's submission with the following words:

> Whilst it is true that pursuant to their rules governing foreign nationals Member States may take measures with regard to workers who are nationals of non-member countries - either by adopting national rules or by negotiating international instruments - which are based on considerations of public policy, public security and public health and which are, as such, their sole responsibility, this does not mean that the whole field of migration policy in relation to non-member countries falls necessarily within the scope of public security.[3]

In particular the Court said that the policies pursued by Member States with regard to migrant workers from non-member countries are liable to affect the employment situation and the improvement of working and living conditions within the Community.[4] Consequently, Member States' policies in this sphere are properly the subject of Commission measures under Article 118.

In adopting this reasoning the Court of Justice ruled that even migration of workers from non-member countries may validly fall within certain limited powers exercisable by the Commission under Article 118 to the extent that the Community's objectives are affected thereby. Nevertheless, issues of public policy, public security and public

[1] Joined Cases 281, 283, 285 and 287/85 [1987] ECR 3203.

[2] *Decision 85/381* (OJ 1985 L217/25).

[3] Joined Cases 281, 283, 285 and 287/85 *Germany, France, Netherlands, Denmark and United Kingdom v Commission* ("*Re Immigration Policy*") [1987] ECR 3203 at p 3253, paragraph 25 of the Court's judgment.

[4] ibid at p 3251, paragraph 16 of the Court's judgment.

health arising from such migration remain the Member States' "sole responsibility", notwithstanding the absence of any Treaty provision expressly reserving this responsibility to the Member States exclusively. This line of reasoning may be said to reflect the existence of a rule protecting the balance established by the scheme of the treaties between the Community institutions and the Member States, subjecting migration and residence rights generally to limitations justified on the grounds of public policy, public security and public health.

The view that such a fundamental constitutional principle exists is, moreover, consistent with the judgment of the Court of Justice in *Society for the Protection of Unborn Children Ireland Ltd v Grogan.*[1] The Society for the Protection of Unborn Children ('SPUC') sought from the Irish High Court an injunction restraining certain officers of student associations from publishing in Ireland information about commercial abortion services available in the United Kingdom. It also sought a declaration that the distribution of such information was unlawful by virtue of Article 40.3.3° of the Irish Constitution.[2] The providers of the United Kingdom abortion services were not involved in the distribution of the information.

The Irish High Court referred several questions to the Court of Justice under Article 177 of the *EEC Treaty*. One of the questions asked whether the activity or process of carrying out an abortion falls within the definition of 'services' provided for in Article 60 of the Treaty.[3]

This question raised the issue of whether the term 'services' has a standard Community-wide meaning independently of the public policy of Member States on the question of abortion. If the Court answered simply "no" then there could be no possibility of persons possessing a right, under the Community's freedom to provide and consume services, to leave or enter Ireland for the purposes of having an abortion.[4] Moreover, even those Member States in which abortions are legal would not need to comply with the Community's rules concerning services in the area of abortions.

[1]Case C-159/90 [1991] ECR I-4685.

[2]Article 40.3.3° of the Irish Constitution provides as follows:

> The State acknowledges the right to life of the unborn and, with due regard to the equal right to life of the mother, guarantees in its laws to respect, and, as far as practicable, by its laws to defend and vindicate that right.

[3]The second and third questions asked whether a Member State may prohibit information about abortion clinics in another Member State and whether a person has a right to distribute such information in Member State A, where abortions are unlawful, about abortion clinics in Member State B, where abortions are lawful under certain conditions.

[4]After the Court of Justice answered this question by saying that the medical termination of a pregnancy is to be considered a service within the meaning of Article 60 if performed in accordance with the law of the Member State in which it was performed, the referring Irish High Court said that "a pregnant woman who is travelling to the United Kingdom for the purposes of an abortion is travelling to avail of a service as defined by the Treaty of Rome": *Society for the Protection of Unborn Children Ireland Ltd (SPUC) v Grogan*, [1993] 1 CMLR 197 at p 202, paragraph 14 of the Court's judgment. In *Attorney General v X* the Irish High Court said that, because a pregnant woman travelling to another Member State for an abortion does so as the recipient of a service for the purposes of the *EEC Treaty*, Ireland could lawfully prevent her from doing so pursuant to its power under Article 8 of *Directive 73/148* to derogate from the right to receive the service on grounds of public policy: [1992] 1 IR 1, [1992] 2 CMLR 277.

Article 59 of the Treaty establishes the freedom to provide services in the European Community. Article 60 goes on to define services for the purposes of the Treaty as services "normally provided for remuneration in so far as they are not governed by the provisions relating to freedom of movement for goods, capital and persons" and which particularly include, *inter alia*, "activities of the professions". Article 66 of the Treaty, which is in the same Chapter as Articles 59 and 60, applies to that Chapter Articles 55 to 58 of the Treaty (in the Chapter dealing with the right of establishment). Article 56(1) of the Treaty provides that the Member States may adopt "special treatment for foreign nationals on grounds of public policy, public security and public health".

In answering the question put by the Irish court, the Court of Justice referred to *Luisi and Carbone v Ministero del Tesoro*[1] for the proposition that medical activities fall within the scope of Article 60. It also noted that termination of pregnancy, as lawfully practised in several Member States, is a medical activity which is normally provided for remuneration and may be carried out as part of a professional activity.[2] The logical conclusion to be drawn from this line of reasoning, although the Court did not spell it out, is that the medical termination of pregnancy is *prima facie* a service within the meaning of Community law. The Court then went on:

> SPUC, however, maintains that the provision of abortion cannot be regarded as being a service, on the grounds that it is grossly immoral and involves the destruction of the life of a human being, namely the unborn child.
>
> Whatever the merits of those arguments on the moral plane, they cannot influence the answer to the national court's first question. It is not for the Court to substitute its assessment for that of the legislature in those Member States where the activities in question are practised legally.
>
> Consequently, the answer to the national court's first question must be that medical termination of pregnancy, performed in accordance with the law of the State in which it is carried out, constitutes a service within the meaning of Article 60 of the Treaty.[3]

Thus, although the medical termination of pregnancy is *prima facie* a service for the purposes of the *EEC Treaty*, a Member State retains a discretion legally to restrict or proscribe it. In that event, the medical termination of pregnancy is not to be regarded as a service for the purposes of the *EEC Treaty* to the extent that it is legally restricted

[1]Joined Cases 286/82 and 26/83 [1984] ECR 377.

[2]Case C-159/90 *Society for the Protection of Unborn Children Ireland Ltd v Grogan* [1991] ECR I-4685 at p I-4739, paragraph 18 of the Court's judgment. Advocate General Van Gerven also pointed out that Article 57(3), to which Article 66 refers, expressly mentions the medical and allied professions (at p I-4708).

[3]ibid at p I-4739, paragraphs 19-21 of the Court's judgment.

or proscribed by a Member State. Consequently there is no uniform Community rule concerning the circumstances in which the medical termination of pregnancy is to be regarded as an Article 60 service. On the contrary, the Member States may, in their legislative discretion, erect widely differing legal régimes governing the provision of such terminations with the consequence that a termination provided in Member State A, and regarded by Community law as a service within the meaning of Article 60, might not be so regarded if performed in Member State B.[1]

Although neither the Court nor the Advocate General, whose opinion the Court substantially accepted, specify why the Member States retain such a discretion in the area of abortion, it is implicit in their reasoning that abortion is a matter of moral judgment and public policy for each Member State to regulate for itself according to law.[2]

In this connection it is significant that neither the Court in its judgment, nor the Advocate General in his opinion, relied on Article 56(1) in answering the question put by the Irish court. Article 56(1), applied through Article 66, permits Member States to provide for "special treatment of foreign nationals on grounds of public policy, public security or public health" in the field of freedom to provide services. The Article says nothing about whether a service, *prima facie* falling within the scope of Article 60, is always to be regarded as a service at all for the purposes of the *EEC Treaty.*

In order to permit Member States to exclude certain services from the scope of Article 60 on moral grounds, as distinct from derogating from the freedom to provide services on the grounds of public morality, it is necessary to imply into the Treaty certain powers reserved to the Member States on matters affecting public policy or public morality. This is effectively, if not expressly, what the Court of Justice did in *Grogan.*[3]

[1]Cf Case C-275/92 *Her Majesty's Customs and Excise v Schindler* [1994] ECR I-1039 at p I-1090, paragraph 32 of the judgment, in which the Court of Justice adopted a similar approach to the question of whether lotteries, the morality of which "is at least questionable", attracted the protection afforded by Article 59 of the *EEC Treaty.*

[2]The requirement that the Member State seeking to remove a service from the scope of Article 60 should actually make the service unlawful is consistent with the approach taken by the Court of Justice in ascertaining whether public policy exceptions to the free movement of persons under Articles 48, 52 and 59 are justified. In Joined Cases 115 and 116/81 *Adoui and Cornuaille v Belgian State* [1982] ECR 1665, the Court of Justice said that such restrictions on the grounds of public policy can only be justified where "repressive measures or other genuine and effective measures intended to combat" the undesired activities of the foreign national have been adopted in respect of the same conduct engaged in by the Member State's own nationals; at p 1708, paragraph 9 of the Court's judgment. The fact that a Member State combats an activity by resort to penal measures is not of itself, however, sufficient to justify restricting a fundamental Community freedom on public policy grounds; Case 16/83 *Prantl* [1984] ECR 1299 at p 1329, paragraph 33 of the Court's judgment (a case involving Article 36 of the *EEC Treaty*).

[3]The judgment of the Court of Justice in *Grogan* is dated 4 October 1991. On 7 March 1991 the European Commission of Human Rights delivered its report in *Open Door Counselling Ltd v Ireland,* App Nos 14234 & 14235/88, (1992) 14 EHRR 131, in which it declared admissible complaints that Irish Supreme Court injunctions restraining the distribution in Ireland of information about commercial abortion services in the United Kingdom constituted breaches of Articles 8 (right to private and family life), 10 (freedom of expression) and 14 (principle of non-discrimination) of the *ECHR.* As in *Grogan,* the persons injuncted had no commercial links with the providers of the services. The European Court of Human Rights gave its

A RESIDUAL CONSTITUTIONAL POWER?

The fact that a power is retained by the Member States does not, however, necessarily imply that it is reserved to them. It is certainly the case that in *Re Immigration Policy* the Court of Justice said that issues of public policy, public security and public health arising from migration into the Community by non-Community nationals remain the Member States' "sole responsibility".[1] This exclusive reservation of power to the Member States exists, however, in an area where the Community's competence is limited to the promotion of "close co-operation between the Member States in the social field".[2] The Member States' exclusive reserve power to limit, on public policy grounds, migration into the Community by non-Community nationals exists therefore in a field which is not the subject of rights conferred on individuals by Community law.

---

judgment on 29 October 1992 (*Open Door Counselling Ltd v Ireland*, Series A No 246, (1993) 15 EHRR 244) in which it held that the injunction violated Article 10 of the *ECHR* because it was disproportionate to the legitimate aim pursued ((1993) 15 EHRR 244 at p 268, paragraph 80 of the Court's judgment). The legitimate aim was the protection of "profound moral values concerning the nature of life" ((1993) 15 EHRR 244 at p 263, paragraph 63 of the Court's judgment). It is unlikely, however, that these developments in Strasbourg would make any difference to the outcome in Luxembourg were the issues in *Grogan* to be reventilated there. Although the Court of Justice has now frequently referred to the *ECHR* in formulating Community principles of fundamental freedoms (eg: Case 36/75 *Rutili v Minister for the Interior* [1975] ECR 1219; Case 130/75 *Prais v Council* [1975] ECR 1589; Case 44/79 *Hauer v Land Rheinland-Pfalz* [1979] ECR 3727; Case 136/79 *National Panasonic (UK) Ltd v Commission* [1980] ECR 2033; Joined Cases 50-58/82 *Administrateur des Affaires Maritimes, Bayonne v Dorca Marina* [1982] ECR 3949; Case 63/83 *R v Kirk* [1984] ECR 2689; Joined Cases 60 and 61/84 *Cinéthèque SA v Fédération nationale des cinémas français* [1985] ECR 2605; Case 222/84 *Johnston v Chief Constable of the Royal Ulster Constabulary* [1986] ECR 1651; Case 222/86 *Union nationale des entraîneurs et Cadres techniques professionnels du football (Unectef) v Heylens* [1987] ECR 4097; Case 12/86 *Demirel v Stadt Schwäbisch Gmünd* [1988] ECR 3719; Case C-260/89 *Elliniki Radiophonia Tileorassi AE v Pliroforissis* [1991] ECR I-2925; Case C-159/90 *Society for the Protection of Unborn Children Ireland Ltd (SPUC) v Grogan* [1991] ECR I-4685), on no occasion has the Court of Justice relied on a judgment of the Court of Human Rights in interpreting it. This would appear to reflect a desire by the Court of Justice to preserve Community law as an instrument of European integration, which objective could be jeopardised by permitting a non-Community institution influence over the development of an important bundle of Community general legal principles (for a critique of the Court of Justice's alleged functional approach to fundamental freedoms, see Jason Coppell and Aidan O'Neill, "*The European Court of Justice: Taking Rights Seriously?*", [1992] 29 CML Rev 669). In any event, in Joined Cases 60 and 61/84 *Cinéthèque SA v Fédération nationale des cinémas français* [1985] ECR 2605 at p 2627, paragraph 26 of the Court's judgment, the Court of Justice emphasised that it has no power to examine national measures for compatibility with Community fundamental freedoms when the national measures concern "an area which falls within the jurisdiction of the national legislator" (this approach has been most recently reaffirmed in Case C-260/89 *Elliniki Radiophonia Tileorassi AE v Pliroforissis* [1991] ECR I-2925 at p I-2964, paragraph 42 of the Court's judgment, where the phrase "national rules which do not fall within the scope of Community law" was used). On the basis of the Court's reasoning in *Grogan* Ireland is entitled to place, and has placed, the provision and receipt of abortion services outside the scope of the Community law on freedom of services. Accordingly, even if Ireland's national measures concerning persons seeking to disseminate information about United Kingdom abortion services are contrary to the *ECHR*, the compatibility of those national measures with the requirements of Community law does not arise for consideration by the Court of Justice while the Court continues to hold that Ireland has effectively removed abortion services from the scope of Community law.

[1] Joined Cases 281, 283, 285 and 287/85 *Germany, France, Netherlands, Denmark and United Kingdom v Commission* ("*Re Immigration Policy*") [1987] ECR 3203 at p 3253, paragraph 25 of the Court's judgment.

[2] Article 118 of the *EC Treaty*.

In fields covered by Community provisions conferring rights on individuals, any public policy powers retained by the Member States are not exclusive and are circumscribed by standards imposed by Community law. Because of the non-exclusive nature of any such Member States' power, and because the expression 'reserve constitutional power' implies the existence of an exclusive power of the Member States, it may be more illuminating to use an expression such as 'residual constitutional power' when describing the possible existence of the Member States' power to derogate from rights conferred on individuals by Community law.

In *Simmenthal SpA v Italian Minister for Finance*[1] the Court of Justice considered, *inter alia*, whether the public health proviso in Article 36 of the Treaty justified Italy in maintaining a system of veterinary checks, and compulsory charges for such checks, on meat imported from other Member States in derogation of the Community provisions on the free movement of goods.

Italy argued that the enactment by the Community of detailed rules concerning the common market for various meat products did not diminish its power, recognised by Article 36 and by the Treaty generally, to take additional regulatory measures in the interests of public health.[2] The Court rejected this submission:

> Article 36 is not designed to reserve certain matters to the *exclusive* jurisdiction of Member States but permits national laws to derogate from the principle of the free movement of goods to the extent to which such derogation is and continues to be justified for the attainment of the objectives referred to in that article.[3]

The limitations on the free movement of goods permitted by Article 36 are themselves limited by virtue of being exceptions to a fundamental Community freedom.[4] This restricted construction on Article 36 was followed up in *Commission v Germany* ("*Re Meat Preparations*")[5] in which the Court of Justice observed:

> Since the restrictive measures authorized by Article 36 derogate from the fundamental principle of the free movement of goods, they are in accordance with the Treaty only in so far as they are "justified", that is

[1]Case 35/76 [1976] ECR 1871.

[2]ibid at p 1882.

[3]ibid at p 1886, paragraph 14 of the Court's judgment (emphasis added). See also Case 5/77 *Tedeschi v Denkavit Commerciale srl* [1977] ECR 1555 at p 1576, paragraph 34 of the Court's judgment; Case 251/78 *Firma Denkavit Futtermittel GmbH v Minister für Ernährung, Landwirtschaft und Forsten des Landes Nordrhein-Westfalen* [1979] ECR 3369 at p 3388, paragraph 14 of the Court's judgment; Case 72/83 *Campus Oil Limited v Minister for Industry and Energy* [1984] ECR 2727 at p 2751, paragraph 32 of the Court's judgment.

[4]Case 13/78 *Joh. Eggers Sohn & Co v Freie Hansestadt Bremen* [1978] ECR 1935 at p 1956, paragraph 30 of the Court's judgment.

[5]Case 153/78 [1979] ECR 2555.

> to say, necessary, in order, in this case, to ensure the protection of human health and life.[1]

Any measures adopted by Member States in reliance on Article 36 must not, therefore, go further than is necessary to meet the objectives permitted by that provision. In other words, Article 36 must be strictly construed[2] and any measures taken pursuant to it must be proportionate to the Article 36 objective sought to be achieved.[3]

The Member States' power to take unilateral measures on public policy grounds may, moreover, be circumscribed or removed by the enactment of Community measures[4] regulating or harmonising the protection of the Member States' protected interests thereby removing the Member States' justification for relying on Article 36.[5] Because the free movement of goods is a fundamental Community freedom granted by the Treaty, secondary Community legislation cannot extend Member States' powers to derogate from the freedom on grounds which are not authorised by Article 36.[6]

Furthermore, although each Member State is in principle free "to determine in accordance with its own scale of values and in the form selected by it the requirements of public morality in its territory",[7] this power must not be employed in such a way as to "constitute a means of arbitrary discrimination or a disguised restriction on trade between the Member States".[8] Therefore "the fact that goods cause offence cannot be regarded as sufficiently serious to justify restrictions on the free movement of goods where the Member State concerned does not adopt, with respect to the same goods manufactured or marketed within its own territory, penal measures or other serious and effective measures intended to prevent the distribution of such goods in its territory".[9]

[1]ibid at p 2564, paragraph 5 of the Court's judgment.

[2]More especially see eg Case 7/68 *Commission v Italy ("Re Export of Art Treasures")* [1968] ECR 423 at p 431; Case 46/76 *Bauhuis v The Netherlands State* [1977] ECR 5 at p 15, paragraph 12 of the Court's judgment.

[3]More especially see eg Case 7/68 *Commission v Italy ("Re Export of Art Treasures")* [1968] ECR 423 at p 431; Case 104/75 *de Peijper* [1976] ECR 613 at 636, paragraph 17 of the Court's judgment; Case 124/81 *Commission v United Kingdom ("Re UHT Milk")* [1983] ECR 203 at p 236, paragraph 16 of the Court's judgment; Case 42/82 *Commission v France ("Re Italian Wine Imports")* [1983] ECR 1013 at p 1047, paragraph 54 of the Court's judgment; Case 261/85 *Commission v United Kingdom ("Re Import Ban on Pasteurised Milk and Cream")* [1988] ECR 547 at p 574, paragraph 12 of the Court's judgment.

[4]eg, directives adopted under Articles 100 or 100a or systems of common organisation of particular markets.

[5]eg, Case 35/76 *Simmenthal SpA v Italian Minister for Finance* [1976] ECR 1871; Case 5/77 *Tedeschi v Denkavit Commerciale srl* [1977] ECR 1555 at pp 1576-1577, paragraph 35 of the Court's judgment; Case 251/78 *Firma Denkavit Futtermittel GmbH v Minister für Ernährung, Landwirtschaft und Forsten des Landes Nordrhein-Westfalen* [1979] ECR 3369 at pp 3388-3389, paragraph 14 of the Court's judgment.

[6]Joined Cases 80 and 81/77 *Société Les Commissionnaires Réunis Sàrl and Sàrl Les Fils de Henri Ramel v Receveur des Douanes* [1978] ECR 927.

[7]Case 34/79 *R v Henn and Darby* [1979] ECR 3795 at p 3813, paragraph 15 of the Court's judgment. This formulation was repeated in Case 121/85 *Conegate Limited v HM Customs and Excise* [1986] ECR 1007 at p 1022, paragraph 14 of the Court's judgment. See also Case C-23/89 *Quietlynn Ltd v Southend Borough Council* [1990] ECR I-3059 at p I-3075, paragraph 29 of the opinion of Advocate General Lenz.

[8]Article 36, second sentence, of the *EC Treaty*.

[9]Case 121/85 *Conegate Limited v HM Customs and Excise* [1986] ECR 1007 at p 1022, paragraph 15 of the Court's judgment.

Virtually identical considerations apply in the field of the freedom of movement conferred on persons under Articles 48, 52 and 59 of the *EC Treaty*. In *Adoui and Cornuaille v Belgian State*[1] the Belgian authorities refused to issue residence permits to two French nationals suspected of being prostitutes. Belgian law did not prohibit prostitution as such although it did make unlawful certain related activities such as soliciting, incitement to debauchery, exploitation of prostitution, the keeping of a disorderly house or brothel and living on immoral earnings. In considering the availability to the Belgian authorities of the public policy provisos in Articles 48(3) and 56(2) of the *EEC Treaty* , the Court of Justice said:

> Although Community law does not impose upon the Member States a uniform scale of values as regards the assessment of conduct which may be considered as contrary to public policy, it should nevertheless be stated that conduct may not be considered as being of a sufficiently serious nature to justify restrictions on the admission to or residence within the territory of a Member State of a national of another Member State in a case where the former Member State does not adopt, with respect to the same conduct on the part of its own nationals repressive measures or other genuine and effective measures intended to combat such conduct.[2]

The Member States are therefore unable to invoke the public policy exceptions in a way which discriminates against nationals of other Member States, thereby ensuring that the fundamental principle against discrimination contained in Article 6 of the *EC Treaty* is observed. Nor are the Member States able to invoke the public policy provisos in order to service economic ends.[3]

It is therefore arguable that the competence of the Member States to limit movement and residence rights on the grounds of public policy, public security and public health is in the nature of a residual constitutional power. This is not to say that the Member States may use any such power in such a way as to impose conditions precedent on the Union citizen's right to move and reside. Rather the power would merely bestow on Member States the opportunity, in individual cases, to impose limitations and conditions on the Union citizen's movement and residence rights where such

[1]Joined cases 115 and 116/81 [1982] ECR 1665.

[2]ibid at p 1708, paragraph 8 of the Court's judgment.

[3]In the case of the free movement of persons:- Article 2(2) of *Directive 64/221*. In the case of the free movement of goods:- Case 7/61 *Commission v Italy* ("*Re Ban on Pigmeat Imports*") [1961] ECR 317 at p 329; reiterated in Case 95/81 *Commission v Italy* ("*Re Advance Payments for Imports*") [1982] ECR 2187 at p 2204, paragraph 27 of the Court's judgment; Case 238/82 *Duphar BV v Netherlands State* [1984] ECR 523 at p 542, paragraph 23 of the Court's judgment; Case 72/83 *Campus Oil Limited v Minister for Industry and Energy* [1984] ECR 2727 at p 2752, paragraph 35 of the Court's judgment; Case 288/83 *Commission v Ireland* ("*Re Potato Imports*") [1985] ECR 1761 at p 1776, paragraph 28 of the Court's judgment.

limitations and conditions are justified on the grounds of public policy, public security and public health.[1]

The insertion of the new Article 100c into the *EC Treaty*, requiring the Council to determine the third countries whose nationals must possess a visa when crossing the Community's external borders, would not prejudice the existence of any residual power of the Member States to limit movement and residence rights on the grounds of public policy, public security and public health. On the contrary, the proposition that there exists such a residual power is reinforced by reference to Article 100c(5) which provides as follows:

> This Article shall be without prejudice to the existence of the responsibilities incumbent upon the Member States with regard to the maintenance of law and order and the safeguarding of internal security.

Even without Article 100c(5) there is nothing in Article 100c which would prejudice the power of Member States to refuse entry to any non-Community national, including those in possession of Community visas, in accordance with their own internal procedures on grounds including, but not limited to, public policy, public security and public health as those terms are understood in Community law. This is because Article 100c does not confer on nationals of non-Community countries any right to enter the territory of the Member States.

Although all the detailed rules for the exercise of the Member States' power in the field of public policy as laid down in *Directive 64/221* would not necessarily apply, any exercise of the Member States' possible residual power would need to conform to the general principles of law which the Court of Justice protects.

In particular the Court of Justice has said that Articles 2(2) and 3 of *Directive 64/221*[2] and Article 8 of *Regulation 1612/68*;[3]

[1]Case 157/79 *R v Pieck* [1980] ECR 2171. This case dealt with the limitations contained in Article 48(3) of the *EEC Treaty*. If, however, this aspect of Article 48(3) is merely an expression of a constitutional principle inherent in the structure of the treaties themselves, the case is useful in understanding the limitations and conditions applicable to the exercise of rights under Article 8a of the *EC Treaty*.

[2]Articles 2 and 3 of *Directive 64/221* provide as follows:

> 2. (1). This Directive relates to all measures concerning entry into their territory, issue or renewal of residence permits, or expulsion from their territory, taken by Member States on grounds of public policy, public security or public health.
> (2). Such grounds shall not be invoked to service economic ends.
> 3. (1). Measures taken on grounds of public policy or of public security shall be based exclusively on the personal conduct of the individual concerned.
> (2). Previous criminal convictions shall not in themselves constitute grounds for the taking of such measures.
> (3). Expiry of the identity card or passport used by the person concerned to enter the host country and to obtain a residence permit shall not justify expulsion from the territory.
> (4) The State which issued the identity card or passport shall allow the holder of such document to re-enter its territory without any formality even if the document is no longer valid or the nationality of the holder is in dispute.

[3]Article 8 of *Regulation 1612/68* provides as follows:

> ... are a specific manifestation of the more general principle, enshrined in Articles 8, 9, 10, and 11 of the Convention for the Protection of Human Rights and Fundamental Freedoms ... and in Article 2 of Protocol 4 of the same Convention, ... which provide, in identical terms, that no restrictions in the interests of national security or public safety shall be placed on the rights secured by the above-quoted articles other than such as are necessary for the protection of those interests 'in a democratic society'.[1]

It seems, therefore, that the provisions referred to in *Directive 64/221* and *Regulation 1612/68* would apply as general principles of Community law regardless of whether they also applied *qua* Community legislation. Accordingly, they would apply to the Member States in exercising any residual power they might possess under the *EC Treaty* to exclude Union citizens seeking to exercise their Article 8a movement and residence rights.[2]

Johnston v Chief Constable: Residual Power Repudiated?

The decision of the Court of Justice in *Johnston v Chief Constable of the Royal Ulster Constabulary*,[3] however, casts doubt upon the existence of any residual constitutional power on the part of Member States to derogate from the Union citizen's fundamental right to move and reside freely.

By 1980 Ms Johnston had for six years been a full-time member of the Royal Ulster Constabulary ("RUC") Reserve when the Chief Constable decided not to renew her contract for full-time duties. She was thereafter placed on part-time duties with a proportionately reduced salary.

There was no suggestion by the Chief Constable that Ms Johnston's performance in the RUC Reserve was unsatisfactory. Rather, the Chief Constable took the view that there was already a sufficient number of women officers available for the duties normally assigned to women. This assessment in turn followed an earlier decision to

---

> **8.** (1) A worker who is a national of a Member State and who is employed in the territory of another Member State shall enjoy equality of treatment as regards membership of trade unions and the exercise of rights attaching thereto, including the right to vote and to be eligible for the administration and management posts of a trade union; he may be excluded from taking part in the management of bodies governed by public law and from holding an office governed by public law. Furthermore, he shall have the right of eligibility for workers' representative bodies in the undertaking.
> (2). The provisions of this Article shall not affect laws or regulations in certain Member States which grant more extensive rights to workers coming from other Member States.

[1] Case 36/75 *Rutili v Minister for the Interior* [1975] ECR 1219 at p 1232, paragraph 32 of the Court's judgment.

[2] Article 8 of *Regulation 1612/68* would not, however, be applicable to persons exercising movement rights under only Article 8a of the *EC Treaty*. The former provision confers certain rights on persons who are employed in a host Member State; any such person would be covered by Article 48 of the *EC Treaty* rather than Article 8a.

[3] Case 222/84 [1986] ECR 1651.

restrict duties involving the use of fire-arms to male officers, thereby reducing the range of duties available to female officers. The Chief Constable was concerned to minimise the risk to female officers arising from the long-running campaign of terrorist attacks against RUC officers in Northern Ireland. This concern manifested itself in a policy of confining women officers to duties where fire-arms were not used. Concern was also expressed by the Chief Constable that the carrying of fire-arms by women officers reduced their effectiveness in areas for which women officers were said to be better suited, such as dealing with families and children. He also took the view that permitting female officers to be armed would constitute a greater departure from the British public's ideal of an unarmed police force.[1]

Acting under Article 235 of the *EEC Treaty*, the Council had adopted *Directive 76/207* ("*Equal Treatment Directive*") providing detailed rules for the implementation of the principle of equal treatment for men and women as regards access to employment, vocational training and promotion, and working conditions.[2]

Article 2(2) of the *Equal Treatment Directive* provides as follows:

> This Directive shall be without prejudice to the right of Member States to exclude from its field of application those occupational activities and, where appropriate, the training leading thereto, for which, by reason of their nature or the context in which they are carried out, the sex of the worker constitutes a determining factor.

The national legislation implementing the *Equal Treatment Directive* in Northern Ireland[3] expressly excluded acts done for the purpose of safeguarding national security or of protecting public safety or public order.[4]

Ms Johnston commenced proceedings in the Northern Ireland Industrial Tribunal challenging the Chief Constable's decisions not to renew her full-time contract and not to give her training in the use of fire-arms. In the course of these proceedings, the Industrial Tribunal referred several questions to the Court of Justice under Article 177 of the Treaty. Included among these was a question asking whether, independently of the meaning to be ascribed to Article 2(2), the Member States are entitled to exclude from the application of the *Equal Treatment Directive* acts of sex discrimination as regards access to employment done for the purpose of safeguarding national security or of protecting public safety or public order.

[1]ibid at p 1665.
[2]The *Equal Treatment Directive* possesses a different material scope from Article 119 of the *EEC Treaty*, which Article provides merely for "the principle that men and women should receive equal pay for equal work". Moreover, Article 119 does not authorise a procedure for the enactment of secondary legislation.
[3]*Sex Discrimination (Northern Ireland) Order 1976* (SI 1976 No 1042 (NI 15)).
[4]ibid, Article 53.

Before the Court of Justice the United Kingdom submitted[1] that the *Equal Treatment Directive* is in principle inapplicable to action taken by the Member States for the purpose of safeguarding national security or for protecting public safety or public order and the Member States are free to exclude such matters from the scope of their legislation on equal treatment. The *EEC Treaty* was said to leave intact the Member States' power to take such measures as they consider necessary or expedient for the protection of the interests referred to. The Court was invited to draw this conclusion from the 'safeguard' clauses in Articles 36, 48, 56, 66, 223 and 224 of the *EEC Treaty*.

It was further submitted by the United Kingdom that the *Equal Treatment Directive* could not be interpreted so as to restrict a power of the Member States which the *EEC Treaty* itself left in place. Accordingly, when confronted by a situation such as that prevailing in Northern Ireland, Member States were said to be free to exclude from their legislation on the implementation of the principle of equal treatment of men and women acts of the kind done by the Chief Constable. The United Kingdom thus advocated the retention of an exclusive reserve power by the Member States in the field of public policy.

The Commission took the view[2] that Article 224 provided the necessary authority for Member States to derogate from the rules established by the *Equal Treatment Directive* on the grounds invoked by the United Kingdom. It was also of the view that, in principle, the situation confronting the national authorities in Northern Ireland at the relevant time justified the application of Article 224. Nothing in Article 224, however, supported the United Kingdom's assertion that the Member States were entitled to do whatever they consider necessary or expedient for the safeguarding of national security or for protecting public safety or public order. Rather, as the "parallel" provisions of Articles 36 and 48(3) of the *EEC Treaty* demonstrated, the discretion afforded to the Member States by Article 224 was subject to judicial supervision both as to the existence of the threat alleged by the Member States and as to the conformity with general principles of Community law, such as proportionality, of the measures adopted by the Member States in response to the alleged threat. The Commission was essentially advocating the existence of a residual constitutional power vested in the Member States for the protection of their public security interests.

Advocate General Darmon[3] thought that the principle of access to effective judicial supervision of measures taken in derogation of Community rights was a general principle of Community law deriving from the fundamental proposition that, "[f]ormed of States based on the rule of law, the European Community is necessarily a Community of law".[4]

[1]Case 222/84 *Johnston v Chief Constable of the Royal Ulster Constabulary* [1986] ECR 1651 at p 1671.
[2]ibid at pp 1674-1675.
[3]ibid esp at pp 1656-1659.
[4]ibid at p 1656.

The Advocate General found it unnecessary expressly to consider the question as to whether there existed in the scheme of the Treaty, and in particular Article 224, a general residual power, possessed by the Member States, entitling them to derogate from the rights detailed in the *Equal Treatment Directive*. This approach was a result of the view that Article 2(2) of the directive enabled the United Kingdom to treat women RUC officers less favourably than their male counterparts on the grounds of public order if the national court could be satisfied that women were more exposed to danger than men in carrying out armed police duties or if the employment of women in such activities could create a greater danger to public order.

Nevertheless, the Advocate General's opinion is premised on the assumption that Member States may take action in derogation of Community rights on grounds of public order. Article 2(2) of the *Equal Treatment Directive* makes no express mention of public order as one of the factors to be taken into consideration in ascertaining whether the nature of a particular type of work or the context in which it is carried out justifies its exclusion from the scope of the directive, yet the Advocate General thought that Article 2(2) justified such derogations.

In discussing the individual's right of access to judicial review of Member States' measures taken in derogation of Community rights, the Advocate General said:

> Although the principle of legality is the cornerstone of the rule of law, it does not exclude consideration of the demands of public order. Indeed, they must be accommodated in order to ensure the survival of the State, whilst at the same time arbitrary action must be prevented. Review by the courts is a fundamental safeguard against such action: the right to challenge a measure before the courts is inherent in the rule of law. ...
>
> Consequently, and subject to review by the courts, the Community legal order expressly incorporates the concept of public order so as to reconcile the proper functioning of the common market with the necessity for the Member States to cope with emergencies which threaten their vital interests.[1]

The Advocate General further remarked that Articles 36, 48 and 224 of the Treaty provided an "illustration" of his analysis.[2]

For the Advocate General, then, Community law necessarily accommodates the Member States' power to take action in derogation of Community rights on public policy grounds if their "vital interests" are threatened. This power derives from the view that the European Community is a community of law composed of States based on the rule of law, that the rule of law can be upheld only through the agency of such

[1] ibid.
[2] ibid.

States, and that States must not be deprived of their ability to combat threats to their survival and, by extension, threats to the survival of the rule of law. Subject to the fundamental principle of Community law ensuring access to judicial supervision in case of derogation by Member States from Community rights, Article 2(2) of the *Equal Treatment Directive* must necessarily be interpreted so as to accommodate the Member States' power to take steps preserving their survival.

Although, according to the Advocate General's opinion, the existence of Article 2(2) made it strictly unnecessary to consider the broader question as to whether the Treaty permits derogations from Community rights on public policy grounds in other contexts, the inescapable implication to be drawn from his line of reasoning is that such derogations are possible, at least when a Member State is confronted with emergencies threatening its vital interests or its survival.

On the closely related question as to whether such a power of derogation is reserved exclusively to the Member States or is held in residue by them until the Community regulates the field with its own rules, it is less easy to divine the Advocate General's view. His insistence however that any such derogation must be subject to judicial supervision and other fundamental principles of Community law, combined with his reliance on Articles 36 and 48 of the Treaty as 'illustrations' of his analysis, suggest that he regarded the Member States as possessing merely a residual power.

The Court of Justice did not, however, embrace any of the relatively broad visions of the Member States' power to derogate from Community rights on public policy grounds advanced by the United Kingdom, the Commission or the Advocate General. Instead, it responded to their views in the following terms:

> It must be observed ... that the only articles in which the Treaty provides for derogations applicable in situations which may involve public safety are Articles 36, 48, 56, 223 and 224 which deal with exceptional and clearly defined cases. Because of their limited character those articles do not lend themselves to a wide interpretation and it is not possible to infer from them that there is inherently in the Treaty a general proviso covering all measures taken for reasons of public safety. If every provision of Community law were held to be subject to a general proviso, regardless of the specific requirements laid down by the provisions of the Treaty, this might impair the binding nature of Community law and its uniform application.[1]

It followed, the Court said, that the Chief Constable's actions must be examined against the exceptional provisions of the *Equal Treatment Directive* in order to determine whether they could be justified on the grounds advanced by the United Kingdom.

[1]ibid at p 1684, paragraph 26 of the Court's judgment.

In conducting this examination, the Court noted that there was nothing in the "nature" of armed police duties which would justify the exclusion of women from performing them. Consequently in order for the Chief Constable to succeed it must be shown, in light of the wording of Article 2(2), that his actions were justified having regard to the "context" in which the duties of armed police officers were carried out in Northern Ireland. The context in which the relevant duties were to be carried out was determined by the environment in which they were to be carried out. In this regard, the Court said,

> ... the possibility cannot be excluded that in a situation characterized by serious internal disturbances the carrying of fire-arms by policewomen might create additional risks of their being assassinated and might therefore be contrary to the requirements of public safety.[1]

Furthermore, in determining the scope of any derogation made on grounds justified by Article 2(2) observance must be made of the principle of proportionality. In this connection the Court said:

> That principle requires that derogations remain within the limits of what is appropriate and requires the principle of equal treatment to be reconciled as far as possible with the requirements of public safety which constitutes the decisive factor as regards the context of the activity in question.[2]

Having thus defined the approach to be taken, the Court of Justice left to the Industrial Tribunal the task of deciding whether, on the facts before it, the Chief Constable's actions were justified under Article 2(2) of the *Equal Treatment Directive*.

Hence the Court of Justice appears to have resolved in the negative the question of whether there exists a reserve or residual constitutional power vested in the Member States by which they may derogate from Community rights on public policy grounds. This is done because the 'safeguard' clauses in Articles 36, 48, 56, 223 and 224 are exceptions to fundamental Community rights which exceptions must be narrowly construed, and that to hold otherwise would be to jeopardise the binding nature of Community law and its uniform application.

Yet there are at least three problems with this resolution of the question.

Firstly, the binding nature and uniform application of Community law would not necessarily be jeopardised by recognising the existence of a residual, as distinct from a reserve, constitutional power of the sort contended for in *Johnston*. As the jurisprudence concerning Article 36 of the Treaty demonstrates, any lack of uniformity caused by differences between national approaches to the limitation of Community

[1]ibid at pp 1686-1687, paragraph 36 of the Court's judgment.
[2]ibid at p 1687, paragraph 38 of the Court's judgment.

rights on public policy grounds can be avoided by the subsequent enactment of uniform Community measures.

Furthermore any deleterious effects on the proper functioning of the common market caused by variations among national measures in consequence of the exercise of a residual power to protect public policy would be substantially limited by judicial supervision. Indeed, in *Johnston* itself the Court of Justice ruled that any derogations from Community rights must be subject to judicial supervision and conform to the numerous general principles of Community law which the Court upholds.

Secondly, there is a fissure between what the Court said in *Johnston* and what it actually did. While it explicitly rejected the existence of a "general proviso covering all measures taken for reasons of public safety", it nevertheless resorted to the concept of public safety as being applicable to the "environment" in which RUC officers performed their work. This was so notwithstanding that the *Equal Treatment Directive* makes no reference to the concept of public safety. The Court nevertheless imported considerations of public safety into its interpretation of the *Equal Treatment Directive*.

The source of this importation is a principle which all liberal legal systems require in order to function as such a legal system at all. The principle that proportionate and judicially reviewable steps, in derogation of some fundamental rights, may be taken when the continuance of democracy, the rule of law or the State itself is threatened is enshrined not only in the *ECHR* but in all the major multilateral treaties on fundamental freedoms.[1] In the Community legal order recognition of this right of self-preservation is, as we shall see, enshrined in Article 224 of the Treaty.

It is thus not surprising that the Court of Justice left the door open for the national tribunal to uphold the Chief Constable's measures while preserving the principle that any such measures must be judicially reviewable. The presence of Article 2(2) of the *Equal Treatment Directive* was convenient in that it permitted the possibility of sustaining the Chief Constable's contested measures without needing to consider in detail the applicability of Article 224 to those measures.

Had Article 2(2) not been present in the *Equal Treatment Directive* the Court of Justice would probably have accepted the Commission's submissions on the effect of Article 224 rather than give an answer which had the effect of obliging the national tribunal to disapply or invalidate the Chief Constable's policy. The national tribunal could still have been left to determine whether the criteria applicable under Article 224 as interpreted by the Court of Justice had been satisfied. This course would have avoided the dangers inherent in the Court of Justice destroying a plank in the United Kingdom's campaign against the serious terrorist situation in Northern Ireland;[2]

[1] In addition to Article 15 of the *ECHR*, see the functionally equivalent provisions in Article 4 of the United Nations *International Covenant on Civil and Political Rights* and Article 27 of the *American Convention on Human Rights*.

[2] In Case 318/86 *Commission v France* ("*Re French Prison and Police Services*") [1988] ECR 3559 at p 3566 the French government sought to justify discriminatory treatment against women in recruitment

dangers not only to the Court and the Community legal order, but also to the lives of female RUC officers.

The third problem is related to the second and concerns the way in which the *Johnston* Court resolved the question as to whether there exists a residual or reserve public policy power on the part of Member States without seriously considering the applicability of Article 224 of the *EEC Treaty,* and the extent to which that provision presupposes the ability of the Member States to derogate from Community rights in certain narrowly conceived circumstances involving emergency situations. This subject deserves separate attention.

Emergency Powers

Article 15(1) of the *ECHR* deals with the exceptional powers of States in emergency situations and provides as follows:

> In time of war or other public emergency threatening the life of the nation any High Contracting Party may take measures derogating from its obligations under this Convention to the extent strictly required by the exigencies of the situation, provided that such measures are not inconsistent with its other obligations under international law.[1]

Reference has already been made to the public policy exceptions which the *ECHR* system permits in respect of the rights contained in Protocol 4 Articles 2(1) (freedom of movement and residence) and 2(2) (freedom to leave any country) and *ECHR* Articles 8 (respect for private and family life, home and correspondence), 9 (freedom of thought, conscience and religion), 10 (freedom of expression), and 11 (freedom of assembly and association). All these provisions also make explicit reference to the taking of the exceptional measures by way of derogation from *ECHR* rights on various grounds, including public safety, where such measures are "necessary in a democratic society".

The thrust of the *ECHR* system of rights is the protection and strengthening of political democracy, the rule of law and civil society in the Contracting States. The

---

procedures to the national police force on the basis that the "tasks entrusted to the police are often very dangerous and require that police officers should always be able to deter troublemakers and resort to physical force" and that this made it "impossible for a large number of women to be appointed to the groups of posts that are responsible for maintaining order". Consequently, the discriminatory procedures were said to be necessitated by "considerations of public interest concerning the organization of the national police force and conditions for maintaining public order in France". France also pleaded that the incorporation of women into the active services of the police force "must be carried out gradually so as not to impair the proper performance of duties which serve public safety" (at p 3581, paragraph 22 of the Court's judgment). The Court of Justice accepted the French argument in principle but considered that Article 2(2) of the *Equal Treatment Directive* could not authorise the French recruitment procedures, those procedures not being susceptible to Commission supervision because they were not transparently for the purpose of excluding specific 'occupational activities' from the directive's rules.

[1] Article 15(2) goes on to exclude from the scope of Article 15(1) the rights contained in Article 2 (right to life, except in respect of deaths resulting from lawful acts of war), Article 3 (freedom from torture and inhuman or degrading treatment or punishment), Article 4(1) (freedom from slavery or servitude) and Article 7 (freedom from retroactive criminal sanction).

reference in Article 15(1) to the "life of the nation" should be construed not simply as a reference to the continuance of the State as a sovereign entity in international law, but also as a reference to the continuance of the *democratic* nation based on the rule of law and civil society.

The Community's closest functional counterpart of Article 15(1) of the *ECHR* is Article 224 of the *EC Treaty*, which provides as follows:

> Member States shall consult each other with a view to taking together the steps needed to prevent the functioning of the common market being affected by measures which a Member State may be called upon to take in the event of serious internal disturbance affecting the maintenance of law and order, in the event of war or serious international tension constituting a threat of war, or in order to carry out obligations it has accepted for the purpose of maintaining peace and international security.

The phrase "which a Member State may be called upon to take" suggests that Article 224 *presupposes* (as distinct from *confers)* the retention by the Member States of a power to take measures of an exceptional nature in derogation of Community rights in the three nominated situations. The Article merely provides for an intergovernmental procedure by which any adverse consequences for the functioning of the common market, caused by the exercise of a Member State's presupposed power, can be jointly overcome.

The obligation to consult other Member States is not imposed only on the Member State taking the exceptional action and is, furthermore, separate from the power to take the exceptional measures in derogation of Community rights. The non-observance of this obligation would not *per se* have the effect of rendering the delinquent Member State's exceptional measures inconsistent with the Treaty.[1] The purpose of such consultations is not to review the continuation or lawfulness of a Member State's emergency measures, but merely to take "together the steps needed to prevent the functioning of the common market being affected by" the exceptional measures. Moreover, the obligation to consult does not necessarily require a Member State to consult its partners before taking the exceptional measures, although the Member States' duty of co-operation would almost certainly require the institution of such consultations as soon as was practicable.

A procedure for challenging the lawfulness of measures taken by a Member State in purported pursuance of Article 224 is provided by Article 225 (second paragraph). The Commission or any Member State may bring directly to the Court of Justice any

[1]The following question was referred to the Court of Justice by the Northern Ireland Industrial Tribunal in Case 222/84 *Johnston v Chief Constable of the Royal Ulster Constabulary* [1986] ECR 1651 at p 1668: "... is it open to an individual to rely upon the fact that a Member State did not consult with other Member States for the purposes of preventing the first Member State from relying on Article 224 of the EEC Treaty". The Court did not find it necessary to answer the question.

matter involving an improper use of the powers provided for in Article 224. This procedure is by way of derogation from the provisions of Articles 169 and 170, and the Court of Justice is required to give its ruling *in camera.*

Whether a situation is sufficiently "serious" as to warrant exceptional measures within the meaning of Article 224 would appear, in the first place, to be a matter of judgment for the Member State concerned. However the Member States' discretion in this regard will be subject to judicial supervision. Such would appear to be the clear implication of Article 225 (second paragraph).

In responding to the Industrial Tribunal's question on the interpretation of Article 224 in *Johnston*, the Court of Justice expressly accepted that the situation in Northern Ireland was one characterised by "serious internal disturbances", but that nothing which had been put before the Court suggested that these disturbances would "make judicial review impossible or that measures needed to protect public safety would be deprived of their effectiveness because of such review by the national courts".[1] Thus, the Court of Justice appeared not to be content to leave to the unfettered discretion of the Member State either the question of the existence of a "serious internal disturbance" or the appropriateness of measures adopted to deal with it.

Furthermore it has been suggested that a national court may make a reference to the Court of Justice "on the impact of Article 224" when a national exceptional measure derogates from Community law.[2] Such a reference, designed to elicit a preliminary ruling concerning the interpretation of Article 224, would seem to be available on the basis of the wording of Article 177.[3]

Thus Article 224 of the *EC Treaty* acknowledges and provides for the existence of a residual power, on the part of the Member States, to take steps derogating from Community rights in the three exceptional situations nominated. The power is better classified as residual, rather than as reserved, for two reasons. Firstly, because of the duty of the Court of Justice and national courts to supervise the power's exercise both as to the existence of one of the three exceptional situations justifying resort to it and as to the appropriateness of the measures adopted in responding to the exceptional situations. Secondly, because Article 235 of the *EC Treaty* would authorise the Community to adopt legislation limiting the impact on the functioning of the common market of national measures adopted in reliance on Article 224.[4]

[1]Case 222/84 *Johnston v Chief Constable of the Royal Ulster Constabulary* [1986] ECR 1651 at p 1692, paragraph 60 of the Court's judgment.

[2]Hans Smit and Peter Herzog, *The Law of the European Economic Community*, 6-216.84.

[3]Indeed in Case 13/68 *SpA Salgoil v Italian Ministry for Foreign Trade* [1968] ECR 453 and in Case 222/84 *Johnston v Chief Constable of the Royal Ulster Constabulary* [1986] ECR 1651 the Court of Justice was asked for an interpretation of Article 224. In *Salgoil* the Court held that a consideration of Article 224 was unnecessary because the Article deals with exceptional cases which are clearly defined and the reference did not fall within any of the exceptional cases. The Court's approach to the reference in *Johnston* has already been mentioned. In neither reference did the Court decline jurisdiction to interpret Article 224.

[4]The only Council measure so far taken against the background of consultations between the Member States under Article 224 occurred in the context of the armed conflict in 1982 between the United

It therefore appears that there is a sphere of residual constitutional power within which the Member States may take measures derogating from rights conferred by Community law. But what is the material scope of that power and can its existence advance our hypothetical argument in favour of Article 8a(2) of the *EC Treaty*, construed narrowly so as to exclude the possibility that it may be used as a basis on which to enact limitations, as the appropriate legal basis for measures adopted under Article 8a(1)?

The three exceptional situations in which Article 224 presupposes the retention by the Member States of a power to derogate from rights conferred by Community law occur where there are (i) serious internal disturbances affecting the maintenance of law and order, (ii) war or serious international tensions constituting a threat of war, and (iii) international obligations undertaken for the maintenance of peace and international security. None of these expressions have yet been the subject of judicial interpretation. Their meanings are, however, reasonably clear.

An internal disturbance need not be of such a magnitude as to actually threaten the life of the nation, however the phrase "the life of the nation" is conceived under the *ECHR*. Provided the disturbance is "serious", it is sufficient that the maintenance of law and order is affected.

Thus it is highly unlikely that merely drunken and disorderly behaviour of the sort that had occurred in *Ministère public v Mutsch*[1] would warrant the taking of exceptional measures even though such behaviour affects the maintenance of law and order. Indeed it would be inappropriate for such an incident to give rise to intergovernmental consultations. Such consultations would be a mandatory consequence of relying on Article 224 as justification for taking exceptional action (eg, expulsion from a Member State's territory) against the perpetrator.

On the other hand expulsion by a Member State from its territory of Community nationals who have engaged in, for example, acts of terrorism or who were known sympathisers of terrorists would almost certainly fall within the ambit of Article 224.

Kingdom and Argentina concerning sovereignty over the Falkland Islands. *Regulation 877/82* (1982 OJ L 102/1), formally enacted under Article 113 after consultations among the Member States held under Article 224, suspended almost all imports from Argentina into the Community. The Regulation was extended several times before being repealed about five weeks after being first enacted (see generally, Geoffrey Edwards, *Europe and the Falkland Islands Crisis 1982*, (1983-84) 22 Journal of Common Market Studies 295). The terms of Article 224 do not, however, require that the steps which must be taken are to be in the form of Community legislation. This follows from the fact that the obligation to consult and take steps is placed on the Member States themselves, rather than on the Council as such. In the interests of responding consistently and coherently, however, Community action would in most conceivable cases be preferable.

[1]Case 137/84 [1985] ECR 2681. Mr Mutsch, a Luxembourg national resident and working in Belgium, had been occupied in a 'pub crawl' whereafter he clashed with members of the Belgian Gendarmerie. The dispute resulted in blows being exchanged and Mr Mutsch was subjected to Belgian criminal proceedings arising from the incident. The issue before the Court of Justice was whether Community law required that Mr Mutsch be treated on a basis of equality with Belgian nationals in determining, under Belgian law, the language in which the criminal proceedings were to be conducted.

Terrorist activity would almost certainly be regarded as a sufficiently serious internal disturbance affecting the maintenance of law and order. Moreover, intergovernmental consultations following the taking of exceptional action against such Community nationals would be most appropriate.[1]

The contrast between these two situations reflects the fact that Article 224 is principally about the protection of national or public security. This is evident not only from the terms of Article 224 itself, but also from the fact that Article 225 provides a common procedure for the supervision of steps taken under both Article 223 (permitted non-disclosure of national security information and permitted protection of national security interests in armaments) and Article 224.

The Court of Justice, it should be pointed out, appears to draw no clear distinction between the concepts of national security and public security.

In *SpA Salgoil v Italian Ministry for Foreign Trade*[2] the Court of Justice said that Articles 36 and 224 of the Treaty "attach particular importance to the interests of Member States"[3] without drawing any distinction between the public security proviso in Article 36 and the national security considerations in Article 224.[4]

The ambiguous nature of the Community law approach to questions of national security became more evident in *R v Thompson, Johnson and Woodiwiss*[5] where the Court of Justice upheld a British ban on the export of coins which had previously been legal tender in the United Kingdom. The ban constituted a derogation from Article 30 of the *EEC Treaty*, but was justified under the terms of Article 36 "because it stems from the need to protect the right to mint coinage which is traditionally regarded as involving the fundamental interests of the State".[6]

In *Campus Oil Limited v Minister for Industry and Energy*[7] Ireland invoked the public policy and public security provisos in Article 36 in justification of its requirement, in derogation of Article 30 of the *EEC Treaty*, that persons marketing petroleum in Ireland buy a fixed proportion of their product from the State owned refinery. Ireland

[1] Particularly as regards any Member States into whose territory the persons are expelled! The consultations under Article 224 would need to focus, however, only on taking together the steps necessary to prevent the functioning of the common market. It is unlikely that the expulsion of people who are not engaged in economic activity within the scope of Articles 48-66 of the *EC Treaty* would adversely affect the functioning of the common market. Of course if the terrorist and his sympathisers were workers, establishees or involved in the supply or consumption of services, they could be expelled under the public security exceptions expressly applicable to Union citizens engaged in those economic activities.

[2] Case 13/68 [1968] ECR 453.

[3] Ibid at p 463.

[4] Although the Court also refrained from drawing any distinction between the public policy and health protection provisos in Article 36 and the matters contained in Article 224, this may have been because the case was disposed of without needing to consider either Article in detail.

[5] Case 7/78 [1978] ECR 2247.

[6] ibid at p 2275, paragraph 34 of the Court's judgment. On this occasion it was the Article 36 public policy proviso which was invoked.

[7] Case 72/83 [1984] ECR 2727.

maintained that its absence of domestic oil supplies combined with its geographical position meant that considerations of public policy and public safety justified a system which ensured the continuing viability of the State's only oil refinery.

In accepting the main thrust of Ireland's submissions, the Court of Justice used language which displays the indeterminate nature of the Community law distinction between public security and national security:

> [P]etroleum products, because of their exceptional importance as an energy source in the modern economy, are of fundamental importance for a country's existence since not only its economy but above all its institutions, its essential public services and even the survival of its inhabitants depend upon them. An interruption of supplies of petroleum products, with the resultant dangers for the country's existence, could therefore seriously affect the public security that Article 36 allows States to protect.[1]

The unity of the concept of public security with notions of national security is further reinforced by the judgment of the Court of Justice in *Richardt*.[2]

Mr Richardt, a French national, had arranged for the export from France to the Soviet Union of a device for the manufacture of memory circuits for computers. The device was legally imported into the Community from the United States, and Mr Richardt possessed all necessary French clearances for its export to the Soviet Union. The Aeroflot flight, intended to convey the device from France to the Soviet Union, was cancelled. On its own initiative and without consulting Mr Richardt, Air France transported the device by road to Luxembourg for the purpose of having it transferred to a Soviet-bound flight from the Grand Duchy.

Customs officials in Luxembourg seized the device on the grounds that its export from Luxembourg to the Soviet Union required a special Luxembourg export licence. The licence was required pursuant to a Luxembourg regulation applicable to certain products originating in, *inter alia*, France or the United States and intended for export to, *inter alia*, the Soviet Union. The attempted unlicensed export of an item for which a licence was required constituted an offence. The Luxembourg regulation was enacted pursuant to arrangements made in the framework of the Co-ordinating Committee for Multilateral Export Controls (CoCom), an intergovernmental organisation whose task is to control the export to communist countries of goods having strategic importance. France possessed similar legislation, but later said that it was unaware of the true

[1] ibid at p 2751, paragraph 34 of the Court's judgment. A similar problem arose in Case 231/83 *Cullet v Centre Leclerc Toulouse* [1985] ECR 305. The French government contended that its system of maintaining minimum retail prices for petrol was justified under Article 36 because, *inter alia*, of a threat to public security which would need to be anticipated on the part of retailers affected by the introduction of unrestricted competition taking action involving social unrest, blockades and violence. The Court of Justice rejected this submission because France had failed to show that, using other means at its disposal, it would be unable to cope with any such threats to public security.

[2] Case C-367/89 [1991] ECR I-4621.

nature of the device (French criminal proceedings were subsequently instituted against Mr Richardt).

The Luxembourg *Cour de Cassation* made a reference to the Court of Justice under Article 177 in which it sought to establish whether Community law required Luxembourg to recognise the arrangements made in France for the export of the device to the Soviet Union notwithstanding that such export would endanger Luxembourg's external security. In the course of replying to the Luxembourg court's reference, the Court of Justice said:

> [T]he concept of public security within the meaning of Article 36 of the Treaty covers both a Member State's internal and its external security. It is common ground that the importation, exportation and transit of goods capable of being used for strategic purposes may affect the public security of a Member State, which it is therefore entitled to protect pursuant to Article 36 of the Treaty.[1]

What is the "external security" of a State other than its national security?[2]

We have already seen how, in *Johnston*, the Court of Justice assimilated the "serious internal disturbances"[3] occasioned by the terrorist campaigns in Northern Ireland to considerations of "public safety".[4] A major terrorist problem of the sort extant in Ulster might just as easily be considered a threat to national security - especially having regard to the aims of those elements among the terrorists who seek the separation of Northern Ireland from the United Kingdom. Indeed by accepting that the internal disturbances in Northern Ireland were serious, the Court implicitly accepted that the preconditions for the exercise of the United Kingdom's powers acknowledged in Article 224 had been fulfilled.

Thus we see that the references to public security in Articles 36, 48(3) and 56 of the Treaty are expressions of the same considerations underlying the idea of "serious internal disturbances affecting the maintenance of law and order" in Article 224. Both sets of provisos are subject to judicial supervision. In particular, the courts are obliged to ensure that the preconditions for their exercise are present and that the general principles of Community law, and especially the principle of proportionality, are complied with.

There are nevertheless at least two, and possibly three, differences between the public security provisos in Articles 36, 48(3) and 56 and the serious internal disturbance proviso in Article 224.

[1]ibid at p I-4652, paragraph 22 of the Court's judgment.

[2]Since the *Richardt* judgment, the Commission has presented a proposal for a regulation on the export of strategic and nuclear goods and technologies from Member States: Com(92) 317 final (31 August 1992).

[3]Case 222/84, *Johnston v Chief Constable of the Royal Ulster Constabulary*, [1986] ECR 1651 at p 1692, paragraph 60 of the Court's judgment.

[4]ibid at p 1687, paragraph 38 of the Court's judgment.

Firstly, the public security provisos apply to the exercise of specific rights under Community law, ie the freedom of establishment and the free movement of goods, workers and services (the last through Article 66). Article 224, on the other hand, recognises a general right by Member States to derogate from Community law at large whenever there are "serious internal disturbances affecting the maintenance of law and order".

Secondly, resort to the serious internal disturbance proviso obliges all the Member States to consult with each other with a view to taking together the steps needed to prevent the common market by being affected by the exceptional measures taken. No such requirement as to consultation exists in the case of the public security provisos.

The third difference, a contingency as to the existence of which it is not possible to be certain on the present state of Community law, concerns the taking of preventive action. As has been demonstrated by *Campus Oil* and *Richardt*, Member States may take action under the public security proviso in order that a threat to public security may be prevented from arising. By contrast, Article 224 envisages action being taken by a Member State "in the event of" a serious internal disturbance. Given that Article 224 will, like the public policy, public security and health provisos be strictly construed,[1] the possibility cannot be ruled out that a Member State will need to be confronted with an actual serious internal disturbance before being entitled to act.[2]

The preferable view is, however, that preventive measures are envisaged by Article 224.[3] This would follow from the proposition that the public safety provisos are but specific manifestations of the more general serious internal disturbance proviso. It would also accord with sound policy considerations. For example, it could hardly be the case that a Member State would be required to admit into its territory a Union citizen who was known to be actively involved in espionage or terrorism on behalf of a hostile third country. It is most unlikely that the Court of Justice would require the host Member State to wait until an act of espionage or terrorism had actually occurred or been attempted before allowing the exceptional action accommodated by Article 224. Any such preventive action would be subject to judicial review under Article 225, and it is precisely this sort of scenario which would make the holding of proceedings *in camera* most appropriate.

A RETURN FROM THE HINTERLAND

We embarked on our journey into the constitutional hinterland of Article 8a of the *EC Treaty* out of a desire to find an answer to a particular question: Does Article 8a(2) of

[1]Case 13/68 *SpA Salgoil v Italian Ministry for Foreign Trade* [1968] ECR 453 at p 463 and Case 222/84 *Johnston v Chief Constable of the Royal Ulster Constabulary* [1986] ECR 1651 at p 1684, paragraph 26 of the Court's judgment.

[2]Article 15 of the *ECHR* would also appear not to authorise the taking of preventive action.

[3]This view is taken, albeit without explanation, by Hans Smit and Peter Herzog; *The Law of the European Economic Community*, 6-216.85.

the *EC Treaty*, understood narrowly as not providing a legal basis for the adoption of provisions restricting the Union citizen's right to move and reside, provide the appropriate legal basis for the adoption of the measures referred to in Article 8a(1)? If the limitations and conditions referred to in Article 8a(1) are not impliedly imposed by the *EC Treaty* generally, then the narrow construction of Article 8a(2) must be wrong. Article 8a(2) must then be capable, notwithstanding the use of the word "facilitating", of serving as a legal basis for the imposition of limitations and conditions on the rights contained in Article 8a(1).

We are now in a position to return from our journey and to address this issue armed with the discoveries we have made.

A reasonable argument can be made out for the proposition that within the structure of the *EC Treaty* there can be found a residual constitutional power vested in the Member States by which they remain entitled to impose limitations and conditions on the Union citizen's rights under Article 8a(1) on the grounds of public policy, public security and the protection of health.[1]

The decision of the Court of Justice in *Johnston*, however, appears to have explicitly rejected the existence of any such power. Nevertheless, the technique employed by the Court in resolving *Johnston* strongly suggests that there remains vested in the Member States a residual constitutional power to derogate from rights conferred under Community law in circumstances narrower than the full range of those contained in Articles 36, 48(3) and 56(1) of the *EC Treaty*. In particular the *Johnston* Court has left open the possibility that the Member States retain a residual constitutional power to derogate from rights conferred under Community law on the much narrower ground of national or public security. Indeed, explicit authority for the existence of this residual power can be found in Article 224 of the *EC Treaty* which recognises the power's existence.

The existence of this truncated residual power is not sufficient, however, to avoid most of the distortions which could arise in Community law were Article 8a(2), as narrowly construed, to be regarded as the appropriate legal basis for the adoption of the measures referred to in Article 8a(1). The very small number of cases in which considerations of national or public security have been ventilated indicates that situations raising such considerations are extremely rare. This can be contrasted to the large body of case law dealing with pleas of public policy or the protection of health.

A Union citizen who was a terrorist or spy, or who perhaps engaged in violent crime, could have his Article 8a(1) rights denied by virtue of the residual power recognised by Article 224. But the Union citizen whose entry into or residence in a host Member State was merely a threat to public health or public policy would not be so exposed.

[1]On grounds of "public health" in the case of the free movement of workers (Article 48(3)), establishers (Article 56(1)) and providers or consumers of services (Article 56(1) through Article 66) and on grounds of "the protection of health and life of humans, animals and plants" in the case the free movement of goods (Article 36).

In respect of these Union citizens a host Member State would probably need more than a residual power to protect their national or public security interests in order to deny the Article 8a(1) rights of movement and residence. Moreover, such a power would not justify a Member State excluding a Union citizen from his rights under Article 8a(1) on the basis that he was not financially independent or that he was not adequately insured for risks to his health.

We might turn to Article 8a(2) as a source of power to enact the limiting and conditioning measures envisaged by Article 8a(1). In order to do so, however, it would be necessary to explain how a provision which authorises the adoption of measures "facilitating" the Union citizen's movement and residence rights could be used in such a way. One solution might be to construe Article 8a(1) as embodying no more than a pledge to introduce a Union citizenship right of free movement, which pledge remains to be redeemed by secondary legislation capable of containing limitations and conditions. Thus construed, legislation adopted under Article 8a(2) could be said to 'facilitate' the 'rights' contained in Article 8a(1). However, as we shall see in Chapter 5, Article 8a(1) does more than merely make a pledge - it operates so as immediately to confer certain substantive rights on Union citizens.

Because the Member States lack a reserve or residual constitutional power to derogate from such rights on grounds of public policy, protection of health and the Union citizen's lack of adequate financial security, alternative means to introduce Community legislation authorising such derogations must be found before resorting to an interpretation of Article 8a(2) which appears to strain its language by permitting it to operate as a legal basis for adopting measures containing derogations.

IN SEARCH OF AN ALTERNATIVE LEGAL BASIS

There are four candidates which immediately present themselves as possibly capable of supplying the alternative means: Articles 6, 100, 100a and 235 of the *EC Treaty*.

Article 100a

Of these provisions, Article 100a - which authorises the Council to "adopt the measures for the approximation of provisions laid down by law, regulation or administrative action which have as their object the establishment and functioning of the internal market" - may be quickly dismissed. Article 100a(2) specifically excludes from the scope of Article 100a "provisions ... relating to the free movement of persons".

There is also the additional possible objection that the movement and residence rights contained in Article 8a are not part of the "internal market" for whose achievement Article 100a is designed. The expression "internal market" would itself seem to imply an entity defined by the undertaking of economic activities. More importantly, Article 7a (second paragraph) of the *EC Treaty* defines the internal market as comprising "an area without internal frontiers in which the free movement of goods, persons, services and capital is ensured in accordance with the provisions of this Treaty". It will be noted that the expression "persons" is used in conjunction with other freedoms of a clearly economic character which implies that the expression is to be given an economic meaning coterminous with workers and establishers. Article 7a of the *EC Treaty* was, moreover, inserted into the *EEC Treaty* (as Article 8a) by the *Single European Act*, ie before the extension of personal movement rights to persons not engaged in economic activities.

Article 3(c) of the *EC Treaty* includes among the activities of the Community "an internal market characterized by the abolition, as between Member States, of obstacles to the free movement of goods, persons, services and capital". Article 3a of the *EC Treaty* moreover provides that "the activities of the Member States and of the Community shall include ... the adoption of an economic policy which is based on the close coordination of Member States' economic policies, on the internal market and on the definition of common objectives, conducted in accordance with the principle of an open market economy with free competition". It would therefore appear that the use of the word "persons" in Article 7a is used in the same sense in which it was employed in the *EEC Treaty* and is not intended to extend to Union citizens who are not engaged in economic activity within the scope of Articles 48-66.[1]

Article 100

Article 100 of the *EC Treaty* authorises the adoption of "directives for the approximation of such laws, regulations or administrative provisions of the Member States as directly affect the establishment or functioning of the common market". The directives are to be adopted by the Council unanimously on a proposal from the Commission and after consulting the European Parliament and the Economic and Social Committee.

The issue needing to be resolved in determining whether Article 100 provides an appropriate legal basis for the adoption of measures limiting and conditioning the Union citizen's right of movement and residence under Article 8a is whether such measures can operate so as to harmonise national legal provisions which "directly affect the establishment or functioning of the common market".

In other words, does the Union citizen's right of movement and residence under Article 8a form part of the common market? The Court of Justice has said that the purpose of the provisions on the free movement of workers "is to assist in the abolition of obstacles to the establishment of a common market in which the nationals of the Member States may move freely within the territory of those states in order to pursue their economic activities".[2] Given that the Union citizen's Article 8a right to move and reside appears to be conferred independently of the performance by the Union

[1] See also, "*The Lifting of Border Controls: Commission Position on the Interpretation of Article 8a of the EEC Treaty*", "Europe" Documents No 1773 of 12 May 1992 in which the Commission argues that Article 8a of the *EEC Treaty* does not extend movement rights beyond those already entitled to enjoy them under other provisions of the *EEC Treaty*. Semble D. Wyatt and A. Dashwood, "*European Community Law*", 3rd ed, p 357.

[2] Joined Cases 35 and 36/82 *Morson and Jhanjan v State of the Netherlands* [1982] ECR 3723 at p 3736, paragraph 15 of the Court's judgment.

citizen of any economic activity, an affirmative answer can be given to this question only if the common market covers Union citizens in their non-economic capacity.

Although the term "internal market" - as employed for example in Article 100a - is defined by the text of the Treaty, no such convenient definition exists for the term "common market". The expression "common market" would however seem to imply an entity defined by the undertaking of economic activities. Indeed, Article 2 of the *EC Treaty* defines the task of the Community in terms of the promotion of a number of essentially economic goals; "a harmonious and balanced development of economic activities, sustainable and non-inflationary growth respecting the environment, a high degree of convergence of economic performance, a high level of employment and social protection, the raising of living standards and the quality of life and economic and social cohesion and solidarity among Member States". All of these goals are to be promoted by, *inter alia*, establishing a common market,[1] thereby implying that the common market is an essentially economic concept.

That the common market whose establishment is required by the *EC Treaty* is an entity characterised by economic activities is reinforced by reference to *Metro SB-Großmärkte GmbH & Co KG v Commission*[2] in which the Court of Justice observed that among the objectives of the *EEC Treaty* was "the creation of a single market achieving conditions similar to those of a domestic market".[3]

Article 7 of the *EC Treaty* lays down a timetable for the progressive establishment of the common market during a transitional period of twelve years, which period expired at the end of 1969. The elimination of customs duties and of charges having equivalent effect on intra-Community trade are required by the Treaty itself to have been abolished by the end of the transitional period,[4] as are quantitative restrictions and measures having equivalent effect on intra-Community trade.[5] These objectives, both economic in nature and affecting the free movement of goods, are clearly part of what constitutes the common market by virtue of being linked to the timetable prescribed for the common market's implementation. Article 9(1) of the *EC Treaty* provides that the Community shall be based on a customs union.

The common market also includes the other economic freedoms fundamental to the Community, ie the free movement of workers, services, capital, and the right of establishment. The Court of Justice in *Levin v Staatssecretaris van Justitie*[6] interpreted Article 48 of the Treaty in such a way as to encompass persons whose employment income was, in the opinion of the host Member State, lower than

[1] Article 2 of the *EC Treaty* also provides that these goals are to be promoted by establishing an economic and monetary union and by implementing the common policies or activities referred to in Articles 3 and 3a.

[2] Case 26/76 [1977] ECR 1875.

[3] ibid at p 1904, paragraph 20 of the Court's judgment. See also Case 270/80 *Polydor Limited v Harlequin Record Shops Limited* [1982] ECR 329 at p 348, paragraph 16 of the Court's judgment.

[4] Articles 13-17 of the *EC Treaty*.

[5] Articles 31-35 of the *EC Treaty*.

[6] Case 53/81 [1982] ECR 1035.

subsistence level, provided the persons are engaged in an effective and genuine employment activity. In so doing the Court said that its interpretation accorded "with the objectives of the Treaty which include, according to Articles 2 and 3, the abolition, as between Member States, of obstacles to the freedom of movement for persons, with the purpose *inter alia* of promoting throughout the Community a harmonious development of economic activities and a raising of the standard of living".[1] Thus the right of free movement for workers was also interpreted in view of an economic objective to be achieved by the establishment of the common market.

In *Walrave and Koch v Association Union Cycliste Internationale*,[2] a case involving the free movement of services, the Court of Justice said that the practice of sport "is subject to Community law only in so far as it constitutes an economic activity within the meaning of Article 2 of the Treaty",[3] thereby implying that the establishment of the common market is an activity with economic objectives. Indeed Article 3 of the *EC Treaty* provides a list of the Community's activities, all essentially economic in character, which are to be undertaken "for the purposes set out in Article 2", one of which is the establishment of the common market. The adoption of measures with a view to facilitating the Union citizenship right of movement and residence is not among the activities nominated by Article 3 for the establishment of the common market.

Furthermore, in *Commission v France* (*"Re French Sailors"*)[4] the Court of Justice observed that Article 2 of the *EEC Treaty* provides the Community with the task of promoting throughout the Community a harmonious development of economic activities by establishing a common market and progressively approximating the laws of the Member States. From this it followed that "[t]he establishment of the common market thus refers to the whole of the economic activities of the Community".[5]

It therefore seems that the common market does not encompass non-economic activity undertaken by Union citizens. Consequently, the Union citizen's non-economic right to move and reside freely within the territory of the Member States does not form part of the common market. It follows that Article 100, authorising the adoption of directives for the approximation of national measures as directly affect the establishment or functioning of the common market, does not provide a legal basis for the adoption of measures limiting or conditioning the Union citizen's right referred to in Article 8a(1) of the *EC Treaty*.

Articles 6 and 235

We will now consider whether either Article 6 or Article 235 of the *EC Treaty* can provide a legal basis for the adoption of measures limiting and conditioning the

[1] ibid at p 1050, paragraph 15 of the Court's judgment.

[2] Case 36/74 [1974] ECR 1405.

[3] ibid at p 1417, paragraph 4 of the Court's judgment. See also Case 13/76 *Donà v Mantero* [1976] ECR 1333 at p 1340, paragraph 12 of the Court's judgment.

[4] Case 167/73 [1974] ECR 359.

[5] ibid at p 369, paragraph 19 of the Court's judgment.

migration rights contained in Article 8a(1). Article 6 (first paragraph) of the *EC Treaty* is identical to Article 7 (first paragraph) of the *EEC Treaty*, and is a directly effective provision[1] of fundamental significance within the framework of Community law.[2]

Articles 6 and 8a Compared. The first paragraph of Article 6 prohibits discrimination on the grounds of nationality of a Member State[3] subject to only two explicit limitations. Firstly, the act or conduct impugned must be within the scope and application of the Treaty.[4] Secondly, the prohibition is subject to any special

[1]This was implicitly the Court of Justice's view as early as Case 14/68 *Wilhelm v Bundeskartelamt* [1969] ECR 1 at pp 15-16, paragraphs 12-13 of the Court's judgment. The direct effect of Article 7 of the *EEC Treaty* was effectively acknowledged in Case 155/73 *Sacchi* [1974] ECR 409 at p 431, paragraph 20 of the Court's judgment, and was first expressly acknowledged in Case 2/74 *Reyners v Belgian State* [1974] ECR 631 at p 651, paragraph 25 of the Court's judgment.

[2]Case 2/74 *Reyners v Belgian State* [1974] ECR 631 at p 651, paragraph 24 of the Court's judgment. See also eg Case 11/77 *Patrick v Ministre des Affaires Culturelles* [1977] ECR 1199 at p 1204, paragraph 9 of the Court's judgment.

[3]Such was the situation in eg Case 152/82 *Forcheri v Belgian State* [1983] ECR 2323 in which it was held that where a Member State organises educational courses relating to vocational training, a breach of Article 7 of the *EEC Treaty* was committed where a national of another Member State was required to pay an enrolment fee which was not payable by the host Member State's own nationals; at p 2336, paragraph 18 of the Court's judgment. Article 7 applied because Article 128 of the *EEC Treaty* authorised the Community to lay down general principles for implementing a common vocational training policy. Although the Treaty did not confer legislative competence over vocational training to the Community, "the opportunity for such kinds of instruction falls within the scope of the Treaty"; at p 2336, paragraph 17 of the Court's judgment. The provision is not expressed to prohibit discrimination on grounds of Member State nationality, but merely of nationality. Nevertheless the phrase "(w)ithin the scope and application of this Treaty" suggests that the prohibition is not intended to extend to nationality discrimination against nationals of non-member countries. See eg Joined Cases 50-58/82 *Administrateur des Affaires Maritimes, Bayonne v Dorca Marina* [1982] ECR 3949 at pp 3958-3959, paragraphs 10-11 of the Court's judgment, Case 238/83 *Caisse d'Allocations Familiales de la Région Parisienne v Meade* [1984] ECR 2631 at p 2638, paragraph 7 of the Court's judgment, Case C-105/89 *Buhari v Institut national d'assurances sociales pour travailleurs indépendants* [1990] ECR I-4211 at p I-4239, paragraph 26 of the Court's judgment.

[4]Thus, the prohibition contained in Article 6 of the *EC Treaty* is inapplicable to situations which are wholly internal to one Member State and which are in no way connected to any situations envisaged by Community law: eg Case 175/78 *R v Saunders* [1979] ECR 1129 at pp 1134-1135, paragraphs 8-11 of the Court's judgment, Joined Cases 35 and 36/82 *Morson and Jhanjan v State of the Netherlands* [1982] ECR 3732 at p 3736, paragraphs 15-16 of the Court's judgment, Case 180/83 *Moser v Land Baden-Württemberg* [1984] ECR 2539 at p 2547, paragraphs 14-15 of the Court's judgment, Case 44/84 *Hurd v Jones (Her Majesty's Inspector of Taxes)* [1986] ECR 29 at p 85, paragraph 55 of the Court's judgment, Case 298/84 *Iorio v Azienda autonoma delle ferrovie dello Stato* [1986] ECR 247 at pp 254-255, paragraphs 13-14 of the Court's judgment, Case C-41/90 *Höfner and Elser v Macrotron GmbH* [1991] ECR I-1979 at p I-2020, paragraph 37 of the Court's judgment, Case C-332/90 *Steen v Deutsche Bundespost* [1992] ECR I-341 at pp I-356 - I-357, paragraph 9 of the Court's judgment, Case C-153/91 *Petit v Office National des Pensions* [1993] 1 CMLR 476 at p 488, paragraph 8 of the Court's judgment. Cf Case C-370/90 *R v Immigration Appeal Tribunal and Surinder Singh ex parte Secretary of State for the Home Department* [1992] 3 CMLR 358. Also outside the scope and application of the *EEC Treaty*, and therefore beyond the reach of the prohibition in its Article 7, were activities which were not of an economic nature within the meaning of Article 2: Case 36/74 *Walrave and Koch v Association Union Cycliste Internationale* [1974] ECR 1405 at p 1417, paragraph 4 of the Court's judgment, Case 13/76 *Donà v Mantero* [1976] ECR 1333 at p 1340, paragraph 12 of the Court's judgment. Thus activities and acts involving, for example, voting in national parliamentary elections or participation in non-remunerative sporting and cultural pursuits would be outside the scope and application of the *EC Treaty* and of the prohibition in Article 6. Although the rights contained in Article 8a of the *EC Treaty* are not dependent on the performance of an economic activity within the meaning of Article 2, they are conferred by the Treaty and are within the scope and application of the Treaty. They would, therefore, be subject to the prohibition contained within Article 6.

provisions contained in the Treaty[1] or in secondary legislation.[2] The Union citizen's right to move and reside will fall within the scope and application of the Treaty if it is construed as conferring either (i) a directly effective right analogous to the rights conferred in Articles 48, 52 and 59, or as (ii) conferring such a right subject to secondary measures which may impose limitations and conditions on the exercise of the right.[3] If, on the other hand, Article 8a is construed as a mere pledge to confer movement and residence rights on Union citizens, which pledge remains to be redeemed by secondary legislation, then there will be nothing to fall within the scope and application of the Treaty until those rights are embodied in secondary legislation.[4]

Article 8a does not itself prescribe any special limitations or conditions on the right it confers. If Article 8a(2) of the *EC Treaty*, because of the word "facilitating", is interpreted as meaning that it cannot be used as a legal basis for the adoption of measures limiting or conditioning the right conferred in Article 8a(1) then Article 8a will not be a 'special provision' for the purposes of imposing such limitations and conditions. Article 6 would thus not be subject to Article 8a for such a purpose.

There is, however, one apparent obstacle to Article 6 providing a legal basis for the adoption of measures limiting or conditioning the Union citizen's right to move and reside freely within the territory of the Member States. The second paragraph of Article 6 is expressed to authorise "rules designed to prohibit" the discrimination forbidden by the first paragraph. If a rule authorises the imposition of limitations and conditions on the ability of a Union citizen to enter or reside within the territory of a Member State of which he is a national, it can hardly be said that such a rule is "designed to prohibit" nationality discrimination in the area of the right conferred by Article 8a(1). Article 6, as a possible legal basis for the adoption of such rules, thus appears to be subject to a disqualification substantially identical to the one apparently afflicting Article 8a(2).

[1] Article 6 must thus give way to any *lex specialis* dealing with nationality discrimination in particular fields. Such *leges speciales* may be found in Articles 37 (State monopolies of a commercial character), 48-51 (free movement for workers), 52-58 (right of establishment), 59-66 (freedom to provide services), 67-73h (free movement of capital), and 132 (association of overseas countries and territories).

[2] In Case 8/77 *Sagulo, Brenca and Bakhouche* [1977] ECR 1495 the Court of Justice held that Community secondary legislation could constitute a "special provision" for the purposes of Article 7 (first paragraph) of the *EEC Treaty*. This finding was inconsistent with the English language version of the provision: "Within the scope and application of *this Treaty* and without prejudice to any special provisions contained *therein* ..." (emphasis added). The German version of the text resembles the English version: "*Unbeschadet besonderer Bestimmungen dieses Vertrags ist in seinem Anwendungsbereich* ...". The language of the case in *Sagulo* was German. The French text of the provision provides, however, as follows; "*Dans le domaine d'application du présent traité, et sans préjudice des dispositions particulières qu'il prévoit* ...". The French version might therefore translate as; "Within the fields covered by this Treaty, and without prejudice to any special provisions envisaged therein". The decision in *Sagulo* is therefore consistent with the French version of Article 7.

[3] See eg Case 152/82 *Forcheri v Belgian State* [1983] ECR 2323, in which access to vocational training programmes was held to be within the scope and application of the Treaty by virtue of Article 128 of the *EEC Treaty* notwithstanding that the Community lacked legislative competence in the field of education and vocational training.

[4] In Chapter 5 it will be demonstrated that Article 8a of the *EC Treaty* is directly effective to confer movement and residence rights on Union citizens subject to secondary measures which may impose limitations and conditions on the exercise of those rights.

Yet the case law affecting Article 6 provides us with the key needed to unlock the puzzle. We shall see that derogations from the non-discrimination principle in Article 6 are permitted when they can be objectively justified.

Objective Justification and Article 6. In *European Parliament v Council ("Re Students' Rights")*[1] the Court of Justice was called upon to decide the validity of *Directive 90/366* on the right of residence for students. In enacting the directive the Council had relied on Article 235 of the *EEC Treaty* as the appropriate legal basis. As the wording of Article 235 itself makes clear, it can provide an appropriate legal basis for legislation only where the Treaty "has not provided the necessary powers". If the Treaty has elsewhere provided the necessary powers for the adoption of legislation, Article 235 may not be used as the legal basis and legislation incorrectly based on Article 235 will be annulled.[2]

The directive had been proposed by the Commission with Article 7 (second paragraph) of the *EEC Treaty* as its legal basis. The second paragraph of Article 7 of the *EEC Treaty* differs from the second paragraph of Article 6 of the *EC Treaty* only in that the former provision required legislation to be adopted in accordance with the co-operation procedure[3] whereas the latter provision requires observance of the procedure referred to in Article 189c of the *EC Treaty*. The two procedures are identical. Hence there is no material difference between the two provisions.

The procedural significance of proposing the directive under Article 7 (second paragraph) as distinct from Article 235 lay in the fact that the co-operation procedure gave the European Parliament more influence over the directive's content than would observance of the consultation procedure required by Article 235. The European Parliament commenced proceedings for annulment of the directive on the grounds that, in employing Article 235 as the legal basis, the Council had violated the European Parliament's prerogatives.[4] The challenge was successful, and the Court of Justice annulled the directive but continued it in force until the entry into force of another directive adopted on the appropriate legal basis.[5]

The contested directive required the Member States to grant a right of residence to nationals of other Member States who were students enrolled in a recognised educational establishment for the principal purpose of following a vocational training course. The right was also to apply to the student's spouse and his dependent

[1] Case C-295/90 [1992] 3 CMLR 281.

[2] Case 45/86 *Commission v Council ("Re Generalised Tariff Preferences")* [1987] ECR 1493 at p 1520, paragraph 13 of the Court's judgment.

[3] The co-operation procedure is set out in Article 149(2) of the *EEC Treaty*.

[4] See Case C-70/88 *European Parliament v Council ("Chernobyl")* [1990] ECR I-2041 at p I-2073, paragraph 27 of the Court's judgment..

[5] The Commission has since made a proposal for a new Council directive (COM (93) 209 final, 14 May 1993) expressed to rest upon the legal base approved by the Court.

children,[1] who were also to be entitled to take up any employed or self-employed activity anywhere within the territory of the host Member State.[2]

Prior to the judgment in *Re Students' Rights*, but after the adoption of the contested directive, the Court of Justice had decided in *Raulin v Minister van Onderwijs en Wetenschappen*[3] that Article 7 of the *EEC Treaty* was effective to confer directly on Member State nationals a right to reside in the territory of a host Member State for the purpose of undertaking a course of vocational training in the host Member State. At the hearing in *Re Students' Rights* the Dutch government and the Council submitted, however, that the directive went beyond a right of residence for the purposes of vocational training by conferring on students a right of free movement similar to that enjoyed by workers. The Court implicitly acknowledged that the directive went beyond what was minimally required for a student to exercise his right to undertake a vocational training course, but said that "rules adopted pursuant to Article 7(2) should not necessarily be limited to regulating rights derived from paragraph (1) of the same Article, but they may also deal with aspects the regulation of which appears necessary for the effective exercise of those rights".[4]

Thus Article 7 of the *EEC Treaty* provided a legal basis for the adoption of rules designed to prohibit nationality discrimination within the scope and application of the Treaty and also to adopt rules to deal with aspects the regulation of which are *necessary for the effective exercise of those rights.* Article 7 (second paragraph) thus appeared to authorise measures merely 'facilitating' a realisation of the directly effective prohibition contained in the first paragraph.

Nevertheless, the directive contained certain limitations and conditions. The student was required to assure the relevant national authority that he had sufficient resources to avoid becoming a burden on the social assistance system of the host Member State during the period of residence and that he and his family were covered by sickness insurance in respect of all risks in the host Member State.[5] The right of residence was to be restricted to the duration of the course.[6] Member States were furthermore ordered not to derogate from the rights contained in the directive save on grounds of public policy, public security and public health.[7]

Given that Article 7 (second paragraph) appears to be merely facilitative in the way indicated, how could it legitimately authorise the adoption of such limitations contained in secondary legislation? The Community's constitutional principles, after all, forbid the valid adoption of secondary legislation if it is inconsistent with a

[1]Article 1.

[2]Article 2(2) (second paragraph).

[3]Case C-357/89 1992 [ECR] I-1027.

[4]Case C-295/90 *European Parliament v Council* ("*Re Students' Rights*") [1992] 3 CMLR 281 at pp 301-302, paragraph 18 of the Court's judgment.

[5]Article 1.

[6]Article 2(1) (first paragraph).

[7]Article 2(2) (third paragraph).

prohibition prescribed by the treaties.[1] Nor can Community secondary legislation be applied in a way which is inconsistent with a fundamental principle of Community law,[2] of which Article 6 of the *EC Treaty* is an example.

This issue was not directly addressed by the Court of Justice in its judgment. Nevertheless, it implicitly accepted the view expressed by Advocate General Jacobs in his opinion to the Court.

The Advocate General argued that, in restricting access to the students' right of residence to the duration of the course and to those who could assure the relevant national authority that they had sufficient resources to avoid becoming a burden on the social assistance system of the host Member State during their period of residence and that they and their families were covered by sickness insurance in respect of all risks in the host Member State, the directive did no more than limit the right of residence to those who were entitled to receive it directly under the effect of Article 7.[3] In these respects, then, no limitations of the Treaty's residence rights for students were actually imposed by the directive.

In connection, however, with the directive's authorisation to limit students' residence rights on grounds of public policy, public security and public health, the directive was doing more than merely recognising the boundaries of the Treaty right. Rather, the directive was expressly authorising derogations from that right. The Advocate General said:

> [M]ember-States are permitted to derogate from the directive on grounds of public policy, public security and public health where ... inequalities of treatment may be objectively justified and therefore permissible under Article 7. In any event, the imposition of a limitation on the rights granted to students by the directive cannot have the effect of taking the rights themselves outside the scope of Article 7.[4]

The prohibition against nationality discrimination contained in Article 6 of the *EC Treaty* can therefore be made subject to derogations contained in secondary legislation enacted under the provision's second paragraph provided such derogations may be "objectively justified". This is so notwithstanding that Article 6 of the *EC Treaty* is a

[1] Thus in Joined Cases 80 and 81/77 *Société Les Commissionnaires Réunis Sàrl and Sàrl Les Fils de Henri Ramel v Receveur des Douanes* [1978] ECR 927 the Court of Justice invalidated a provision of a Council regulation to the extent that it purported to authorise Member States to impose charges having an effect equivalent to customs duties in the field of the Community wine market contrary to the prohibitions in Articles 13(2) and 38-46 of the *EEC Treaty*.

[2] Thus in Case 63/83 *R v Kirk* [1984] ECR 2689 the Court of Justice disallowed the giving of effect to a Council regulation purporting retrospectively to validate national penal laws which national laws were not valid at the time they were enacted by the Member States. The Court said that to hold otherwise would be to violate the fundamental Community principle, as enshrined in all the Member States' legal systems and in Article 7 of the *ECHR*, that penal provisions should not be given retrospective effect.

[3] Case C-295/90 *European Parliament v Council* ("*Re Students' Rights*") [1992] 3 CMLR 281 at p 295.

[4] ibid.

directly effective provision of fundamental significance within the framework of Community law, that it is in unconditional terms, and that its second paragraph is expressed to authorise the adoption of legislation "designed to prohibit" nationality discrimination.

The idea that the rule against nationality discrimination in Article 6 of the *EC Treaty* is, or can be made, subject to derogations which are objectively justified is not a new one and did not originate in *Re Students' Rights.*

In *Wilhelm v Bundeskartelamt,*[1] a case decided in 1969, the Court of Justice was asked to consider whether the conduct of the German authorities responsible under national law for combating cartels had violated Article 7 of the *EEC Treaty* in penalising the German participants in an unlawful price-fixing agreement when the non-German participants were not so penalised. The non-German participants did not operate in German territory and the German authorities lacked the jurisdictional authority to impose penalties on them.

The Court of Justice said that Article 7 forbade Member States from applying their laws on cartels differently on the ground of the nationality concerned. The provision did not, however, proscribe "disparities in treatment or the distortions which may result ... from divergences existing between the laws of the various Member States, so long as the latter affect all persons subject to them, in accordance with objective criteria and without regard to their nationality".[2]

What the Court meant by the expression "objective criteria" is not made completely clear by the judgment. At the very least, however, a criterion is objective if it applies without regard to the person's nationality. The implication would appear to be that two persons of different nationality may be treated differently in similar circumstances if there is a nationality-neutral factor objectively justifying different treatment. In the instant case, the discrimination was due to the fact that the German nationals were amenable to the national authority's territorial powers whereas the non-German nationals were not, and there was no intention in proceeding against the German nationals of discriminating against them simply because they were German.

The necessary implication in *Wilhelm* seems to be that a sufficiently important consideration of public policy (*in casu* the preservation of market competition) can justify *de facto* discrimination on grounds of nationality provided that the person's nationality is not the basis of and is not the real reason for the discrimination.

In *Anklagemyndigheden v Kerr,*[3] for example, a Danish law which temporarily prescribed a catch quota for the Greenland fisheries, which quota was based on established patterns of fishing activity and discriminated in favour of certain Member

[1]Case 14/68 [1969] ECR 1.
[2]ibid at p 16, paragraph 13 of the Court's judgment.
[3]Case 287/81 [1982] ECR 4053.

States and of Greenlanders, was held not to violate Article 7 of the *EEC Treaty* because it was aimed at conserving a scarce economic resource and the "Danish authorities allocated the quotas in accordance with objective criteria, taking into account, in the first place, the needs of the coastal population, and secondly, the need to maintain a situation temporarily created in the region in question".[1]

Not every consideration of public policy will, however, be sufficiently serious as objectively to justify measures which discriminate between individuals on grounds of their Community nationality. Thus in *Boussac Saint-Frères SA v Gerstenmeier*[2] the Court of Justice rejected a submission by the German government that a German law making it procedurally simpler to recover certain debts expressed in German currency rather than in foreign currency was objectively justified and therefore not in covert breach of Article 7 of the *EEC Treaty*.

The German government said that the objective justification existed because its computer system, through which the simplified system was handled, could not be made economically to process claims for debts expressed in foreign currency and that it would need to process such claims manually if the simplified procedure were to accommodate them. The Court did not say why the German law was not objectively justified on this basis[3] (the law was held to be in conformity with Article 7 of the *EEC Treaty* on another basis), but presumably it was because the public interest in not incurring the additional expense in modifying the computer system or in processing claims manually did not outweigh the less favourable procedural treatment accorded to creditors seeking to enforce debts expressed in foreign currencies.

Similarly in *Lenoir v Caisse d'allocations familiales des Alpes-Maritimes*[4] the Court of Justice held that a Community rule requiring Member States to pay to certain of their nationals living in other Member States only "family allowances" in a narrow sense, but not certain other family benefits (such as a school expenses allowance and a family supplement allowance), did not discriminate against individuals on grounds of their Community nationality. The exclusion of the other benefits was objectively justified:

> If the legislation of the Member State by which the pension is payable grants periodical cash benefits to the recipient's family exclusively by reference to the number and, where appropriate, the age of the members of the family, the grant of such benefits continues to be justified wherever the recipient and his family reside. By contrast, benefits of another kind or subject to other conditions, as in the case, for example, of a benefit intended to cover certain costs incurred at the beginning of the school year, are in most cases closely linked with the

[1]ibid at pp 4076-4077, paragraph 30 of the Court's judgment.
[2]Case 22/80 [1980] ECR 3427.
[3]ibid at p 3436, paragraph 12 of the Court's judgment.
[4]Case 313/86 [1988] ECR 5391.

> social environment and therefore with the place where the persons concerned reside.[1]

In so reasoning the Court appears to have accepted the submission of the French government that non-payability of the other benefits abroad is justified by their very nature. According to the French government, if it were to make such benefits payable to its nationals abroad the result would be a distortion of "their very nature because they are designed to compensate for certain very specific family expenses incurred in and governed by local conditions in connection with a particular cost of living, so that they may prove, if transported to another place, abnormally advantageous or inadequate".[2] Thus the Community regulation did not violate Article 7 of the *EEC Treaty* because it applied criteria which neither overtly nor covertly depended upon the individual's nationality and because it served a public interest in ensuring that a social security benefit was not paid in circumstances where it did not discharge its purpose.

It therefore seems that measures may be adopted under Article 6 (second paragraph) of the *EC Treaty* which derogate from the fundamental and directly effective principle enshrined in Article 6 (first paragraph) where those derogations are objectively justified. This remains so notwithstanding that Article 6 (first paragraph) is expressed in unconditional terms, and that its second paragraph is expressed merely to authorise the adoption of legislation "designed to prohibit" nationality discrimination.

A measure is objectively justified although it represents a *de facto* derogation from the principle against nationality discrimination if it applies criteria which are nationality-neutral, if the real purpose of the measure is not to discriminate on grounds of nationality and if a sufficiently important public interest is served. The avoidance of administrative inconvenience or expense is not a sufficiently important public interest (*Gerstenmeier*), although objectives such as the conservation of limited economic resources (*Kerr*), the integrity of the social security system (*Lenoir*), the preservation of conditions of market competition (*Wilhelm*) and the protection of public policy, public security and public health (*Re Students' Rights*) would, at least in certain contexts, appear to be sufficient.

Objective Justification and Article 8a. It has already been observed that as a candidate for a legal basis authorising the adoption of measures limiting or conditioning the Union citizen's right of movement and residence, Article 6 (second paragraph) appears to be subject to a disqualification substantively identical to the one seemingly afflicting Article 8a(2). The former provision is expressed to authorise the adoption merely of "rules designed to prohibit" nationality discrimination within the scope and application of the Treaty, whereas the latter provision is expressed to authorise the adoption of "provisions with a view to facilitating" the Union citizen's right of movement and residence. Given the similar textual difficulties apparently obstructing the employment of either provision as the legal basis for the adoption of measures

[1]ibid at p 5424, paragraph 16 of the Court's judgment.
[2]ibid at p 5403, paragraph 9 of the supplementary report for the hearing.

limiting the rights contained in Article 8a(1), the restrictions permissible on the principle against nationality discrimination are potentially instructive in helping to understand the operation of Article 8a(2).

If a provision such as Article 6 (second paragraph) can authorise the adoption of measures limiting the application of the principle against nationality discrimination, why can Article 8a(2) not be used to adopt measures limiting the Union citizen's right of movement and residence in like circumstances? In other words why can Article 8a(2) not be employed as the legal basis for the adoption of measures limiting the Union citizen's right of movement and residence when such limitation is 'objectively justified'?

Objective Justification and Economic Freedom of Movement. It is instructive to note, in this context, that restrictions justified by reference to certain criteria, similar to the 'objective criteria' employed in the context of limiting the rule against nationality discrimination, may also be applied to the free movement of economically active persons under the *EC Treaty*.

Thus in *van Binsbergen v Bestuur van de Bedrijfsvereniging voor de Metaalnijverheid*[1] the Court of Justice said that, in principle, a Member State could impose on Community nationals providing services on its territory "specific requirements ... where they have as their purpose the application of professional rules justified by the *general good* - in particular rules relating to organization, qualifications, professional ethics, supervision and liability - which are binding upon any person established in the State in which the service is provided, where the person providing the service would escape from the ambit of those rules being established in another Member State".[2]

The Court went on to discuss whether it was compatible with Community law for a national rule to require lawyers, wishing to appear before the *Centrale Raad van Beroep*, to be established in the Netherlands. In this connection the Court said:

> [T]he requirement that persons whose functions are to assist the administration of justice must be permanently established for professional purposes within the jurisdiction of certain courts or tribunals cannot be considered incompatible with the provisions of Articles 59 and 60, where such requirement is *objectively justified* by the need to ensure observance of professional rules of conduct connected, in particular, with the administration of justice and with respect for professional ethics.[3]

[1]Case 33/74 [1974] ECR 1299.

[2]ibid at p 1309, paragraph 12 of the Court's judgment (emphasis added).

[3]ibid at p 1310, paragraph 14 of the Court's judgment (emphasis added). In using these words the Court was stating a proposition of principle. The Court went on to find that the principle could be satisfied by measures less restrictive of the freedom to provide services than those actually adopted by the national authorities.

Similarly, in *Gullung v Conseils de l'ordre des avocats du barreau de Colmar et de Saverne*[1] the Court of Justice said that measures restricting the right of establishment, by prescribing a requirement of registration in the jurisdiction where a lawyer is seeking to practice, ensure the observance of moral and ethical principles and the disciplinary control of the activity of lawyers thereby pursuing "an objective worthy of protection".[2]

It therefore seems that the freedom to provide services may in principle be restricted where to do so is objectively justified by the general good, which general good includes the observance of professional rules of conduct. The scope of the general good is not, however, restricted to this objective.

The protection of the integrity of a Member State's social security system may, as we have seen, provide objective justification for departing from the principle of nationality non-discrimination prescribed by Article 6 of the *EC Treaty* (*Lenoir*).

The cohesion of a Member State's system of taxation may, in appropriate circumstances, similarly warrant a derogation from the principle of equal treatment in the exercise of the Community's economic migration rights. In *Bachmann v Belgian State*,[3] Belgian law permitted individuals to deduct from their occupational income voluntary sickness and invalidity insurance contributions they had paid to an insurance company recognised by Belgium. Individuals were also allowed to deduct pension and life insurance contributions paid in Belgium. Mr Bachmann was a German national employed in Belgium. Before arriving in Belgium, he concluded in Germany sickness and invalidity insurance contracts and life assurance contracts and made contributions on those contracts. When he sought to deduct these contributions from the occupational income he had earned in Germany before his migration to Belgium, the Belgian authorities refused because the voluntary sickness and invalidity insurance contributions had not been paid to an insurance company recognised by Belgium and because the life insurance contributions were not paid in Belgium. Mr Bachmann commenced proceedings in Belgium against the decision of the taxation authorities and the *Cour de Cassation* sought a preliminary ruling on whether the relevant provisions of Belgian revenue law were compatible with, *inter alia*, Article 48 of the *EEC Treaty*.

One of the arguments advanced by the Belgian government was that the cohesion of its taxation system was at stake. Under Belgian law there existed a connection between

[1]Case 292/86 [1988] ECR 111.

[2]ibid at p 140, paragraph 29 of the Court's judgment. See also Joined Cases 110 and 111/78 *Ministère Public v van Wesemael* [1979] ECR 35 in which the Court of Justice made similar remarks in relation to a Belgian provision requiring the licensing of fee-charging employment agencies providing services within Belgium. The Court said that such agencies may, in principle, be made subject to "specific requirements imposed on persons providing services ... where they have as their purpose the application of professional rules, justified by the *general good* ... which are binding upon any person established in the said State, in so far as the person providing the service is not subject to similar requirements in the Member State in which he is established"; ibid at p 52, paragraph 28 of the Court's judgment (emphasis added).

[3]Case C-204/90 [1992] ECR I-249.

the deductibility of contributions and a liability to taxation on sums payable by insurers under life assurance and pension contracts. If contributions were deducted from the insured's income, the sums payable by the insurers were taxed at source. Conversely, if contributions were not deducted from income, the insurers' payments were free of tax. In this connection the Court of Justice observed that "in such a tax system the loss of revenue resulting from the deduction of life assurance contributions from total taxable income - which includes pensions and insurance payable in the event of death - is offset by the taxation of pensions, annuities or capital sums payable by the insurers".[1]

The Court of Justice held that legislation of a Member State which makes the deductibility of sickness and invalidity insurance contributions and pensions and life assurance contributions conditional on those contributions being paid in that State is contrary to Article 48 of the Treaty.

The practical difficulties, however, associated with proceeding against insurers located in another State, the absence of effective legal mechanisms which would guarantee the Belgian authorities the ability to recover at source tax on insurance payouts, and the possibility of exposing the insured to the burdens of double-taxation meant that "as Community law stands at present, it is not possible to ensure the cohesion of such a tax system by means of measures which are less restrictive than those at issue" between Mr Bachmann and the Belgian authorities.[2] The result was that the impugned Belgian taxation laws were allowed:

> [I]n the field of pensions and life assurance, provisions such as those contained in the Belgian legislation at issue are justified by the need to ensure the cohesion of the tax system of which they form part, and ... such provisions are not, therefore, contrary to Article 48 of the Treaty.[3]

In *Bachmann*, as in other cases, we see the Court of Justice permitting derogations from the principle of equal treatment in the application of the Community's economic movement rights which derogations are not sought to be justified on the basis of the public policy, public security and public health grounds authorised by Articles 48(3), 56(1) or 66.

There are other examples of Community citizens being treated differently in the exercise of their economic movement rights on grounds that are unconnected with public policy, public security or public health. Nationals of other Member States may be excluded from membership of national sporting teams in derogation of the Community rules about nationality discrimination, the free movement of workers and

[1] ibid at p I-282, paragraph 22 of the Court's judgment.
[2] ibid at p I-283, paragraph 27 of the Court's judgment.
[3] ibid at pp I-283 - I-284, paragraph 28 of the Court's judgment.

services and the right of establishment[1] provided any such measure remains "limited to its proper objective".[2] Member States are furthermore entitled to impose upon Community nationals and those accommodating them a requirement to report their presence to local authorities because "Community law has not excluded the power of Member States to adopt measures enabling the national authorities to have an exact knowledge of population movements affecting their territory",[3] although the time limit within which the foreigner's presence must be reported is not permitted by Community law to be unreasonably short.[4] A Member State's policy of promoting and protecting its national and official language also justifies a derogation from the Community's free movement of workers, such that an applicant for a State teaching post can be denied appointment on the basis that he fails to demonstrate a reasonable minimum proficiency in the language.[5]

The Public Interest. These seemingly indistinct derogations from the economic free movement of persons are not merely co-extensive with the concept of public policy, public security and public health. Rather, as *Re Students' Rights* indicates, public policy is part of a wider category of related concepts justifying derogation from the free movement of persons under the Treaty. This wider category of concepts might conveniently be referred to as the 'public interest',[6] which term encompasses not only public policy,[7] but also the other apparently *ad hoc* bases for validly derogating from

[1]This analysis explains the Court's handling of Case 13/76 *Donà v Mantero* [1976] ECR 1333 in which the Court held that the *EEC Treaty* did not "prevent the adoption of rules or of a practice excluding foreign players from participation in certain matches for reasons which are not of an economic nature, which relate to the particular nature and context of such matches and are thus of sporting interest only, such as, for example, matches between national teams from different countries"; at p 1340, paragraph 14 of the Court's judgment. See also Case 36/74 *Walrave and Koch v Association Union Cycliste Internationale* [1974] ECR 1405 at p 1418, paragraph 8 of the Court's judgment.

[2]Case 13/76 *Donà v Mantero* [1976] ECR 1333 at p 1340, paragraph 15 of the Court's judgment. See also Case 36/74 *Walrave and Koch v Association Union Cycliste Internationale* [1974] ECR 1405 at p 1418, paragraph 9 of the Court's judgment.

[3]Case 118/75 *Watson and Belmann* [1976] ECR 1185 at p 1198, paragraph 17 of the Court's judgment. In successfully defending the national legislation impugned in this case, the Italian government referred to considerations which can be classified as public interest and public policy; ibid at pp 1192-1193. Advocate General Trabucchi also said that the national legislation was in furtherance of a "genuine public interest ... in checking the presence of aliens on the national territory"; ibid at p 1210.

[4]Case C-265/88 *Messner* [1989] ECR 4209 at pp 4224-4225, paragraphs 10-12 of the Court's judgment.

[5]Case C-379/87 *Groener v Minister for Education* [1989] ECR 3967 especially at pp 3993-3994, paragraphs 19-21 of the Court's judgment. The Court of Justice did not formulate a more general principle supporting its decision in this case. It is, however, at least possible to understand the case as falling within the same *genus* as the other cases mentioned in the same paragraph on the basis that a policy protecting and promoting the official language is one justified by an overriding general good or public interest. Indeed, Advocate General Darmon said that the "preservation of languages is one of those questions of principle which one cannot dismiss without striking at the very heart of cultural identity"; ibid at p 3982, paragraph 19 of the opinion.

[6]It has been suggested that when Community law allows indirect discrimination because there is an "objective reason" for it, it is because the otherwise unlawful discrimination rests "on some rational ground, not inconsistent with Community law, on which it might be justified": Nicholas Green, Trevor C. Hartley and John A. Usher, "*The Legal Foundations of the Single European Market*" (1991), at p 140.

[7]In Case C-379/87 *Groener v Minister for Education* [1989] ECR 3967 Advocate General Darmon said that the power of Member States to impose certain restrictions, based on the posession of a minimum competency in the official national language, on the free movement of workers did not derive from the Member States' powers concerning public policy as expressed in Article 48(3) of the *EEC Treaty*; ibid at p 3985, paragraph 35 of the opinion. See also the previous footnote.

the Community's free movement of economically active persons on grounds assimilable to objective justification or to the general good.[1]

Indeed, the Court of Justice has itself perceived these sorts of seemingly indistinct considerations as falling within the conceptual rubric of the public interest. In *Commission v Germany* ("*Re Insurance Services*")[2] the Court of Justice was called upon to decide whether Germany had failed to fulfil its obligations under Articles 59 and 60 of the *EEC Treaty* in maintaining national laws requiring the providers of insurance and leading insurance services to be both officially registered in Germany and to be established on German territory.

The Court said that Member States may impose on the provision of services, and having regard to their particular nature, "specific requirements ... which have as their purpose the application of rules governing such activities" and which restrict the freedom to provide services "only by provisions which are justified by the *general good* and which are applied to all persons or undertakings operating within the territory of the State in which the service is provided in so far as that interest is not safeguarded by the provisions to which the provider of a service is subject in the Member State of his establishment".[3] It followed that the national requirements as to registration and establishment "may be regarded as compatible with Articles 59 and 60 of the EEC Treaty only if it is established that in the field of activity concerned there are imperative reasons relating to the *public interest* which justify restrictions on the freedom to provide services, that the *public interest* is not already protected by the rules of the State of establishment and that the same result cannot be achieved by less restrictive means".[4]

[1]The concept of the public interest as a ground justifying certain kinds of restrictions on the free movement of persons is also apt to encompass the objectively justified limitations permissible on the rule against nationality discrimination. There, it will be recalled, a measure is objectively justified although it represents a *de facto* derogation from the principle against nationality discrimination if it applies criteria which are nationality-neutral, if the real purpose of the measure is not to discriminate on grounds of nationality and if a sufficiently important public interest is served.

[2]Case 205/84 [1986] ECR 3755.

[3]ibid at p 3803, paragraph 27 of the Court's judgment (citing Joined Cases 110 and 111/78 *Ministère public v van Wesemael* [1979] ECR 35 and Case 279/80 *Webb* [1981] ECR 3305) (emphasis added). See also the following cases dealing with similar issues and decided on the same day: Case 220/83 *Commission v France* [1986] ECR 3663 at p 3708, paragraph 17 of the Court's judgment, Case 252/83 *Commission v Denmark* [1986] ECR 3713 at p 3748, paragraph 17 of the Court's judgment, and Case 206/84 *Commission v Ireland* [1986] ECR 3817 at p 3849, paragraph 17 of the Court's judgment. In otherwise virtually identical passages, the Court of Justice used the expression "general interest" rather than "public interest" in Case C-154/89 *Commission v France* ("*French Tourist Guides*") [1991] ECR I-659 at p I-686, paragraph 14 of the Court's judgment, Case C-180/89 *Commission v Italy* ("*Italian Tourist Guides*") [1991] ECR I-709 at pp I-722-723, paragraph 17 of the Court's judgment, Case C-198/89 *Commission v Greece* ("*Greek Tourist Guides*") [1991] ECR I-727 at pp I-740-741, paragraph 18 of the Court's judgment.

[4]Case 205/84 *Commission v Germany* ("*Re Insurance Services*") [1986] ECR 3755 at p 3803, paragraph 29 of the Court's judgment (emphasis added). See also the following cases dealing with similar issues and decided on the same day: Case 220/83 *Commission v France* [1986] ECR 3663 at pp 3708-3709, paragraph 19 of the Court's judgment, Case 252/83 *Commission v Denmark* [1986] ECR 3713 at p 3748, paragraph 19 of the Court's judgment, and Case 206/84 *Commission v Ireland* [1986] ECR 3817 at p 3849, paragraph 19 of the Court's judgment.

There is No Alternative

It therefore appears that Article 8a(2) of the *EC Treaty* provides an appropriate legal basis for the adoption of certain measures restricting the exercise of the rights referred to in Article 8a(1), notwithstanding that Article 8a(2) is expressed to authorise the adoption of provisions "facilitating" the exercise of the rights referred to in Article 8a(1). This result follows from the combination of two considerations.

Firstly, Article 6 (second paragraph) of the *EC Treaty*, which is a fundamental and directly effective provision of the Treaty and which is textually similar to Article 8a(2) in that it is expressed to authorise the adoption of rules "designed to prohibit" nationality discrimination, itself provides a legal basis for the adoption of provisions limiting and conditioning the application of the rule against nationality discrimination. Any such rule must be objectively justified. It will be so justified if it applies criteria which are nationality-neutral, if the real intention of the measure is not simply to derogate from the right conferred in the Article's first paragraph and if a sufficiently important public interest is served.

Secondly, the provisions of the *EC Treaty* conferring freedom of movement on economically active persons (ie in respect of workers, establishment and services) are themselves subject to certain restrictions permissible under Community law. These restrictions certainly include the limitations permitted expressly by the Treaty itself on grounds of public policy, public security and public health. These are not, however, the only permissible restrictions. Certain limitations are also permitted if they are objectively justified, or if they serve the general good or on similar grounds. In other words, and perhaps less prosaically, they will also be justified if they serve a sufficiently important public interest.

Having regard to the fact that restrictions on the rule against nationality discrimination on grounds of public policy, public security and public health are permissible when they are objectively justified, the same restrictions would, in the public interest, be applicable to the provisions guaranteeing the free movement of economically active persons under the *EC Treaty* even if they were not expressly provided for in Articles 48(3), 56(1) and 66.

The suitability of Article 8a(2) to the task of providing a legal basis for the adoption of restrictions on the rights contained in article 8a(1) precludes the availability of both Articles 6 and 235 for the same purpose. As we have seen, Article 6 will apply only "without prejudice to any special provisions contained" in the Treaty while Article 235 may not be employed as a legal basis for the adoption of measures unless the "Treaty has not provided the necessary powers". On the present analysis, Article 8a(2) provides the necessary powers for the adoption of measures restricting the Union citizen's movement and residence rights, albeit within certain parameters. To that extent it therefore precludes the employment of Article 235 as an appropriate legal basis and is a "special provision" disqualifying the use of Article 6 (second paragraph).

There is no alternative to the use of Article 8a(2) as a legal basis for the adoption of certain measures restricting the Union citizen's right to move and reside because there is no need for one: Article 8a(2) itself provides the legal basis, notwithstanding that it is expressed to authorise the adoption of provisions "facilitating" the rights contained in Article 8a(1).

Summary and Conclusion

We are now in a position to formulate an answer to the questions posed at the outset of this Chapter: To what limitations and conditions, if any, are citizens of the Union subject in exercising their Article 8a rights of movement and residence within the territory of the Member States? In particular are they subject to, or can they be made subject to, the limitations on the grounds of public policy, public security and public health to which persons exercising migration rights under Articles 48-66 of the *EC Treaty* are presently subject? Furthermore, can they be made subject to conditions concerning financial self-sufficiency and health insurance if not engaged in economic activity within the scope of Articles 48-66?

Firstly, it is apparent from the very wording of Article 8a(1) ("subject to the limitations and conditions laid down in this Treaty and by the measures adopted to give it effect") that the rights guaranteed therein are not absolute and unqualified. Moreover, even if one were to infer that the use of the word "facilitating" in Article 8a(2) accorded the rights in Article 8a(1) an absolute quality, one would quickly collide with the paradoxes and legal distortions attendant upon treating the broader category of Union citizens more favourably in the exercise of movement and residence rights than the narrower sub-categories of workers, establishers and participants in the supply and consumption of services.

The proximate solution to this difficulty is to recognise that the Union citizen's movement and residence rights are subject to the limitations and conditions imposed on nationals of Member States exercising rights under *Directive 90/365* (residence rights for former employees and former self-employed persons), *Directive 90/366* (residence rights for students) and especially *Directive 90/364* (residence rights for persons of independent means). Consequently, Union citizens exercising their Article 8a rights will be subject to the limitations and conditions laid down in these three directives, including restrictions justified on grounds of public policy, public security and public health and subject to satisfying the national authorities as to their financial self-sufficiency and health insurance status in accordance with the requirements of the three directives.

Yet the proximate solution cannot be completely satisfying for, standing alone, it fails to allow for the possibility of subjecting the Union citizen's movement and residence rights to restrictions if the three directives were to be repealed through the legislative process or annulled through the judicial process. It also fails to allow for the possibility, after the coming into force of the *Union Treaty*, of imposing restrictions not already contained in the three EEC directives.

A reasonable argument can be made out for the proposition that within the structure of the *EC Treaty* there can be found a residual constitutional power vested in the Member States by which they remain entitled to impose limitations and conditions on the Union citizen's rights under Article 8a(1) on the grounds of public policy, public security and the protection of health.

The decision of the Court of Justice in *Johnston*, however, appears to have explicitly rejected the existence of any such power. Nevertheless, the technique employed by the Court in resolving the issues in *Johnston* strongly suggests that there remains vested in the Member States a residual constitutional power to derogate from rights conferred under Community law on the ground of national or public security (but not on the grounds of public policy and public health). This analysis of the Court's technique has the advantage of being harmonious with Article 224 of the *EC Treaty* which presupposes the existence of such a power. The existence of this much truncated residual power is not sufficient, however, to avoid most of the distortions which could arise in Community law were Article 8a(2), as narrowly construed and in the absence of the three EEC movement and residence directives, to be regarded as the appropriate legal basis for the adoption of the measures referred to in Article 8a(1).

We might, in reaction to this difficulty and in spite of the apparent textual obstacles, be tempted to turn immediately to Article 8a(2) as a source of power to enact the limiting and conditioning measures envisaged by Article 8a(1). In order to do so, however, it is first necessary to explain how a provision which on its face authorises the adoption of measures "facilitating" the Union citizen's movement and residence rights could be employed in such a way. At the very least it is necessary to show that there is simply no alternative to Article 8a(2) for the achievement of our necessary purpose. This means that because the Member States lack a reserve or residual constitutional power to derogate from the Union citizen's movement and residence rights on grounds of public policy, protection of health and the Union citizen's lack of adequate independent financial security, alternative means to introduce Community legislation authorising such derogations must be eliminated before resorting to an interpretation of Article 8a(2) which appears to strain its language by permitting it to provide such a legal basis.

An examination of the possible alternative legal bases in Articles 100 and 100a of the *EC Treaty* shows them both to be unsuitable. Article 100 is unsuitable because it authorises the adoption of directives for the approximation of such national measures as directly affect the establishment or functioning of the common market. The Union citizen's right of movement and residence under Article 8a does not form part of the common market. Article 100a is unsuitable because Article 100a(2) specifically excludes from the scope of Article 100a "provisions ... relating to the free movement of persons". There is also the additional possible objection that the movement and residence rights contained in Article 8a do not form part of the "internal market" for whose achievement Article 100a is designed.

Still assuming for textual reasons that Article 8a(2) is not available as a legal basis for the adoption of provisions restricting - as distinct from 'facilitating' - the Union citizen's right to move and reside, Article 6 (second paragraph) of the *EC Treaty* would appear to be available for the purpose. The rights contained in Article 8a, because Article 8a(1) operates as more than a mere pledge to confer movement and residence rights in secondary legislation,[1] are clearly within the "scope and application" of the *EC Treaty* for the purposes of Article 6 (first paragraph).

Notwithstanding that Article 6 (second paragraph) is expressed to authorise the adoption of rules "designed to prohibit" nationality discrimination, we have seen that it is apt to provide a legal basis for the adoption of rules authorising derogations from the principle of nationality non-discrimination on grounds of public policy, public security and public health, where such derogations are 'objectively justified' (*Re Students' Rights*). A measure is objectively justified although it represents a *de facto* derogation from the principle against nationality discrimination if it applies criteria which are nationality-neutral, if the real purpose of the measure is not to discriminate on grounds of nationality and if a sufficiently important public interest is served. Thus a derogation against the principle of nationality non-discrimination may be objectively justified on grounds of public policy, public security and public health, but it may also be so justified on other grounds involving a sufficiently important public interest.

Yet if Article 6 (second paragraph) can serve, despite its apparent textual inability, as a legal basis for the adoption of rules authorising certain derogations from the principle against nationality non-discrimination in the field of Union citizens' movement and residence rights, there would appear to be no good reason why Article 8a(2), subject to a very similar apparent textual inability, could not likewise serve. This view is reinforced by the fact that the economic movement rights accorded to Member State nationals under the *EC Treaty* are similarly subject to certain conditions justified in the public interest.

The suitability of Article 8a(2) to the task of providing a legal basis for the adoption of certain restrictions on the rights contained in Article 8a(1) precludes the availability of both Articles 6 and 235 for a co-extensive purpose, the former being "without prejudice to any special provisions contained" elsewhere in the Treaty and the latter being available as a legal basis only where the Treaty "has not provided the necessary powers".

Hence in spite of the apparent textual difficulty standing in the way, Article 8a(2) turns out after all to provide a legal basis for the adoption of provisions restricting the rights referred to in Article 8a(1). The Union citizen's movement and residence rights

[1]See Chapter 5.

may be restricted by provisions adopted under Article 8a(2) where such provisions are objectively justified in the public interest. Restrictions may be so justified when considerations of public policy, public security and public health are at stake.

Just as the freedoms of movement accorded to persons under Articles 48-66 of the *EC Treaty* are intended to give effect to, or are specific manifestations of, the principle against nationality discrimination in Article 6,[1] falling as they do within the scope and application of the Treaty, so are the rights contained in Article 8a. A measure may therefore be objectively justified although it represents a *de facto* derogation from the principle against nationality discrimination if it applies criteria which are nationality-neutral, if the real purpose of the measure is not to discriminate on grounds of nationality and if a sufficiently important public interest is served. The avoidance of administrative inconvenience or expense is not a sufficiently important public interest, although objectives such as the conservation of limited economic resources, the integrity of the social security and taxation systems, and the preservation of conditions of market competition would, at least in certain contexts, appear to be sufficient. Furthermore, "Community law has not excluded the power of Member States to adopt measures enabling the national authorities to have an exact knowledge of population movements affecting their territory".[2]

Although the public interest may, in certain objectively justified circumstances, warrant the limitation or conditioning of the rights conferred by Article 8a, they may not be restricted to the extent of being entirely negated.[3] Nor can such limitations operate so as to "cause an obstacle to the freedom of entry and residence provided for in the Treaty".[4]

Given, now, that the Union citizen's movement and residence rights may be limited on grounds of public policy, public security and public health when such limitations

[1]See eg Case 63/86 *Commission v Italy* ("*Re Access to Social Housing*") [1988] ECR 29 at p 52, paragraph 12 of the Court's judgment and Case 305/87 *Commission v Greece* ("*Re Immovable Property*") [1989] ECR 1461 at p 1472, paragraph 14 of Advocate General Jacobs' opinion.

[2]Case 118/75 *Watson and Belmann* [1976] ECR 1185 at p 1198, paragraph 17 of the Court's judgment. The Court of Justice in this case preferred not to categorise the Member States' power to require Community nationals to report their presence to local authorities as a restriction on the Community right of free movement of persons and services. Nevertheless, to the extent that the national measure in question placed administrative formalities in the way of exercising the right, it can at least rationally be classified as a form of condition or restriction. See also Case 8/77 *Sagulo, Brenca and Bakhouche* [1977] ECR 1495 at p 1503, paragraph 4 of the Court's judgment.

[3]In Case 118/75 *Watson and Belmann* [1976] ECR 1185 at p 1199, paragraph 20 of the Court's judgment, the Court of Justice said that a penalty of deportation for failure by a Community national to report his presence to local authorities as required by national law was "incompatible with the provisions of the Treaty since ... such a measure negates the very right conferred and guaranteed by the Treaty". See also Case 157/79 *R v Pieck* [1980] ECR 2171 at p 2187, paragraph 18 of the Court's judgment.

[4]Case 8/77 *Sagulo, Brenca and Bakhouche* [1977] ECR 1495 at p 1506, paragraph 12 of the Court's judgment. The German courts were enjoined, in deciding upon a penalty for failure by Community nationals to comply with administrative formalities permitted by Community law and attaching to the EEC rights of movement and residence, to use their "judicial discretion to impose a punishment appropriate to the character and objective" of the freedom of personal movement provisions in the *EEC Treaty*; ibid. See also Case 157/79 *R v Pieck* [1980] ECR 2171 at p 2187, paragraph 19 of the Court's judgment and Case C-265/88 *Messner* [1989] ECR 4209 at p 4224, paragraph 8 of the Court's judgment.

are objectively justified, it remains only to determine whether the exercise of these rights may be made subject to the citizen satisfying the host Member State's authorities that he is financially self-sufficient and covered by health insurance if not engaged in economic activity within the scope of Articles 48-66.

The principal purpose of any such restriction would be to protect a host Member State's public revenue from calls which could otherwise be made on it by Union citizens who, while not engaged in economic activity within the scope of Articles 48-66, are unable adequately to provide for themselves and their families.[1] This is clearly an economic objective. We have already seen that Member States are unable to invoke the express public policy, public security and public health provisos in the Treaty if the purpose of the restriction is to serve an economic end.[2] There is no reason in principle why the same inability would not apply to Member States seeking to limit, on implied public interest grounds, a Community national's economic migration rights under Articles 48-66. Any ability to restrict economic migration rights for economic purposes would tend to negate the very *raison d'être* of the Community, just as it does when the Member States have unsuccessfully sought to restrict the free movement of goods for the same purposes.[3]

But the Union citizen's movement and residence rights under Article 8a of the *EC Treaty* are not of an economic nature. They do not depend on the Union citizen being a worker, establisher or a provider or consumer of services. Nor, as we have already seen, do they form part of the common market or, probably, of the internal market.

Furthermore requirements as to financial self-sufficiency and health insurance are for the purpose of ensuring that beneficiaries of the right of movement and residence do not become an unreasonable burden on the public finances of the host Member State. In this connection the cohesion of the national taxation system is a public interest whose protection may objectively justify a derogation from the principle of equal treatment for Union citizens exercising their movement and residence rights.

The rights conferred on Union citizens by Article 8a may therefore be made subject to a condition that the beneficiary possess sufficient resources and be possessed of health insurance such that neither he nor any members of his family who are not themselves

[1] The rights of movement and residence granted by each of *Directive 90/364* (persons of independent means), *Directive 90/365* (pensioners) and *Directive 90/366* (students) are subject to the beneficiaries satisfying the host Member State that they have sufficient resources to avoid becoming a burden on its social assistance system (Article 1 of each directive). Each directive provides, in its preamble, that the beneficiaries of the movement and residence rights "must not become an unreasonable burden on the public finances of the host Member State".

[2] In the case of the free movement of persons see Article 2(2) of *Directive 64/221*.

[3] Eg:- Case 7/61 *Commission v Italy* ("*Re Ban on Pigmeat Imports*") [1961] ECR 317 at p 329; reiterated in Case 95/81 *Commission v Italy* ("*Re Advance Payments for Imports*") [1982] ECR 2187 at p 2204, paragraph 27 of the Court's judgment; Case 238/82 *Duphar BV v Netherlands State* [1984] ECR 523 at p 542, paragraph 23 of the Court's judgment; Case 72/83 *Campus Oil Limited v Minister for Industry and Energy* [1984] ECR 2727 at p 2752, paragraph 35 of the Court's judgment; Case 288/83 *Commission v Ireland* ("*Re Potato Imports*") [1985] ECR 1761 at p 1776, paragraph 28 of the Court's judgment.

Union citizens[1] will become a burden on the social assistance system of the host Member State.

Community legislation adopted under Article 8a(2) may therefore authorise Member States to refuse admission to and expel Union citizens who are nationals of other Member States on grounds of public policy, public security and public health or because such Union citizens lack sufficient resources and health insurance to avoid being a burden on the social assistance system of the host Member State.

Member States may adopt their own measures protecting their interests in these fields as regards Article 8a migrants even in the absence of regulating Community legislation. Any such national measures will be subject to Community supervision so that they must be proportionate to the interests sought to be protected and must not be a disguised form of nationality discrimination. Furthermore, the provisions of Articles 2(2) and 3 of *Directive 64/221* will apply as general principles of Community law which must be respected by any national measures adopted.

If, therefore, a Member State wished to exclude or expel a person exercising movement rights under Article 8a, it could not do so in order to service economic ends,[2] or on grounds not based exclusively on the individual's personal conduct,[3] or solely on the basis of the person's previous criminal record.[4] Nor can a Member State expel a Union citizen simply because the identity card or passport used by him to enter the host Member State's territory has expired.[5]

Article 224 of the *EC Treaty* may, however, justify a departure from some of these restraints where there is a serious internal disturbance affecting the maintenance of law and order, in the event of war or serious international tension constituting a threat of war, or in order to carry out obligations it has accepted for the purpose of maintaining peace and international security. A sadly commonplace example might be a Member State's decision to perform an act of mass expulsion of real or apparent football supporters from another Member State where large-scale international football hooliganism results in a serious internal disturbance affecting the maintenance of law and order. In such circumstances, Article 224 would probably justify a Member State's failure to examine each instance of expulsion on its individual merits.

[1]In Case C-295/90 *European Parliament v Council* ("*Re Students' Rights*") [1992] 3 CMLR 281 at p 302, paragraph 19 of the judgment, the Court of Justice said that "the right of residence conferred upon the spouse and dependent children (by *Directive 90/366*) appears to be an essential element for genuine exercise of the student's right of residence". It is therefore very arguable that the student's spouse and dependent children have a right to reside with their student spouse or parent as a result of the direct effects of Article 7 of the *EEC Treaty* and independently of the directive.

[2]Article 2(2).

[3]Article 3(1).

[4]Article 3(2).

[5]Article 3(3).

CHAPTER 5

DIRECT EFFECT OF CITIZENSHIP MIGRATION RIGHTS

It has been said that the "right of free movement and the right of residence are ... the foundations of Union citizenship".[1] The purpose of this Chapter is to determine whether the Union citizen's right to move and reside freely in the territory of the Member States laid down in Article 8a of the *EC Treaty* is directly effective. The importance of the issue is obvious, for a directly effective Article 8a confers a new constitutional movement right which may be enforced by national courts at the suit of Union citizens. Furthermore, such commentary as presently exists concerning Article 8a has not addressed its possible direct effect.

Textual Difficulties

As the discussion in the previous Chapter revealed, the interpretation of Article 8a of the *EC Treaty* is not without its difficulties. In particular, it is not obvious from the English version of the text whether the provision actually confers any substantive rights which Union citizens may call upon national courts to protect. In other words, it is not immediately apparent from a perusal of the English version of Article 8a whether the provision is directly effective.

There are three textual difficulties associated with the English language version of Article 8a which impact upon the question of its direct effect.

The difficulty which first presents itself arises from the unusual juxtaposition of the prepositions "in" and "by" in the phrase "subject to the limitations and conditions laid down *in* this Treaty and *by* the measures adopted to give it effect". Did the draftsman mean that every citizen of the Union possesses the right to move and reside freely within the territory of the Member States *by* (ie through the agency of) the measures adopted to give it effect, and subject to the limitations and conditions laid down in the Treaty? Or did he mean that every citizen of the Union possesses the right to move and reside freely within the territory of the Member States, subject to the limitations and conditions laid down in the Treaty and also subject to the limitations and conditions laid down in the measures adopted to give it effect? If the former interpretation is correct, Article 8a is probably not directly effective. If, on the other hand, the latter interpretation is the correct one, a much stronger case for direct effect can be made out.

Another difficulty arises from the use of the word "effect". Is the draftsman saying that until the 'measures' are 'adopted' the right to move and reside is not effective, in the

[1]David O'Keeffe, "*Union Citizenship*", in David O'Keeffe and Patrick M Twomey (eds), "*Legal Issues of the Maastricht Treaty*" (1994), p 87 at p 90.

sense of not being operative (the narrow meaning of "effect")? Or is he simply saying that the measures to be adopted are for the purpose of implementing or applying the right to move and reside granted by the first limb of Article 8a(1) (the broad meaning of "effect")? In the former case, Article 8a is not directly effective. In the latter case it probably is.

Finally there is the question as to the noun to which the pronoun "it", in the phrase "measures adopted to give it effect", refers. Is "it" a reference to the noun "right" or to the noun "Treaty"? If the measures to be adopted are to give effect to the "right to move and reside freely in the territory of the Member States", then Article 8a might not be directly effective (if one adopts the narrow reading of the word "effect"). If, on the other hand, the measures to be adopted are to give effect to the Treaty, then it is a much more general provision referring to any measure made under the Treaty including, for example, the provisions to be adopted under Article 8a(2). Such an interpretation is not inconsistent with Article 8a's direct effect.

The English version of Article 8a permits of three possible interpretations. Firstly, Article 8a could be construed as meaning that it immediately grants a right to move and reside, which right is to be elaborated in secondary measures and which is subject only to the limitations and conditions laid down elsewhere in the Treaty. This construction might conveniently be referred to as the 'strong interpretation' of Article 8a.

Article 8a could also be the subject of a 'weak interpretation' in which it is construed as expressing merely a commitment to confer movement and residence rights on Union citizens the terms of which are to be found in measures giving effect to the right to move and reside, which measures may also contain unspecified limitations and conditions, and subject to limitations and conditions laid down elsewhere in the Treaty.

Finally, Article 8a might be understood as meaning that it immediately grants a right to move and reside subject to unspecified limitations and conditions contained or to be contained in measures giving effect to that right and also subject to limitations and conditions laid down elsewhere in the Treaty. This could be referred to as the 'intermediate interpretation' of Article 8a.

The strong interpretation is, having regard to the conclusions we reached in Chapter 4, unlikely to be correct, for it would preclude adopting any secondary legislation limiting or conditioning the Union citizen's right to move and reside. Furthermore, it would mean that such provisions as limit the right are to be found elsewhere in the Treaty. On the other hand, both the weak and intermediate interpretations are perfectly consistent with the conclusions of Chapter 4. The claims of all three interpretations will, nevertheless, be considered.

The Jurisprudential and Philosophical Basis of Direct Effect

This method of formulating the possible interpretations of Article 8a is of assistance in helping to understand whether, or to what extent, the provision is directly effective. In the context of discussing the direct effect of provisions of the *EEC Treaty*, former Judge Pescatore divided the Treaty provisions effectively into two broad groups.[1]

Firstly there are those provisions which Judge Pescatore placed in a "positive list" and which are directly effective. The other group consists of provisions in a "negative list" which are not directly effective. There is also a hybrid category which consists of provisions which, upon a detailed analysis of their terms, are seen to contain elements some of which are directly effective and some of which are not. The provisions in the "positive list" outnumber those in the "negative list". Why should this be so?

In reviewing the development of the doctrine of direct effect up until 1983, Judge Pescatore (as he then was) advanced the view that the Court of Justice was impelled by a legal philosophy which regarded the direct effectiveness of legal rules as their normal status and that this philosophy decisively influenced the Court's response to arguments concerning the direct effectiveness of individual Treaty provisions. He summarised the Court's philosophy in the following terms:

> This philosophy is very simple indeed. It means that legal rules, by their very nature have a practical purpose. Any legal rule is devised so as to operate effectively ... . If it is not operative, it is not a rule of law. The task of lawyers is therefore not to thwart effects of legal rules, but to help in putting them into operation. In other words, practical operation for all concerned, which is nothing else than "direct effect," must be considered as being the normal condition of any rule of law. The non-operation of a rule of law appears thus to be not an ordinary phenomenon, but a real antinomy in the legal system. In other words, "direct effect" must be presumed, it has not to be established *a priori*. To return to medical comparisons, I would say that "direct effect" is the normal state of health of the law; it is only the absence of direct effect which causes concern and calls for the attention of legal doctors. ...
>
> Effectiveness is the very soul of legal rules and therefore I think that it is not excessive to say that any legal rule must be at first sight presumed to be operative in view of its object and purpose. ...
>
> "[D]irect effect" is nothing but the ordinary state of the law. Questions will therefore arise only in those exceptional cases where the implementation of a given Community rule, whatever its source and

[1]Pierre Pescatore, "*The Doctrine of 'Direct Effect': An Infant Disease of Community Law*", (1983) 8 European Law Review 155.

> whatever its form, meets some obstacle in law or in fact which even the best-intentioned lawyer feels it difficult to overcome.[1]

Indeed, according to Judge Pescatore, the judges of the Court of Justice first embarked upon the path of direct effect in *NV Algemene Transport- en Expeditie Onderneming van Gend & Loos v Nederlandse administratie der belastingen*[2] not because they regarded technical arguments as decisive, but because they had "*une certaine idée de l'Europe*" of their own.[3]

This "*idée*" is made explicit in the Court's judgment in *van Gend & Loos* where, in a celebrated passage, it said that "the Community constitutes a new legal order of international law for the benefit of which the states have limited their sovereign rights, albeit within limited fields, and the subjects of which comprise not only Member States but also their nationals".[4] According to Judge Pescatore, this conception of the Community legal system;

> ... is the consequence of a democratic ideal , meaning that in the Community, as well as in a modern constitutional state, Governments may not say any more as they are used to doing in international law: "L'Etat, c'est moi." Far from it; the Community calls for participation of everybody, with the result that private individuals are not only liable to burdens and obligations, but that they have also prerogatives and rights which must be legally protected. It was thus a highly political idea, drawn from a perception of the constitutional system of the Community, which is at the basis of *Van Gend & Loos* and which continues to inspire the whole doctrine flowing from it.[5]

In analysing claims that a Treaty provision is directly effective, the Court of Justice therefore commences with certain jurisprudential and philosophical assumptions which favour a finding of direct effect. The jurisprudential assumption is that legal rules are by their nature ordinarily to be regarded as directly effective. The philosophical assumption is that the Community legal system treats those who are subject to the duties it imposes as analogous to citizens in a democratic state who possess effective rights and prerogatives as well as duties and obligations. Given that Article 8a deals with one of the rights of Union citizenship *per se*, it is to be expected that in considering the provision's direct effectiveness the Court of Justice will be especially sensitive to the implications flowing from the philosophical assumption.

[1] ibid at pp 155 and 177.
[2] Case 26/62 [1963] ECR 1.
[3] Pierre Pescatore, op cit, p 157.
[4] Case 26/62 *NV Algemene Transport- en Expeditie Onderneming van Gend & Loos v Nederlandse administratie der belastingen* [1963] ECR 1 at p 12. See also Case 6/64 *Costa v ENEL* [1964] ECR 585 at p 593.
[5] Pierre Pescatore, op cit, p 158 (footnote omitted).

Three Technical Criteria for Direct Effect

Although these assumptions significantly inform the attitude taken by the Court of Justice to a claim of direct effect, the resolution of such a claim is not inevitably determined by them. In other words, they cannot really be regarded as "decisive" as Judge Pescatore suggests.[1] In particular, there are certain well-established technical requirements which must be satisfied before a Community legislative provision can be regarded as directly effective.

All the principal provisions on the free movement of economically active persons in the *EC Treaty*, Article 48 (workers), Article 52 (establishment) and Article 59 (services), have been held to be directly effective.[2]

Advocate General Mayras, in *Reyners v Belgian State*,[3] has usefully summarised the technical criteria to be applied in establishing whether a rule of Community law may be regarded as directly effective:

> 1. The first condition which the case law establishes is that the rule must be sufficiently clear and precise. ...
>
> 2. The second criterion of direct applicability lies in the unconditional character of the Community standard, the implementation of which must not be subject to any fundamental condition. ...
>
> 3. There remains a third condition. The Community standard must be perfected; it must be sufficient in itself. Its implementation must not depend on measures being subsequently taken by Community Institutions or Member States with discretionary power in the matter.[4]

FIRST CRITERION: CLARITY AND PRECISION

Article 8a of the *EC Treaty* would appear easily to satisfy the first of Advocate General Mayras' technical requirements. There is little room to quibble as to the meaning of the term "the right to move and reside freely within the territory of the Member States". Clearly, the drafters of the provision have in mind that Union citizens shall be entitled to enter, establish a residence or residences in, and travel within the territory of any Member State of which they are not a national on a basis of equality with the host Member State's own nationals. This aspect of Article 8a is unaffected by the choice one makes among the strong, weak and intermediate interpretations of the provision.

[1]ibid, p 157.
[2]Case 41/74 *van Duyn v Home Office* [1974] ECR 1337 (workers); Case 2/74 *Reyners v Belgian State* [1974] ECR 631 (establishment); Case 33/74, *van Binsbergen v Bestuur van de Bedrijfsvereniging voor de Metaalnijverheid* [1974] ECR 1299 (services).
[3]Case 2/74 [1974] ECR 631.
[4]ibid at pp 659, 660, 661.

The second and third of the Advocate General's technical requirements are, however, not so obviously satisfied.

SECOND CRITERION: UNCONDITIONAL CHARACTER

It is clear from the terms of Article 8a that the rights it contains are "subject to the limitations and conditions laid down" in the *EC Treaty*. What are these limitations and conditions and do they operate so as to deprive Article 8a of the quality which would bring it within Advocate General Mayras' second technical requirement for direct effect?

A perusal of the *EC Treaty* will demonstrate that there are no limitations and conditions which are expressed to apply to Union citizens *per se*. The Treaty does, however, contain limitations and conditions on the right to move and reside enjoyed by nationals of Member States[1] *qua* workers (Articles 48(3) and 48(4)), establishees (Articles 55 (first paragraph) and 56(1)) and those engaged in the supply or receipt of services (Article 66). The reference in Article 8a(1) to "limitations and conditions laid down in this Treaty" must be a reference at least to the limitations and conditions laid down in Articles 48(3), 48(4), 55 (first paragraph), 56(1) and 66 if it is to have any meaning at all.

Union citizens who are engaged in economic activities falling within the scope of Articles 48-66 of the *EC Treaty* continue, therefore, to be subject to the limitations and conditions applicable to the freedom of movement and residence attaching to those economic activities. Thus a Union citizen who seeks to enter or remain in the territory of a Member State of which he is not a national for the purposes of, for example, undertaking paid employment could be excluded on grounds of, for example, public health under Article 48(3). This remains so notwithstanding any right to move and reside derived from his status as a Union citizen.

The existence of these limitations and conditions, however, does not operate so as to place Article 8a outside Advocate General Mayras' second requirement for direct effect. These exceptional provisions permit restrictions on the rights to which they refer on grounds of public policy, public security and public health,[2] employment in the public service[3] and activities connected with the exercise of official authority.[4]

In *Reyners* Advocate General Mayras expressly rejected the view that the limitations on grounds of public policy, public security and public health can affect the direct effect of the provisions to which they refer. This was so because "[s]uch reservations

[1] It will be recalled that Article 8(1) of the *EC Treaty* extends citizenship of the Union to "(e)very person holding the nationality of a Member State".

[2] Articles 48(3), 56(1) and 66.

[3] Article 48(4).

[4] Articles 55 (first paragraph) and 66.

... are very limited".[1] There is no reason in principle, however, why a limited reservation could not operate so as to deprive a provision of Community law of its unconditional character. All reservations, short of a general one to derogate in any circumstances and on any grounds whatever, are limited in some way, and the Advocate General gives no guidance on how to distinguish a "very limited" reservation from a merely limited one for the purpose of deciding when it operates to deny direct effect to a legislative provision..

A more satisfactory basis for identifying reservations which do not deprive a provision of Community law of its direct effect was supplied shortly after Advocate General Mayras' *Reyners* opinion in the judgment of the Court of Justice in *van Duyn*. The Court made the following remarks in discussing whether the provisos contained in Article 48(3) of the *EEC Treaty* deprive Article 48 of direct effect:

> Paragraph 3, which defines the rights implied by the principle of freedom of movement for workers, subjects them to limitations justified on grounds of public policy, public security or public health. The application of these limitations is, however, subject to judicial control, so that a Member State's right to invoke the limitations does not prevent the provisions of Article 48, which enshrine the principle of freedom of movement for workers, from conferring on individuals rights which are enforceable by them and which the national courts must protect.[2]

The test to be applied in determining whether a proviso is of such a nature as to deprive a provision of Community law of the unconditional character which it requires in order to be directly effective is therefore not one of examining how 'limited' is the proviso. Rather, attention must be paid to whether the proviso is "subject to judicial control". If a proviso is not subject to judicial control, then it will deprive a provision of Community law of the unconditionality it requires in order to be directly effective. Conversely, if the proviso is subject to judicial control then it will not deprive a provision of Community law of the unconditionality it requires in order to be directly effective.

Judge Pescatore strikes a similar chord when he says that "in the last analysis ... the prerequisite of the unconditional character and the sufficient degree of Community provisions, in order to be recognised as having 'direct effect', boil [*sic*] down to a question of justiciability".[3]

[1]Case 2/74 [1974] ECR 631 at p 660.

[2]Case 41/74 *van Duyn v Home Office* [1974] ECR 1337 at p 1347, paragraph 7 of the Court's judgment. See also Case 36/75 *Rutili v Minister for the Interior* [1975] ECR 1219 at p 1231, paragraph 27 of the Court's judgment.

[3]Pierre Pescatore, op cit, p 176.

The decision of the Court of Justice in *van Duyn v Home Office*[1] makes it clear that the public policy, public security and public health limitations contained in the *EEC Treaty*, and continued in the *EC Treaty*, are justiciable in that they are subject to judicial control. Furthermore the freedoms of movement for persons covered by Articles 48, 52 and 59 have all been held directly effective notwithstanding the public policy, public security and public health limitations permitted by the *EEC Treaty*. It follows that the existence of these limitations does not operate so as to deprive Article 8a of the direct effect which it may be presumed to possess.

As to the limitations concerning the public service and the exercise of official authority, Advocate General Mayras has correctly pointed out that they "restrict the scope of the principle of equality of treatment, but do not bring its direct applicability into question".[2]

THIRD CRITERION: PERFECTED COMMUNITY STANDARD

Article 8a therefore satisfies the first two of Advocate General Mayras' three requirements for direct effect. It remains only to determine whether Article 8a meets the third requirement. Is it perfected? Does its implementation depend on measures being taken by the Community's institutions or by Member States with discretionary power in the matter? Of the three criteria for direct effect, this is the most difficult to determine.

Resolving the Textual Ambiguities: Language

It is at this point that the ambiguities in the English text of Article 8a, which were pointed out at the beginning of this Chapter, fall to be confronted.

If the weak interpretation of Article 8a is the correct one, then the Union citizen's right to move and reside freely within the territory of the Member States is not perfected and cannot be directly effective. It will be recalled that the weak interpretation posits Article 8a as expressing merely a commitment to confer movement and residence rights on Union citizens the terms of which are to be found in measures giving effect to the right, which measures may also contain unspecified limitations and conditions, and subject to limitations and conditions laid down elsewhere in the Treaty. Such an interpretation would have Article 8a function as a mere pledge, the redemption of which would depend entirely upon legislative action by the Community institutions. Clearly Article 8a, conceived in such a way, could not be regarded as perfected and independent of measures being subsequently taken by Community institutions with discretionary power in the matter.

Any case for the weak interpretation of Article 8a commences with the handicap arising from the existence of the Court of Justice's jurisprudential and philosophical assumptions predisposing it to findings of direct effect. Any such case would need,

[1]Case 41/74 [1974] ECR 1337 at p 1347, paragraph 6 of the Court's judgment.
[2]Case 2/74 *Reyners v Belgian State* [1974] ECR 631 at p 660.

moreover, to be a convincing one if it is to prevail in the face of two rival interpretations each of which is more harmonious with the Court's assumptions.

English. The weak interpretation of Article 8a depends essentially on a grammatical proposition in the English version of the text which relies on treating the phrase "subject to the limitations and conditions laid down in this Treaty and" as a subordinate clause. The supposed principal clause in Article 8a(1) would then read as follows: "Every citizen of the Union shall have the right to move and reside freely within the territory of the Member States ... by the measures adopted to give it effect". If there are no measures, there is no right. The institutions charged with adopting the secondary measures are, on this analysis, given considerable discretion as to the scope and conditions of any right conferred by those measures adopted under Article 8a.

Article 8a, construed in accordance with the weak interpretation, would resemble the non-directly effective Article 67(1) of the *EC Treaty*, which requires the Member States to abolish certain restrictions on capital movements "to the extent necessary to ensure the proper functioning of the common market" thereby leaving the relevant Community institutions considerable discretion in its implementation.[1]

The grammatical proposition upon which the weak interpretation of the English version of Article 8a depends is, however, unsustainable. This is firstly because, as we shall see, the grammatical proposition underpinning a weak interpretation of the English version of Article 8a(1) is not available when one examines the other language versions of the text. Secondly, the phrase "subject to the limitations and conditions laid down in this Treaty and" does not make sense as a subordinate clause. The phrase "by the measures adopted to give it effect" cannot therefore be read as being part of a principal clause with the opening phrase of Article 8a(1). Hence, the grammatical proposition necessary for a weak interpretation of Article 8a is not really available in the English version of the text. We shall see that the proposition does not even arise in the other language versions.

The strong interpretation would have Article 8a operate in a fashion similar to the directly effective freedom of movement provisions in Articles 48, 52 and 59 of the *EC Treaty*. On this analysis, any legislation adopted under Article 8a(2) can serve - as in the case of secondary legislation implementing the directly effective freedom of movement provisions in Articles 48, 52 and 59 - only to determine "the scope and detailed rules for the exercise of rights conferred directly by the Treaty".[2]

[1]Case 203/80 *Casati* [1981] ECR 2595.

[2]Case 48/75 *Royer* [1976] ECR 497 at p 512, paragraph 28 of the Court's judgment. By contrast, Article 48(3)(d) of the *EEC Treaty* confers on workers a right to remain in the territory of a Member State after having been employed there "subject to conditions which shall be embodied in implementing regulations". This implies that the right in question may be restricted, rather than merely facilitated, by the foreshadowed regulations. Restrictions on the right contained in Article 48(3)(d) were imposed by Article 2(1) of *Regulation 1251/70* (OJ Sp Ed 1970, L 142/24, p 402) which has the effect of excluding from enjoyment of the right several categories of persons who would otherwise fall within the scope of the Treaty provision.

The strong interpretation could be supported by pointing to the strong and apparently analogous provisions in Articles 48, 52 and 59.

Furthermore, it could be argued that the positioning of Article 8a within the new Part Two of the *EC Treaty* establishing, defining and constitutionalising Union citizenship, tends to indicate that it, no less than the free personal movement provisions covered by Articles 48-66 of the Treaty, is a fundamental Community freedom.

Finally, such an argument might run, if Article 8a(2) provides the procedure by which the measures referred to in Article 8a(1) are to be adopted, then those measures may not operate so as to limit or restrict the Union citizen's right of movement and residence because Article 8a(2) authorises the adoption of only those measures "facilitating the exercise of the rights referred to in" Article 8a(1). This view of Article 8a(2) assumes, however, that Article 8a(1) confers a perfected Community right, and this is the very issue which needs to be resolved. If the true interpretation of Article 8a(1) is the weak one, then Article 8a(2) can 'facilitate' the exercise of the rights referred to in Article 8a(1) by making any provision for their exercise, even a provision subject to limitations and conditions.

The strong interpretation of Article 8a would, however, have a radical impact on the constitutional nature of the Community. Its adoption would mean that all Union citizens, regardless of their involvement in any economic activity, would have a directly effective and unabridgeable Community right to move and reside in the territory of Member States whose nationality they do not possess. The strong interpretation of Article 8a would make it an even 'stronger' provision that Articles 48, 52 and 59 all of which are made subject to limitations and conditions on the grounds of public policy, public security and public health by the express terms of the Treaty itself. In one move, Union citizenship would thus acquire one of the most fundamental attributes of citizenship in a democratic nation-state.

Such an outcome would not be required by the objectives of Article 7a of the *EC Treaty*, since that provision does not extend migration rights to persons not already covered by other provisions of the Treaty. Rather, to the extent that it is relevant to the free movement of persons, Article 7a merely requires at most the removal of physical barriers at internal borders for all persons within the Community without conferring additional movement and residence rights on any person.[1]

[1]See eg, "*The Lifting of Border Controls: Commission Position on the Interpretation of Article 8a of the EEC Treaty*", "Europe" Documents No 1773 of 12 May 1992; D. Wyatt and A. Dashwood, "*European Community Law*", 3rd ed, p 357; C.W.A. Timmermans, "*Free Movement of Persons and the Division of Powers between the Community and its Member States: Why do it the intergovernmental way?*", in Henry G. Schermers et al (eds), "*Free Movement of Persons in Europe*" (1993), p 352 at pp 354-356.

The ambiguity in the English text of Article 8a(1) may be resolved, however, by reference to the equivalent texts in the other official language versions.[1]

German and Danish. The German version[2] of the text makes it clear that Union citizens possess a right to move and 'remain' ("*sich ... aufzuhalten*") freely in the territory of the Member States, subject to the limitations and conditions as provided for in the Treaty and as provided for in the 'implementing measures' ("*Durchführungsvorschriften*"). The German version of the text does not permit of an interpretation which would preclude the *Durchführungsvorschriften* referred to in Article 8a(1) from containing limitations and conditions on the Union citizen's right to move and reside.

Furthermore, the German text cannot be interpreted as meaning that the right to move and reside is granted 'by' (in the sense of 'through the agency of') the *Durchführungsvorschriften.* Rather, the German version uses the phrase "*vorbehaltlich der in diesem Vertrag und in den Durchführungsvorschriften vorgesehenen Beschränkungen und Bedingungen*" (literally 'subject to the limitations and conditions foreseen *in* this Treaty and *in* the implementing measures').

In any event the German version does not easily accommodate an interpretation which assigns to the *Durchführungsvorschriften* the function of redeeming a mere pledge to confer migration rights on Union citizens. Rather, the use of the word "*Durchführungsvorschriften*" strongly implies that the measures to be adopted are for the purpose merely of implementing or executing a general rule already in existence.

[1]Article S of the *Union Treaty* provides that the Treaty's single original texts in the Danish, Dutch, English, French, German, Greek, Irish, Italian, Portuguese and Spanish languages are equally authentic. The drafters of the *Union Treaty* did not, however, take advantage of the opportunity to update the equivalent provision of the *EC Treaty* - Article 248 - which provides that the Treaty is equally authentic in merely the Dutch, French, German and Italian languages (semble Article 225 of the *Euratom Treaty* and Article 49 of the *Merger Treaty*). This provision has remained unaltered since the establishment of the European Economic Community in 1958. Nevertheless in Case 283/81 *Srl CILFIT v Ministry of Health* [1982] ECR 3415, a case involving the interpretation of Article 177 of the *EEC Treaty*, the Court of Justice said "it must be borne in mind that Community legislation is drafted in several languages and that the different language versions are all equally authentic" and that "(a)n interpretation of a provision of Community law thus involves a comparison of the different language versions"; at p 3430, paragraph 18 of the Court's judgment. In Case 150/80 *Elefanten Schuh GmbH v Jacqmain* [1981] ECR 1671 the Court of Justice was called upon to interpret Article 18 of the *Convention on Jurisdiction and the Enforcement of Judgments in Civil and Commercial Matters*. In so doing, the Court referred to "the different language versions of Article 18"; at p 1685, paragraph 14 of the Court's judgment. Advocate General Sir Gordon Slynn had, in the same case, referred the Court to the Dutch, English, French, German, Italian and Irish versions of the provision; at pp 1693-1694. Like the *EC Treaty*, the *Convention on Jurisdiction and the Enforcement of Judgments in Civil and Commercial Matters* is expressed to be authentic in only the Dutch, French, German and Italian languages; Article 68. The *ECSC Treaty* is expressed to be official in the French language only; Article 100 (first paragraph).

[2]The German version of Article 8a(1) provides as follows: "*Jeder Unionsbürger hat das Recht, sich im Hoheitsgebiet der Mitgliedstaaten vorbehaltlich der in diesem Vertrag und in den Durchführungsvorschriften vorgesehenen Beschränkungen und Bedingungen frei zu bewegen und aufzuhalten.*"

The Danish version[1] of Article 8a(1) is to almost identical effect as the German version, with the minor exception that the Danish verb corresponding to the German "*sich aufzuhalten*" (Danish, *opholde*) can mean either 'to reside' or 'to remain'.

Dutch. The Dutch version[2] of Article 8a(1) provides that every citizen of the Union has the right 'to travel' ("*te reizen*") and 'to remain' ("*te verblijven*") freely in the territory of the Member States, subject to the limitations and conditions 'which are adopted' ("*die ... zijn vastgesteld*") 'by this Treaty and the measures for the execution thereof' ("*bij dit Verdrag en de bepalingen ter uitvoering daarvan*"). In the Dutch version, the word for 'thereof' ("*daarvan*") can refer only to the noun for 'Treaty' ("*Verdrag*"), given that both are contained in the same subordinate clause. Accordingly the 'measures' ("*bepalingen*") are for the execution of the Treaty, and not of the right to move and reside. Furthermore the use of the word "*uitvoering*", meaning 'execution' or 'implementation' strongly suggests that Article 8a(1) directly confers a right and that the *bepalingen* are merely for the purpose of providing detailed rules for its application.

Spanish and Portuguese. The Spanish version[3] of Article 8a(1) provides that all Union citizens hold the right to move and reside freely in the territory of the Member States 'subject to the limitations and conditions foreseen in the present Treaty and in the measures adopted for its application' ("*con sujeción a las limitaciones y condiciones previstas en el presente Tratado y en las disposiciones adoptadas para su aplicación*").

It is significant that the phrase '*in* the measures adopted for its application', rather than '*by* the measures adopted for its application', is used. The Spanish version very strongly indicates that the *disposiciones* may contain limitations and conditions on the Union citizen's extant right to move and reside and are not for the purpose of conferring that right. Indeed the word "*disposiciones*" is better translated as 'implementing measures' (the same as the German "*Durchführungsvorschriften*") rather than as 'measures making the right effective'.

Furthermore the use of the word "*aplicación*" shows that in the Spanish version the Union citizen possesses a completed right to move and reside and that the *disposiciones* serve the purpose of merely giving "the scope and detailed rules for the exercise of rights conferred directly by the Treaty".[4] The Spanish text therefore supports the proposition that Article 8a itself gives effect to the Union citizen's migration rights.

[1]The Danish version of Article 8a(1) provides as follows: "*Enhver unionsborger har ret til at færdes og opholde sig frit på medlemsstaternes område med de begrænsninger og på de betingelser, der er fastsat i denne Traktat og i gennemførelsesbestemmelserne hertil.*"

[2]The Dutch version of Article 8a(1) provides as follows: "*Iedere burger van de Unie heeft het recht op het grondgebied van de Lid-Staten te reizen en te verblijven, onder voorbehoud van de beperkingen en voorwaarden die bij dit Verdrag en de bepalingen ter uitvoering daarvan zijn vastgesteld.*"

[3]The Spanish version of Article 8a(1) provides as follows: "*Todo ciudadano de la Unión tendrá derecho a circular y residir libremente en el territorio de los Estados miembros, con sujeción a las limitaciones y condiciones previstas en el presente Tratado y en las disposiciones adoptadas para su aplicación.*"

[4]Case 48/75 *Royer* [1976] ECR 497 at p 512, paragraph 28 of the Court's judgment.

The Portuguese version[1] of Article 8a(1) is to almost identical effect as the Spanish version, with the minor exception that in the Portuguese version the Union citizen is given a right to 'remain' (Portuguese, "*permanecar*") rather than a right to 'reside' (Spanish, "*residir*").

Irish. The Irish version[2] of Article 8a(1) provides that all Union citizens hold the right to move and reside freely in the territory of the Member States 'subject to the limitations and the conditions which are (being) laid down in this Treaty and in the measures (being) adopted to give it application' ("*faoi réir na dteorainneacha agus na gcoinníollacha dá bhforáiltear sa Chonradh seo agus sna forálacha arna nglacadh lena chur chun feidhme*").

Thus, like the Spanish and Portuguese versions, the Irish version uses the phrases '*in* this Treaty' ("*sa Chonradh seo*") and '*in* the measures' ("*sna forálacha*"), thereby indicating that the measures are for the purpose of expressing limitations and conditions on the right to move and reside rather than for the purpose of making that right effective. Furthermore the word "*feidhme*" is better translated as 'application' or 'execution', or in accordance with the broad meaning of "effect" in the English version.. The phrase "*lena chur chun feidhme*" therefore means 'to give it application' or 'to give it execution' and is not satisfactorily rendered as the phrase, 'to make it effective'. It is to the same effect as the Spanish phrase "*para su aplicación*".

French and Italian. The French[3] and Italian[4] versions state that Union citizens possess a right to move and 'remain' (French, "*séjourner*"; Italian, "*soggiornare*") freely in the territory of the Member States, subject to the limitations and conditions 'foreseen *by* the present Treaty' (French, "*prévues par le présent Traité*"; Italian, "*previste dal presente trattato*"). The French version then adds 'and *by* the measures adopted for its application' ("*et par les dispositions prises pour son application*"), while the Italian version adds 'and *by* the measures adopted in application of the same' ("*e dalle disposizioni adottate in applicazione dello stesso*").

Thus whereas the English version of Article 8a(1) juxtaposes the prepositions "in" and "by", and the Spanish, Portuguese and Irish versions use only prepositions corresponding to "in", the French and Italian versions use only prepositions

[1]The Portuguese version of Article 8a(1) provides as follows: "*Qualquer cidadão da União goza do direito de circular e permanecar livremente no território dos Estados-membros, sem prejuízo das limitações previstas no presente Tratado e nas disposições adoptades em sua aplicação.*"

[2]The Irish version of Article 8a(1) provides as follows: "*Beidh an ceart ag gach saoránach den Aontas gluaiseacht agus cónaí faoi shaoirse ar chríoch na mBallstát, faoi réir na dteorainneacha agus na gcoinníollacha dá bhforáiltear sa Chonradh seo agus sna forálacha arna nglacadh lena chur chun feidhme.*"

[3]The French version of Article 8a(1) provides as follows: "*Tout citoyen de l'Union a le droit de circuler et de séjourner librement sur le territoire des Etats membres, sous réserve des limitations et conditions prévues par le présent Traité et par les dispositions prises pour son application.*"

[4]The Italian version of Article 8a(1) provides as follows: "*Ogni cittadino dell'Unione ha il diritto di circolare e di soggiornare liberamente nel territorio degli Stati membri, fatte salve le limitazioni e le condizioni previste dal presente trattato e dalle disposizioni adottate in applicazione dello stesso.*"

corresponding to "by". The difficulty with the English version arises from the juxtaposition, and is resolved when either of the two prepositions is employed in both parts of the relevant phrase. Moreover, it is resolved in the same way whichever of the two prepositions is uniformly employed. In the Spanish, Portuguese and Irish versions, as we have seen, the right to move and reside is subject to the limitations and conditions foreseen *in* the Treaty and *in* the measures adopted for its application. In the French and Italian versions, the right to move and reside is subject to the limitations and conditions foreseen *by* the Treaty and *by* the measures adopted for its application. In both the Spanish-Portuguese-Irish versions and the French-Italian versions the phrase means that the limitations and conditions on the Union citizen's right to move and reside are to be found in, or are laid down by, the Treaty and the measures adopted to give it effect.

The French and Italian versions, no less than the Spanish, Portuguese and Irish versions, therefore suggest that the measures referred to in Article 8a(1) of the English version may contain limitations and conditions on the Union citizen's right to move and reside. Moreover, they suggest that those measures are for the purpose of containing such limitations and conditions, and not for the purpose of making the right to move and reside 'effective'.

Similarly, the word "*dispositions*" in the French version and the word "*disposizioni*" in the Italian version has the same meaning as the word "*disposiciones*" in the Spanish version. The French and the Italian versions are therefore saying that the Union citizen has certain Treaty-conferred movement and residence rights which are subject to limitations and conditions prescribed by the Treaty and also prescribed, or to be prescribed, by the measures adopted giving the scope and detailed rules for the exercise of those rights.

Furthermore, the use of the word "*application*" in the French version and of the word "*applicazione*" in the Italian version has the same meaning and serves the same purpose as the use of the word "*aplicación*" in the Spanish version, so that the "*dispositions*" of the French version and the "*disposizioni*" of the Italian version merely give the scope and detailed rules for the exercise of rights conferred directly by the Treaty.

Greek. The Greek version[1] of Article 8a(1) signifies that the pronoun in the English phrase "measures adopted to give it effect" refers back to the noun "Treaty", rather than to the noun "right". This is because the Greek equivalent of the English pronoun "it" ("της" - literally 'of it') in the phrase "διαταξεις που θεσπιζονται για την εφαρμογη της" (literally 'measures which are adopted for the implementation of it') can refer only to a noun of feminine gender. The word corresponding to "Treaty" in the Greek version ("συνθηκη") is of feminine gender, whereas the Greek word

[1]The Greek version of Article 8a(1) provides as follows: "Καθε πολιτης της 'Ενωσης εχει το δικαιωμα να κυκλοφορει και να διαμενει ελευθερα στο εδαφος των κρατων μελων, υπο την επιφυλαξη των περιορισμων και με τις προυποθεσεις που προβλεπονται στην παρουσα συνθηκη και στις διαταξεις που θεσπιζονται για την εφαρμογη της."

corresponding to "right" ("δικαιωμα") is neuter. Accordingly, the "measures adopted" in the English version are to 'implement' the Treaty, and not the right of movement and residence.

The Greek version also provides that the right to move and reside is subject to the "περιορισμων και με τις προυποθεσεις που προβλεπονται στην παρουσα συνθηκη και στις διαταξεις που θεσπιζονται για την εφαρμογη της" (literally 'limitations and with the conditions which are proposed *in* the present Treaty and *in* the measures which are adopted for the application of it'). Thus the διαταξεις ('measures'), like the *disposiciones* in the Spanish version, may contain limitations and conditions on the Union citizen's extant right to move and reside and are not for the purpose of conferring that right; the right is not conferred *by* the διαταξεις. This is also indicated by the use of the word "εφαρμογη" ('application'), which corresponds to the broad meaning of "effect" in the English text, to the word "*uitvoering*" in the Dutch version, to the word "*feidhme*" in the Irish version, and to the word "*aplicación*" in the Spanish version and words of identical derivation in the French, Italian and Portuguese versions.

Both the strong and weak interpretations of Article 8a(1) would, by reference to its different language versions, therefore seem to be excluded. The intermediate interpretation, by contrast, tends to be confirmed.

Resolving the textual ambiguities: Context
The impression that the intermediate interpretation of Article 8a is correct is further reinforced by resort to a contextual and teleological interpretation.

Limits to Literal Interpretation. A comparison of the various language versions of an ambiguous Community legal text is an important, and possibly critical, starting point in establishing its true meaning. In interpreting Community treaties it is not sufficient, however, merely to adopt a literal approach to the texts, even where the various language versions are referred to.[1] In particular an ambiguity in one of the language versions of a Community legal text may be resolved by reference to the other language versions, but the Court will endeavour to reconcile its interpretation of the various language versions with the objectives of the measure in question.[2]

[1]Case 6/60 *Humblet v Belgian State* [1960] ECR 559 at p 575. The Court referred to the Dutch, French and German versions of Article 16 of the *Protocol on the Privileges and Immunities of the European Coal and Steel Community*.

[2]Eg. Case 16/65 *Firma C Schwarze v Einfuhr- und Vorratsstelle für Getreide und Futtermittel* [1965] ECR 877 at p 889, where the French, Italian and Dutch versions of *Regulation 19* were employed to support an interpretation of the German version which corresponded to the principles laid down in Article 9(2) of the *EEC Treaty* extending the customs union to products coming from third countries which are in free circulation in the Member States; Case 29/69 *Stauder v City of Ulm, Sozialamt* [1969] ECR 419 at pp 424-425, paragraphs 3-4 of the Court's judgment, where the French and Italian versions of *Decision 69/71* were employed to support an interpretation of the German and Dutch versions which accorded with a liberal approach to the rights contained therein, which liberal approach corresponded to the necessity to minimise the impact of restrictions on individual freedoms to the extent consistent with achieving the objectives pursued by the decision; Case 9/79 *Wörsdorfer v Raad van Arbeid* [1979] ECR 2717 at p 2724, paragraphs 6-8 of the Court's judgment, where all the other language versions were employed to support an interpretation of the Dutch version of *Regulation 574/72* which accorded with the principle of equal

Furthermore, the Court of Justice has said that the elimination of linguistic discrepancies by way of simply comparing various language versions may run counter to the requirements of legal certainty, inasmuch as one or more of the texts involved may have to be interpreted in a manner at variance with the natural and usual meaning of the words. Consequently, according to the Court, it is preferable to explore the possibility of solving the points at issue without giving preference to any one of the texts involved.[1] But how is this to be achieved?

Intention, Context and Objectives. An early lead was given in *Stauder v City of Ulm, Sozialamt.*[2] The Court of Justice said that "the necessity for uniform application and accordingly for uniform interpretation makes it impossible to consider one version of the text in isolation but requires that it be interpreted on the basis of the real intention of its author and the aim he seeks to achieve, in the light in particular of the versions in all four languages".[3]

Somewhat more detailed guidance was given in *Srl CILFIT v Ministry of Health*[4] in which the Court of Justice said "every provision of Community law must be placed in its context and interpreted in the light of the provisions of Community law as a whole, regard being had to the objectives thereof and to its state of evolution at the date on which the provision in question is to be applied".[5]

---

treatment for men and women; Case 316/85 *Centre public d'aide sociale de Courcelles v Lebon* [1987] ECR 2811 at pp 2838-2839, paragraph 23 of the Court's judgment, where the German and Greek language versions of *Regulation 1612/68* were employed to support an interpretation of the French version which accorded with the principle that provisions establishing the free movement of workers must be construed broadly; In Case 8/77 *Sagulo, Brenca and Bakhouche* [1977] ECR 1495 the Court of Justice held that Community secondary legislation could constitute a "special provision" for the purposes of Article 7 (first paragraph) of the *EEC Treaty.* This finding was inconsistent with the English language version of the provision: "Within the scope and application of *this Treaty* and without prejudice to any special provisions contained *therein* ..." (emphasis added). The German version of the text resembles the English version: "*Unbeschadet besonderer Bestimmungen dieses Vertrags ist in seinem Anwendungsbereich* ...". The language of the case in *Sagulo* was German. The French text of the provision provides, however, as follows; "*Dans le domaine d'application du présent traité, et sans préjudice des dispositions particulières qu'il prévoit* ...". The French version might therefore translate as; "Within the fields covered by this Treaty, and without prejudice to any special provisions envisaged therein". The decision in *Sagulo* is therefore consistent with the French version of Article 7.

[1]Case 80/76 *North Kerry Milk Products Ltd v Minister for Agriculture and Fisheries* [1977] ECR 425 at p 435, paragraph 11 of the Court's judgment.

[2]Case 29/69 [1969] ECR 419.

[3]ibid at p 424, paragraph 3 of the Court's judgment. The reference to "all four languages" should be seen in the context of the fact that in 1969 the Community was still comprised of only the original six Member States in respect of which there were four official languages. In a similar vein the Court of Justice, confronted with divergences between several language versions of two Regulations in the field of the common agricultural policy in Case 61/72 *Mij PPW International NV v Hoofdproduktschap voor Akkerbouwprodukten* [1973] ECR 301 said that "(n)o argument can be drawn ... from any linguistic divergences between the various language versions, or from the multiplicity of the verbs used in one or other of these versions, as the meaning of the provisions in question must be determined with respect to their objective": at p 310, paragraph 14 of the Court's judgment.

[4]Case 283/81 [1982] ECR 3415.

[5]ibid at p 3430, paragraph 20 of the Court's judgment.

The application of these criteria assist in confirming the validity of the intermediate interpretation of Article 8a already suggested by an examination of the texts in the various official language versions.

It should firstly be observed that there is no risk, in comparing the English version of the text with the other language versions in the way herein suggested, that the English version may have to be interpreted in a manner at variance with the natural and usual meaning of its words. The English version is ambiguous and a comparison with the other language versions merely assists in resolving the ambiguity. On the other hand to interpret the other language versions, in accordance with either the strong or weak interpretations of the English text, would be to construe them in a manner at variance with the natural and usual meaning of their words. The Court of Justice will however interpret a Community Treaty provision in one or more, or even most, languages contrary to their ordinary and natural meaning if another language version is more compatible with the provision's objectives.[1]

The Preamble. The *Union Treaty* did not amend the preamble to the *EEC Treaty*, which preamble therefore remains unaltered in the *EC Treaty*.[2] The preamble consists of ten recitals. Seven of them, the second to eighth, refer to undoubtedly economic objectives.[3] The ninth recital refers to a liberal political aim in the realm of

[1]In Case 150/80 *Elefanten Schuh GmbH v Jacqmain* [1981] ECR 1671 the Court of Justice was called upon to interpret Article 18 of the *Convention on Jurisdiction and the Enforcement of Judgments in Civil and Commercial Matters*. In so doing, the Court disregarded the word "solely" in the English version and its cognates in the Danish, Dutch, German and Italian versions. Instead the Court preferred the French and Irish versions of the provision in which no equivalent word existed. Thus Article 18 which in English (supported by the Danish, Dutch German and Italian versions) provides that "a court of a Contracting State before whom a defendant enters an appearance shall have jurisdiction" but that "(t)his rule shall not apply where appearance was entered solely to contest the jurisdiction", was interpreted as if the word "solely" were entirely absent. Defendants are thereby allowed to contest the national court's jurisdiction even where a defendant's appearance raises issues of substance in addition the national court's jurisdiction. The Court of Justice preferred the French and Irish versions of the text because they were "more in keeping with the objectives and spirit of the Convention" because "under the law of civil procedure of certain Contracting States a defendant who raises the issue of jurisdiction and no other might be barred from making his submissions as to the substance if the court rejects his plea that it has no jurisdiction" and that "(a)n interpretation of Article 18 which enabled such a result to be arrived at would be contrary to the right of the defendant to defend himself in the original proceedings, which is one of the aims of the Convention"; at p 1685, paragraph 14 of the Court's judgment.

[2]In Case C-260/89 *Elliniki Radiophonia Tileorassi AE v Pliroforissis* [1991] ECR I-2925 at p I-2948, paragraph 47(a) of the opinion, Advocate General Lenz said that the preamble to and Article 2 of the *EEC Treaty* "enunciate general obligations of the Member States and the Community institutions and their main function is thus to furnish criteria for interpretation which may be of use in applying specific provisions relating to concrete measures". This was the approach effectively adopted by the Court of Justice in Opinion 1/76 [1977] ECR 741 in which the second recital in the preamble to the *EEC Treaty* was used to help interpret Article 228(1); at p 758, paragraph 11 of the Court's judgment. According to *Halsbury's Laws of England*, 4th edition, 1976, volume 52 at paragraph 1.09: "Whilst the preamble, as such, represents only a broad programme without containing mandatory rules or legally binding obligations, it may nevertheless be called in aid of interpretation of provisions of the treaty as being part of the travaux préparatoires". See also Stefan Schepers, "*The Legal Force of the Preamble to the EEC Treaty*", (1981) 6 ELRev 356.

[3]Economic and social progress of the Member States by common action to eliminate the barriers which divide Europe; constant improvement of the living and working conditions of the Member States' peoples; concerted action in order to guarantee steady expansion, balanced trade and fair competition; strengthening the unity of the Member States' economies and ensuring their harmonious development by reducing differences existing between the various regions and the backwardness of the less favoured

international relations,[1] and the tenth recital formally records the Member States' decision to establish a European Economic Community.[2]

None of these recitals can be construed as supporting the strong interpretation of the English version of Article 8a. On the contrary the second to eighth recitals tend to reinforce the fundamentally economic intentions of the Member States in establishing the Community, thereby making it unlikely that they intended to confer an unqualified non-economic movement and residence right in their territories on nationals of other Member States.

The preamble's first recital records the Member States' determination to lay the foundation of an ever closer union among the peoples of Europe. This recital might, at least at first glance, seem to provide some support for the strong interpretation of the English version of Article 8a. After all, the bestowal of a strong right of movement and residence on Union citizens could be said to strengthen the foundations of an ever closer union among the peoples of Europe. However, as Judge Mancini has pointed out in connection with the *EEC Treaty*:

> [W]hile the American Declaration of Independence spoke of '*one people*' dissolving the bonds which connected them with '*another people*', the preamble of the Rome Treaty recites that the contracting parties are 'determined to lay the foundations of an ever closer union among the *peoples* of Europe'. ...
>
> Treaties are basically different from constitutions. ... As a rule, treaties devise systems of checks and balances whose main function is to keep under control the powers of the organisation which they set up. In the case of the Rome Treaty these differences are emphasised by two highly significant characteristics. The Treaty does not safeguard the fundamental rights of the individuals affected by its application, nor does it recognise, even in an embryonic form, a constitutional right to European citizenship. Europe cannot confer citizenship; this remains the prerogative of the Member States. By the same token, individual citizens of a Member State are entitled to move from their State to another Member State exclusively by virtue of their being workers, self-employed persons or providers of services, that is *qua* units of production factor.[3]

---

regions; contributing to the progressive abolition of restrictions on international trade by means of a common commercial policy; confirmation of the solidarity which binds Europe and the overseas countries and desiring to ensure the development of their prosperity, in accordance with the principles of the United Nations Charter.

[1] Preserving and strengthening peace and liberty and calling upon the other peoples of Europe who share the Member States' ideal to join in their efforts.

[2] The drafters of the *Union Treaty* did not replace the reference to the European Economic Community in the tenth recital to the preamble with a reference to the European Community.

[3] Federico Mancini, "*The Making of a Constitution for Europe*", (1989) 26 CMLRev 595 at p 596 (emphasis in the original).

Judge Mancini goes on in the same article to argue that the "main endeavour" of the Court of Justice has been to remove or reduce these two main differences between constitutions and treaties, as far as the *EEC Treaty* was concerned, by seeking to "constitutionalise" the Treaty. Nevertheless, by speaking of the *peoples* of Europe the preamble of the *EC Treaty* preserves the emphasis which has always existed in the Treaty's preamble on Europeans being primarily members of several national communities rather than being primarily members of a single European society, whatever other conclusions might be drawn from other provisions of the Treaty.[1]

Furthermore, although Article 8a the *EC Treaty* does not require the beneficiaries of the right it confers to move and reside to be "units of production factor", Article 8(1) reserves to the Member States the power to determine who, *prima facie*, are to enjoy the status of Union citizen by making Union citizenship dependent on tenure of the nationality of a Member State.

Nevertheless, the Member States' determination to lay the foundation of an ever closer union among the peoples of Europe is consistent with granting an effective non-economic movement and residence right which is, or can be made, subject to limitations and conditions consistent with their objectively justifiable interests.

Consequently, it cannot be said that the preamble's first recital supports the strong interpretation of the English version of Article 8a. On the other hand, it is consistent with the intermediate interpretation.

The Community's Basic Objectives. In attempting to interpret Article 8a of the *EC Treaty* in the context of the Treaty's fundamental aims and objectives, it is impossible to leave Article 2 of the Treaty out of the equation.[2] Being in Part One ("Principles")

[1]The *Union Treaty* likewise speaks of the Member States' desire "to deepen the solidarity between their peoples while respecting their history, their culture and their traditions" (fourth recital to the preamble), their resolution to "continue the process of creating an ever closer union among the peoples of Europe" (eleventh recital to the preamble) and their view that the *Union Treaty* "marks a new stage in the process of creating an ever closer union among the peoples of Europe" (Article A (second paragraph)). Construing Article A the *Bundesverfassungsgericht* (Germany's federal constitutional court) said, in *Brunner v The European Union Treaty* (Cases 2 BvR 2134/92 and 2159/92) [1994] 1 CMLR 57 at p 89, paragraph 51 of the Court's judgment: "The Union Treaty (as explained) establishes a federation of States for the purpose of realising an ever closer union of the peoples of Europe (organised as States) and not a state based on the people of one European nation. ... Given that subject-matter, the question raised ... as to whether the Constitution allows or prohibits German membership of a European state does not arise. All that has to be scrutinised is the Act assenting to German membership of a federation of States".

[2]Article 2 of the *EC Treaty* is, except for minor changes, identical to Article 2 of the *EEC Treaty*. In Case C-260/89 *Elliniki Radiophonia Tileorassi AE v Pliroforissis* [1991] ECR I-2925 at p I-2948, paragraph 47(a) of the opinion, Advocate General Lenz said that the preamble to and Article 2 of the *EEC Treaty* "enunciate general obligations of the Member States and the Community institutions and their main function is thus to furnish criteria for interpretation which may be of use in applying specific provisions relating to concrete measures". This approach is consistent with the view of the Court of Justice that Article 2 of the *EEC Treaty* is not directly effective; eg Case C-339/89 *Alsthom Atlantique SA v Compagnie de construction mécanique Sulzer SA* [1991] ECR I-107 at p I-123, paragraphs 8-9 of the Court's judgment, and Case C-260/89 *Elliniki Radiophonia Tileorassi AE v Pliroforissis* [1991] ECR I-2925 at p I-2963, paragraphs 39-40 of the Court's judgment. Article 2 of the *EEC Treaty* was employed to interpret specific Treaty provisions in Case 6/72 *Europemballage Corporation v Commission* [1973] ECR

of the Treaty it is one of the fundamental provisions of the Community legal order.[1] It is also a fundamental provision of the Treaty because it lays down the Treaty's basic objectives. The European Community has six basic objectives:

(i) The promotion throughout the Community of a harmonious and balanced development of economic activities.

(ii) Sustainable and non-inflationary growth (while) respecting the environment.

(iii) A high degree of convergence of economic performance.

(iv) A high level of employment and of social protection.

(v) The raising of the standard of living and of the quality of life.

(vi) Economic and social cohesion and solidarity among the Member States.

These six objectives replace the five objectives previously contained in Article 2 of the *EEC Treaty*. A comparison of Article 2 of the *EC Treaty* with Article 2 of the *EEC Treaty* reveals that only the *EC Treaty* objective of achieving a high level of employment and social protection is a substantively new addition to the fundamental objectives of the Community.[2]

In *Commission v France* ("*Re French Sailors*")[3] the Court of Justice said that the "fundamental provisions applicable to the whole complex of economic activities" (*in casu* Article 74 relating to the common transport policy) "are of prime importance to the objectives of the Treaty" which are provided for in Articles 2 and 3 of the Treaty,[4]

---

215 at p 244, paragraph 24 of the Court's judgment (Article 2 helps define the limits on competition permitted by the Treaty), Joined Cases 6 and 7/73 *Istituto Chemioterapico Italiano SpA v Commission* [1974] ECR 223 at p 252, paragraph 32 of the Court's judgment (the prohibitions in Articles 85 and 86 of the *EEC Treaty* must be interpreted and applied in the light of Article 2 which gives the Community the task of promoting harmonious development of economic activities), and in Case 167/73 *Commission v France* ("*Re French Sailors*") [1974] ECR 359 at p 370, paragraph 24 of the Court's judgment (the reference in Article 74 of the *EEC Treaty* to the "objectives of this Treaty" is a reference *inter alia* to Article 2).

[1]Case 43/75 *Defrenne v Société Anonyme Belge de Navigation Aérienne Sabena* [1976] ECR 455 at p 474, paragraph 28 of the Court's judgment, referring specifically to Article 7 of the *EEC Treaty* (Article 6 of the *EC Treaty*) which is also in Part One.

[2]The new objective of promoting throughout the Community a harmonious and balanced development of economic activities replaces the corresponding old objective merely in insisting that the development be balanced as well as harmonious. The new objective of achieving sustainable and non-inflationary growth (while) respecting the environment replaces the corresponding old objective of continuous and balanced expansion. The new objective of a high degree of convergence of economic performance replaces the corresponding old objective of greater stability. The new objective of raising the standard of living and of the quality of life replaces the corresponding old objective of an accelerated raising of the standard of living. Finally, the new objective of economic and social cohesion and solidarity among the Member States replaces the corresponding old objective of closer relations between the States belonging to the Community.

[3]Case 167/73 [1974] ECR 359.

[4]ibid at p 370, paragraph 24 of the Court's judgment.

thereby indicating that the objectives of the Community are primarily economic. The inclusion in the *EC Treaty* of the new objective of a high level of employment and of social protection does not alter this aspect of Article 2's character.

Similarly in *Walrave and Koch v Association Union Cycliste Internationale*,[1] it was emphasised by the Court of Justice that "[h]aving regard to the objectives of the Community, the practice of sport is subject to Community law only in so far as it constitutes an economic activity within the meaning of Article 2 of the Treaty".[2]

The Court of Justice also pointed out in *Re French Sailors* that Article 2 of the Treaty provides the Community with the task of promoting throughout the Community a harmonious development of economic activities by establishing a common market and progressively approximating the laws of the Member States.[3] From this it followed that "[t]he establishment of the common market thus refers to the whole of the economic activities of the Community".[4] By reasoning in this way the Court focused not only on the Community's basic objectives, but also on the means prescribed by Article 2 for their realisation. The means prescribed by Article 2 of the *EEC Treaty* are not substantively different from those prescribed by Article 2 of the *EC Treaty*.[5] The Court has also said that the common market "involves the elimination of all obstacles to intra-Community trade in order to merge the national markets into a single market bringing about conditions as close as possible to those of a genuine internal market".[6]

It therefore appears that, notwithstanding the removal of the word "Economic" from the Community's name, its basic objectives presently remain economic. Certainly, Article 2 of the *EC Treaty* does not prescribe the establishment of Union citizenship as one of the Community's basic objectives or as one of the means to achieve the basic objectives.

The Community's basic objectives do not, therefore, provide a context in which the strong interpretation of the Union citizen's non-economic migration right under Article 8a can confidently be advanced.

[1]Case 36/74 [1974] ECR 1405.

[2]ibid at p 1417, paragraph 4 of the Court's judgment.

[3]Case 167/73 *Commission v France* ("*Re French Sailors*") [1974] ECR 359 at p 369, paragraph 18 of the Court's judgment.

[4]ibid at p 369, paragraph 19 of the Court's judgment.

[5]The means prescribed by Article 2 of the *EEC Treaty* are, as indicated by *Re French Sailors*, the establishment of a common market and the progressive approximation of Member States' economic policies. Article 3 of the *EEC Treaty* also provides for certain activities "(f)or the purposes set out in Article 2". Article 2 of the *EC Treaty* preserves the establishment of a common market as a means to achieve the Community's basic objectives, but replaces the progressive approximation of Member States' economic policies with the achievement of an economic and monetary union and the activities referred to in Articles 3 and 3a. Article 3 of the *EC Treaty* closely resembles Article 3 of the *EEC Treaty*, and Article 3a of the *EC Treaty* prescribes activities specifically associated with the objective of economic and monetary union.

[6]Case 15/81 *Gaston Schul Douane Expediteur BV v Inspecteur de Invoerrechten en Accijnnzen, Roosendaal* [1982] ECR 1409 at pp 1431-1432, paragraph 33 of the Court's judgment.

The Community's Activities. The Community's activities are prescribed by Articles 3 and 3a of the *EC Treaty*, which activities are among the means nominated by Article 2 for the achievement of the Community's basic objectives. Here, too, we find no support for the proposition that the strong interpretation of the English version of Article 8a is supported by the fundamental aims and objectives of the *EC Treaty*. The activities listed by Article 3, twenty-one in number, are all clearly economic or socio-economic in nature and extend, by way of illustration, to such things as the elimination of customs duties between Member States,[1] ensuring that competition in the common market is not distorted,[2] establishing an environment policy[3] and contributing to a high level of health protection.[4]

Only two of the nominated activities bear upon the free movement of persons. Article 3(c) nominates "an internal market characterized by the abolition ... of obstacles to the free movement of goods, persons, services and capital" and Article 3(d) nominates "[m]easures concerning the entry and movement of persons in the internal market as provided for in Article 100c". Both these provisions link free personal movement to the internal market which, as we have already seen, is an economic concept. Moreover Article 100c of the *EC Treaty* is concerned with migration into the Community by persons who are not Union citizens.

Finally, neither the establishment of Union citizenship nor the Union citizen's right of movement and residence are among the activities listed in Articles 3 and 3a, the undertaking of which are required for the achievement of the Community's basic objectives.

Consequently it cannot be said that, in viewing Article 8a in the context of the Treaty's fundamental aims and objectives, Articles 2, 3 and 3a of the *EC Treaty* support the strong interpretation of the English version of Article 8a.

Nor can any support for the strong interpretation necessarily be drawn from the draftsman's decision to position Article 8a, together with the Treaty's other citizenship provisions, in its own Part (Part Two) of the Treaty. By positioning Article 8a in this way, the draftsman avoided placing it in Part One ("Principles") where it would have been regarded as one of the fundamental provisions of the Community legal order.[5]

Indeed there is not even a passing reference to Union citizenship anywhere in Part One of the *EC Treaty*. On the other hand the truly strong freedom of economic movement provisions in Articles 48, 52 and 59 of the *EC Treaty* are, as we have seen, adumbrated by Article 3(c) which is in Part One of the Treaty and which prescribes activities the undertaking of which are required to achieve the Treaty's basic objectives.

[1] Article 3(a).
[2] Article 3(g).
[3] Article 3(k).
[4] Article 3(o).
[5] Case 43/75 *Defrenne v Société Anonyme Belge de Navigation Aérienne Sabena* [1976] ECR 455 at p 474, paragraph 28 of the Court's judgment.

European Unity. Article 1 (first paragraph) of the *Single European Act*, however, provides that the "European Communities and European Political Co-operation shall have as their objective to contribute together to making concrete progress towards European unity". Might this reference to "European unity" as the Community's objective imply that the fundamental purpose of the *EC Treaty* transcends economics, thereby providing some support for the strong interpretation of Article 8a?

European unity, while remaining a somewhat enigmatic concept in terms of its implications for possible future political developments, appears at this stage of the development of Community law to be a distillation of the various objectives and tasks of the Community and of the intergovernmental activities of the Member States. It does not presently compel adoption of the view that the objective necessitates the achievement of a full-scale political union, which objective could justify the conferment of movement and residence rights on Union citizens equivalent to those enjoyed by the citizens of a democratic nation-state.

Citizenship and the Union Treaty. The *rôle* of the *Union Treaty*, as it concerns citizenship of the Union, is not restricted to inserting Articles 8-8e into the *EC Treaty*. The preamble to the *Union Treaty* records the Member States' resolve "to establish a citizenship common to the nationals of their countries".[1] Article B furthermore sets the Union the objective "to strengthen the protection of the rights and interests of the nationals of its Member States through the introduction of a citizenship of the Union".[2] It might be tempting to employ these two provisions of the *Union Treaty* as a basis for arguing that the migration rights conferred by Article 8a of the *EC Treaty* are fundamental and that they should therefore be construed in accordance with the 'strong' interpretation.

Article L of the *Union Treaty*, however, forbids the Court of Justice from exercising its powers under the *EC Treaty* in respect of either of the relevant provisions of the *Union Treaty*. Furthermore, Article M of the *Union Treaty* provides that neither that Treaty's preamble nor its Article B, *inter alia*, "shall affect the Treaties establishing the European Communities or the subsequent Treaties and Acts modifying or supplementing them". Thus although the establishment of Union citizenship is of central importance for the European Union, its significance at this level is political rather than juridical and does not affect the work of the Court of Justice in interpreting and applying the law of the European Community.

Accordingly, the strong interpretation of the English version of Article 8a of the *EC Treaty* is supported by reference neither to the several official language versions of the provision, nor by reference to the fundamental aims and objectives of the Treaty, nor by having regard to the provision's context in the Treaty.

[1]Eighth recital.
[2]Third indent.

Weak or Intermediate Interpretation? We are left, then, with a choice between the weak and intermediate interpretations of the English version of Article 8a.

It has already been shown that the weak interpretation depends essentially on a grammatical ambiguity which is resolved by reference to the other official language versions in a way inconsistent with the validity of the weak interpretation, but consistent with the intermediate interpretation.

All the official language versions of Article 8a(1) are, moreover, expressed to confer a 'right' on Union citizens.[1] Furthermore Article 8(2) of the *EC Treaty*, in all the language versions, states that Union citizens "shall enjoy the rights conferred by this Treaty" or words to identical effect. These references in the treaties to rights tend to suggest that Article 8a is conferring on Union citizens something of substance which is not merely declarative of a commitment the realisation of which is wholly dependent upon future legislative action. This approach sits more easily with the basic philosophical and jurisprudential assumptions of the Court of Justice concerning the direct effect of provisions of Community law and tends to rule out the weak interpretation possibly assignable to the English version of Article 8a.

Furthermore, the procedure prescribed by Article 8a(2) of the *EC Treaty* for the adoption of provisions with a view to facilitating the rights contained in Article 8a(1) tends to support a finding of direct effect. Before any such provisions can be adopted, they must be assented to by the European Parliament *and* unanimously approved by the Council. This is a uniquely rigorous legislative procedure indicating both the importance of Article 8a and of the measures to be adopted under it.

Thus it would appear that the ambiguity in the English version of Article 8a is more accurately resolved by assigning to it the intermediate interpretation, so that the provision is to be understood as meaning that it immediately grants to Union citizens a right to move and reside subject to limitations and conditions contained in measures giving effect to the right and subject to limitations and conditions laid down elsewhere in the Treaty. Such an interpretation is also strongly suggested by the several official language versions of the text.

Conclusion

Is it possible that Article 8a, thus understood, can be directly effective? Put more abstractly, can a provision of Community law which confers a right on individuals yet permits the enactment of unspecified limitations and conditions on the exercise of that right be regarded as directly effective? This in turn raises the question as to whether the Community standard created by such a provision is sufficient in itself inasmuch as its implementation is not dependent on measures being subsequently taken by Community institutions or Member States with discretionary power in the matter.

[1] Danish, *ret*; Dutch, *recht*; French, *droit*; German, *Recht*; Greek, δικαιωμα; Irish, *ceart*; Italian, *diritto*; Portuguese, *direito*; Spanish, *derecho*.

In this connection it is firstly instructive to recall our earlier consideration of Article 6 of the *EC Treaty*.[1] It will be remembered that Article 6 is a directly effective provision of fundamental significance within the framework of Community law and that its second paragraph authorises the adoption of rules "designed to prohibit" nationality discrimination. Notwithstanding this textual restriction on the character of the rules which may be adopted under the authority of Article 6 (second paragraph), it nevertheless permits the adoption of rules limiting or conditioning the principle against nationality discrimination where such rules may be objectively justified in the public interest. The requirement that the limitations and conditions be 'objectively justified' signifies that they are subject to judicial control. Included among such rules may be provisions permitting derogation on the grounds of public policy, public security and public health. This feature of Article 6 does not operate so as to deprive it of its directly effective character.

In this connection it is also helpful to recall that limitations and conditions on the fundamental Community movement rights granted by Articles 48, 52 and 59 of the *EC Treaty* do not operate so as to deprive those provisions of their direct effect while those limitations and conditions remain subject to judicial control.

Notwithstanding that Article 8a(2) is expressed to authorise the adoption of "provisions with a view to facilitating the exercise of the rights referred to in" Article 8a(1), it too is apt to authorise the enactment of provisions limiting or conditioning the right granted by Article 8a(1) where such measures are objectively justified, and therefore subject to judicial control. Among the limitations and conditions on the Union citizen's right to move and reside which provisions adopted under Article 8a(2) may authorise are those which are objectively justified on grounds of public policy, public security and public health. Because the right conferred by Article 8a is not an economic one and is not part of the common market or the internal market, limitations and conditions on its exercise may also be objectively justified on economic grounds, such as the protection of host Member States' social assistance systems.[2]

[1]Chapter 4.

[2]It might conceivably be objected that Article 6 of the *EC Treaty* does not provide a valid analogy to Article 8a for the purposes of establishing that the latter authorises the adoption of merely objectively justified limitations and conditions on the rights contained in Article 8a(1). After all, such an argument might run, Article 6 (second paragraph) does not expressly authorise the adoption of measures limiting or conditioning the principle against nationality discrimination. This contrasts with the terms of Article 8a(1) which expressly envisages that the measures adopted to give effect to the Union citizen's movement and residence rights may include limitations and conditions. It could be said to follow that Article 8a authorises the adoption of limiting and restricting measures which go beyond the merely objectively justified. If this were so, the measures would not be susceptible to judicial control and would therefore be outside the reach of judicial control. The logical consequence is that Article 8a is deprived of the direct effect which it would otherwise possess. This objection would, however, be wrong for two reasons. Firstly although Article 8a(1) expressly envisages that measures to be adopted may contain limitations and conditions, the measures must also "give effect" to the Union citizen's right to move and reside. A measure which permitted the imposition of conditions which were not susceptible to judicial control would not be giving effect to the Article 8a(1) right, for it would permit the complete frustration of the right. We have already seen, in the context of economic migration rights, that limitations and conditions must not operate so as to negate the very right which the Treaty itself confers (Case C-265/88 *Messner* [1989]

A limitation or condition which is subject to judicial control does not, as we have seen, deprive a provision of Community law of its direct effect. Therefore measures adopted under Article 8a(2) which enable Member States to exclude Union citizens from their territories on grounds of public policy, public security and public health or on other objectively justified grounds - such as the protection of their social assistance systems - will not operate so as to deprive Article 8a of its direct effect.

Accordingly, both the language and context of Article 8a indicate that it is directly effective. The fact that it is subject to judicially supervised limitations and conditions does not deprive it of direct effect.

ECR 4209). Secondly Article 48(3)(d) of the *EC Treaty* provides an example of a directly effective provision which nevertheless expressly authorises the adoption of conditions. The direct effect of Article 48 generally is a well established feature of Community law (eg Case 41/74 *van Duyn v Home Office* [1974] ECR 1337). In Case 75/63 *Hoekstra v Bestuur der Bedrijfsvereniging voor Detailhandel en Ambachten* [1964] ECR 177, decided before the enactment of *Regulation 1251/70* laying down the conditions foreshadowed in Article 48(3)(d), the Court of Justice said that Article 48(3)(d) already applied to persons likely to remain in the territory of a Member State after having been employed there (at p 185). Similarly, in Case 316/85 *Centre public d'aide sociale de Courcelles v Lebon* [1987] ECR 2811, Advocate General Lenz said he was convinced by a Commission argument that "since the former migrant worker's right to remain is expressly mentioned in Article 48(3)(d) of the EEC Treaty it can have no lesser rank than the worker's right to freedom of movement" (at p 2825, paragraph 23 of the opinion). Restrictions on the right contained in Article 48(3)(d) were imposed by Article 2(1) of *Regulation 1251/70* (OJ Sp Ed 1970, L 142/24, p 402) which has the effect of excluding from enjoyment of the right several categories of persons who would otherwise fall within the scope of the Treaty provision. These restrictions are therefore more in the nature of "limitations" than "conditions". Nevertheless the Court of Justice has, in several cases, assumed the validity of *Regulation 1251/70*.That the ability to remain in the territory of a host Member State after having been employed there is a right guaranteed by the Treaty is, moreover, recognised by the preamble to *Regulation 1251/70*. Accordingly, a directly effective Treaty provision may, in principle, be subject to limitations and conditions to be contained in secondary legislation provided the right conferred by the Treaty is not negated.

APPENDIX

§ 1. United Kingdom declaration on nationality upon signing the *Treaty of Accession 1972.*

At the time of signature of the Treaty of Accession, the Government of the United Kingdom of Great Britain and Northern Ireland makes the following declaration:

"As to the United Kingdom of Great Britain and Northern Ireland, the terms 'nationals', 'nationals of Member States' or 'nationals of Member States and overseas countries and territories' wherever used in the Treaty establishing the European Economic Community, the Treaty establishing the European Atomic Energy Community or the Treaty establishing the European Coal and Steel Community or in any of the Community acts deriving from those Treaties, are to be understood to refer to:

(a) persons who are citizens of the United Kingdom and Colonies or British subjects not possessing that citizenship or the citizenship of any other Commonwealth country or territory, who, in either case, have the right of abode in the United Kingdom, and are therefore exempt from United Kingdom immigration control;

(b) persons who are citizens of the United Kingdom and Colonies by birth or by registration or naturalization in Gibraltar, or whose father was so born, registered or naturalized."

§ 2. United Kingdom declaration on nationality upon the entry into force of the *British Nationality Act 1981.*

In view of the entry into force of the British Nationality Act 1981, the Government of the United Kingdom of Great Britain and Northern Ireland makes the following Declaration which will replace, as from 1 January 1983, that made at the time of signature of the Treaty of Accession by the United Kingdom to the European Communities:

'As to the United Kingdom of Great Britain and Northern Ireland, the terms "nationals", "nationals of Member States" or "nationals of Member States and overseas countries and territories" wherever used in the Treaty establishing the European Economic Community, the Treaty establishing the European Atomic Energy Community or the

Treaty establishing the European Coal and Steel Community or in any of the Community acts deriving from those Treaties, are to be understood to refer to:

(a) British citizens;

(b) persons who are British subjects by virtue of Part IV of the British Nationality Act 1981 and who have the right of abode in the United Kingdom and are therefore exempt from United Kingdom immigration control;

(c) British Dependent Territories citizens who are acquire their citizenship from a connection with Gibraltar.'

The reference in Article 6 of the third Protocol to the Act of Accession of 22 January 1972, on the Channel Islands and the Isle of Man, to 'any citizen of the United Kingdom and Colonies' is to be understood as referring to 'any British citizen'.

§ 3. Danish declaration on citizenship of the Union made at the European Council meeting at Edinburgh on 11-12 December 1992.

1. Citizenship of the Union is a political and legal concept which is entirely different from the concept of citizenship within the meaning of the Constitution of the Kingdom of Denmark and of the Danish legal system. Nothing in the Treaty on European Union implies or foresees an undertaking to create a citizenship of the Union in the sense of citizenship of a nation-state. The question of Denmark participating in any such development does, therefore, not arise.

2. Citizenship of the Union in no way in itself gives a national of another Member State the right to obtain Danish citizenship or any of the rights, duties, privileges or advantages that are inherent in Danish citizenship by virtue of Denmark's constitutional, legal and administrative rules. Denmark will fully respect all specific rights expressly provided for in the Treaty and applying to nationals of the Member States.

3. Nationals of the other Member States of the European Community enjoy in Denmark the right to vote and to stand as a candidate at municipal elections, foreseen in Article 8b of the European Community Treaty. Denmark intends to introduce legislation granting nationals of the other Member States the right to vote and to stand as a candidate for elections to the European Parliament in good time before the next elections in 1994. Denmark has no intention of accepting that the detailed arrangements

foreseen in paragraphs 1 and 2 of this Article could lead to rules detracting from the rights already given in Denmark in that matter.

4. Without prejudice to the other provisions of the Treaty establishing the European Community, Article 8e requires the unanimity of all the Member States of the Council of the European Communities, ie all the Member States, for the adoption of any provision to strengthen or to add to the rights laid down in Part Two of the EC Treaty. Moreover, any unanimous decision of the Council, before coming into force, will have to be adopted in each Member State, in accordance with its constitutional requirements. In Denmark, such adoption will, in the case of a transfer of sovereignty, as defined in the Danish Constitution, require either a majority of 5/6 of Members of the Folketing or both a majority of the Members of the Folketing and a majority of voters in a referendum.

INDEX